The Toscanini Phenomenon

The Man and His Audience
"The world has been very fortunate. . . . Toscanini's music has been available for a long time."

Toscanini's Musicianship
"Toscanini revealed new and hitherto unknown possibilities of virtuosity and clarity in orchestral playing. . . . Toscanini continued to show us new and unexpected things about great music which, in the hands of other conductors, we thought we knew fully and completely."

The Recordings
". . . documents in sound which Toscanini has left for the generations who will never hear him in a concert hall."

Toscanini's Repertory
". . . the process by which Toscanini selected the music he was to perform was essentially emotional. . . ."

ROBERT CHARLES MARSH

TOSCANINI

ART OF

AND THE
CONDUCTING

New, Revised Edition

COLLIER BOOKS

NEW YORK, N.Y.

Toscanini and the Art of Conducting originally appeared under the title *Toscanini and the Art of Orchestral Performance*

This Collier Books edition is published by arrangement with J. B. Lippincott Company

Collier Books is a division of The Crowell-Collier Publishing Company

First Collier Books Edition 1962

Library of Congress Catalog Card Number: 62-15808

Contents

Preface

PORTIONS of this book are appearing here in their fourth edition and under their third title. All four editions differ from one another. The two most closely related are the American and British printings of 1956, although the latter publication corrects some factual errors of the American version. Both these texts are entitled *Toscanini and the Art of Orchestral Performance*. *Toscanini Der Meisterdirgent*, which appeared in Switzerland in 1958, is a German translation which eliminates the record listings of Chapter III. I was not permitted to see either the German text or a single sheet of proof prior to publication, and I waive any personal responsibility for the distinctive errors in this volume.

Thomas Mann once described the publication of a book as the beginning of its "earthly life," and a writer can surely wonder how, in any sense, he can presume to revise his thoughts once they have been circulated in print. Must not any such process seem a presumptuous bid for the forgiveness of youthful indiscretion?

What I wrote about Toscanini in 1954 and 1955 was a true expression of the person I was in those years: an academic man who was groping for a larger and more rewarding way of life. Returning to this text seven years later I was concerned by many instances in which I had been guilty of bad writing or bad judgment, false conjecture or factual error. The present text has been thoroughly revised and edited on the basis of whatever wisdom I have acquired in six seasons as music critic of a large metropolitan newspaper.

In preparing the new version I must thank a number of persons who in reviews and letters pointed out the failings of the original. Although I cannot name them all, I am in their debt. Chief of the benevolent Beckmessers has been the Maestro's son, Mr. Walter Toscanini. Without his aid there never would have been a book in the first place, and he has since gone over the text with me, pointing out mistakes and setting them right. These searches have taken us to the Toscanini family papers, and whenever possible I have worked directly from the documents themselves. No polite verbal formula conveys proper gratitude for that sort of co-operation.

I must also thank Mr. John Corbett, resident engineer of the Riverdale Project, who gave me a week of his time in preparing the revisions. Mr. Robert Hupka came to my rescue by reading the proofs for Chapter 3 and finding any number of gross and subtle errors. Mr. Harlin Quist of Collier Books proved himself the right kind of editor to have in moments of crisis and confusion.

During the preparation of the original text Mr. George R. Marek supplied data on the date and place of recording sessions as preserved in the RCA-Victor engineering files. However, neither RCA-Victor nor the National Broadcasting Company have provided any assistance in the preparation of this revision.

Reading the reviews of the American edition I found certain misunderstandings about my background and career. During the dozen years when I was primarily a specialist in mathematical logic, I corresponded in an intermittent manner with Mr. B. H. Haggin, who was then music critic for *The Nation*. He gave me a certain amount of advice when I first started work on this book, but he was never in any sense responsible for any part of its contents. Only after our correspondence had ceased and I had more or less completed my work on a book called *Logic and Knowledge* (London and New York, 1956), did I begin to think seriously of becoming a professional music critic. I had studied music since childhood, but I had never undertaken any systematic investigation of the problems and methods of music criticism. It was not until after most of the work on the first edition of this book had been completed, in the autumn of 1955, that I began rigorous preparation on the broad scale necessary for a career of critical writing. These studies completed my work at Trinity College of the University of Cambridge and were directed informally by Dr. Hubert S.

Middleton, whose influence upon British music criticism was deeply felt throughout much of the present century.

The full effect of Middleton's teachings was not clear to me until after his death, but the more experience I have as a critic the more aware I become of the wisdom of his counsels and the force of his lectures in the shaping of my viewpoint. If I were to name my mentor, there is no doubt in my mind but that Middleton was the man.

Chicago, 1962

ROBERT CHARLES MARSH

Toscanini and the Art of Conducting

Chapter 1

The Man and His Audience

1

THE CAREER of Arturo Toscanini contains all the elements of a successful novel except one: it is too fabulous to be plausible. That a poor boy should rise quickly to the top of his profession and remain there for over half a century, retiring with his skill virtually unimpaired and the devotion of his public at the highest pitch is the stuff of a film scenario. Our sensitivity to social realities causes us to doubt its possibility as an actual life pattern; but in this case the exceptional and the actual are the same.

Arturo Toscanini was born on the twenty fifth of March, 1867, in Parma, which was then (as now) a reasonably good-sized city in northern Italy. Claudio Toscanini, his father, was a tailor, and he and his wife, Paola Montani, both represented working-class families that depended on agriculture or employment as craftsmen for subsistence. There were no musicians among them and no direct evidence of art in the blood, except perhaps Claudio Toscanini's dislike for the drudgery and routine of his craft which had led him to abandon his needle and cutting bench for a career in Garibaldi's army as a youth and made him vulnerable to shaky, if imaginative, ventures in later years. Whatever his failings as a parent, he gave his son a love for liberty and an impassioned dedication to the idea of democracy that was to shape the course of his life.

Arturo was the first of four children. Three sisters were born during his early childhood, and his favorite among them, Narcisa, died in 1878, two years after he became a student at the conservatory. With them he shared the life of the Oltretorrente, the working class quarter where the two younger of his sisters grew to maturity.

13

Paola Toscanini was the strong member of the family. She too sewed, and she cared for her children as best she could, taught them to be honest, to work hard, and to stand up to their misfortunes rather than be overcome by them. Her handsome, cheerful, husband could not provide her with the way of life known to the rest of her family, but in spite of her difficulties she tried to meet her relatives as a peer, and demanded of her children that they conceal their poverty and hunger. Apart from this she was too deeply involved in reviewing the unfortunate consequences of her situation to offer her children much affection or aid. Arturo had the ability to follow her guidance and better himself, but his sisters were unable to extricate themselves from their environment, and their failure came to occupy her thoughts more than his success.

Young Arturo was quick to learn to read and insatiable in his desire for books. The rapidity with which he could memorize things and the skill with which, when he finally got access to a piano in the home of one of his teachers, he played operatic airs of the day, led to the conclusion that he should become a musician. He was unsuccessful in obtaining a scholarship to the Royal School of Music at Parma but the family budget under the unusual strain yielded the fees, and at the age of nine he left his demanding, unaffectionate mother and indifferent father and took up a way of life with rigid discipline demanding complete dedication to music. Two years later, in 1878, he was granted a scholarship which he held to the end of his studies. His parents accepted his departure from the household and did not visit him at the conservatory. He worked unceasingly, winning honors for 'cello, piano, and composition on his graduation. The prescribed course did not take all his time, and when his assigned work was done he read scores.

The Toscanini that emerged from the Parma conservatory in 1885 was a musician of recognized competence who had had the practical experience of conducting a small orchestra of his fellow students and playing in the pit orchestra of Parma's Teatro Regio during five spring carnival seasons. (His zeal for Wagner goes back to a performance of

Lohengrin in which he played in 1884.) He returned to his family as its head. His father gave in without a struggle; his mother accepted him in his new role, with pride probably mixed with meaner emotions.

He did not stay at home long. The impresario Claudio Rossi engaged him to play the 'cello and serve as assistant chorus master and vocal coach with an Italian opera company going to Brazil for the winter season.

The debut of the greatest Italian conductor of our time took place, therefore, not in Italy but in the Americas: in Rio de Janeiro on June 30, 1886. He was nineteen, and the whole affair reads like fiction. The principal conductor of the company was a Brazilian, Leopoldo Miguez. After two months in Sao Paulo, where the performances had been bad, the company arrived in Rio, where they got no better. After two notably unsuccessful presentations of *Aïda,* Miguez bet on the chauvinism of the audience to save himself, and, sending a statement to the newspapers, he placed the blame on the Italian singers (most of whom were well-established artists) and walked out. When the assistant conductor appeared in the pit for the third performance he was forced to retreat before the din from the house. So was the impresario, who tried to make a speech. The chorus master then attempted to start the performance, with the same lack of success.

Toscanini heard none of this since, as he used to tell of the event, he was "playing the piano with a girl." However, as the hour for the performance past, his conscience got the better of him and he went to the theater. He was the only remaining member of the company qualified to conduct, and under the persuasion of the singers and his fellows in the orchestra (somehow I feel that not a great deal of persuasion was necessary) he took up the stick, entered the pit, and led the opera from memory. Much has always been made of the latter accomplishment, although Toscanini never thought anything of it. He had been engaged in the preparation of the opera, and he had heard two performances within the week. Why shouldn't the score be well fixed in his mind?

The performance, in any case, was a success and the critic of the *Gazeta de Noticias* found Toscanini "a full-fledged and reliable conductor . . . worthy of waving the baton." A career was under way.

Before leaving Brazil Toscanini led eighteen operas from the repertory of the day (among them Gounod's *Faust* and the *Rigoletto* and *Il Trovatore* of his beloved Verdi). When he returned to Italy in the autumn the next step was not clearly marked out for him. The Italian public were indifferent to what had taken place in distant Rio, and there were no bids awaiting the young Maestro. The singers, however, knew what he had done, and through Nicola Figner, who had been the tenor of Rossi's troop, Toscanini was engaged to give Alfredo Catalani's *Edmea* at Turin. His Italian debut on November 4, 1886, in a city where his reputation was to grow almost yearly during the twelve seasons to come, was a tame and orderly affair compared with his first Brazilian appearance, but it was a success, and Catalani (for whom he always retained the most sincere loyalty and affection) showed himself to be a good judge of musicians by predicting that Toscanini was on his way to an "extraordinary career."

Toscanini's first Turin season (at the Teatro Carignano) was a makeshift one, based largely upon the fact that the conductor engaged for the theater was late in arriving. Indeed, Toscanini's final task in Turin that year was getting the orchestra ready for a production of *The Flying Dutchman* which the other man was to direct. This only happened once. Toscanini returned to Turin regularly, and, after 1895, he was at the Teatro Regio with the prerogatives of one who was a Maestro in his own right. At the close of his conducting assignment in 1886, however, Toscanini took up his 'cello, and went to Milan. On the occasion of the first performance of Verdi's *Otello* on February 5, 1887, Toscanini was present as neither conductor nor spectator, but as the second desk 'cellist. La Scala was then, as it is today, the leading operatic theater in Italy, and as Toscanini sat in the pit that first season it is possible he imagined that he would be able to make a career there; but he could hardly have conceived the nature of his relationship with the house in his various periods there, or the way that relationship would end.

His career as an orchestra player, however, was about over. The following season brought him engagements as a conductor, first in Casale Monferrato, which in those days could hardly be regarded as a center of the lyric stage, and then in Verona, a city of some importance. He was on his way through the theaters of the provinces and the smaller cities, broken by an occasional visit to a larger place such as Turin or the Teatro dal Verme in Milan, gaining the experience which these opera houses (and their counterparts in Central Europe) provided by way of practical training to nearly every great singer and conductor of our time. In the twelve seasons he spent acquiring a reputation, between 1886 and 1898, he appeared in twenty Italian cities and towns. (He left the Italian circuit briefly in 1890 to appear in Barcelona.) From 1892, when he gave three operas (including a première) at Rome, his apprenticeship can be regarded as definitely over. The fact that he achieved full professional stature while in his early twenties indicates a phenomenal natural aptitude for conducting which even a short period of experience could turn into mastery of the art. Of the operas he prepared in the years between his debut and 1898, only about half are known outside Italy, and of the seven world premières he gave only two, *Pagliacci* (Milan, 1892) and *La Bohème* (Turin, 1896), were of scores heard in many of the world's opera houses today. In the winter season of 1895-96 he applied himself to weightier matters, the first Italian performance of *Die Götterdämmerung,* in Turin, December 22, 1895.

The main stream of Italian music was opera; symphonic works came second, and it was a rare operatic conductor who was engaged to lead symphony concerts. It was, therefore, not until March 20, 1896, nearly ten years after his debut, that Toscanini, five days short of his twenty-ninth birthday appeared on the stage of the opera house in Turin to lead a program that sounds much the same as those he offered throughout his later career: Brahms' *Tragic Overture,* the *Entry of the Gods into Valhalla* from *Das Rheingold,* a Wagnerian excerpt he did not play in any of his American concerts after 1921, the Tchaikovsky *Nutcracker*

Suite, and the great *C Major Symphony, No. 9,* of Franz Schubert.[1] Later in the spring he gave four symphonic programs at La Scala in Milan. He played Haydn, Beethoven, Schubert, Brahms, Tchaikovsky, Wagner—all composers he continued to play until his retirement—plus some lesser music, a certain amount of which remained in his repertory along with the major compositions. During the following season he returned to operatic scores, but in 1898 he again turned to symphonic music and gave forty-three concerts (including the first Italian performance of the recent *Pathétique Symphony* of Tchaikovsky) during the International Exposition at Turin.

At thirty he was a man of position and recognized stature. In June, 1897, he married Carla de Martini, the daughter of a Milan banker. Their first child, Walter, was born in March of the following year. His family life, as his private life in the years before his marriage, was now completely divorced from that of his parents and sisters, with whom he had only the most tenuous links. They never attended his performances and were not present at his wedding.

In the autumn of 1897 La Scala remained closed, for the city fathers of Milan had ended the subsidy on which the theater relied. By the summer of 1898, however, a new committee took over the management of the house. Giulio Gatti-Casazza and Toscanini were called to assume the administrative and artistic direction of the theater, and from that point onward it was obvious that Toscanini was the foremost Italian conductor of the day. He was then thirty-one and, with twelve years of conducting behind him, had arrived at the highest position in the musical life of his country.

Toscanini's first period at La Scala ran five years. As had been the case in his previous engagements, he had a loyal and appreciative public, but there were also detractors and critics, musicians he drove too hard, singers he offended, and members of the audience who wanted encores and

[1] Previously he had given a short concert in Venice in 1895, but apparently not of the type one would regard today as a program of symphonic music.

similar indulgences, on hand to speak against him. No self-less, hard-driving man is ever completely popular, and those who did not share Toscanini's dedication to music found it somewhat oppressive at times.

In addition to Italian operas he offered a representative selection of Wagner; *Die Meistersinger* (with which he opened his first season), *Siegfried, Lohengrin,* and *Tristan und Isolde.* Among his other productions was the first Italian performance of another score of Tchaikovsky, *Eugene Onegin.*

It was customary to give four symphony concerts at the close of the opera season at La Scala, rather meager fare by American standards, but to the Italian public music was primarily opera and ballet. In 1900, at the end of the season, Toscanini took the La Scala Orchestra on a short tour of northern Italy with considerable success. Parma welcomed him with enthusiasm.

There was a devoted audience for Italian opera in South America, and it was natural that Toscanini should want to appear there. The fact that the Argentine winter season ran from National Day, May twenty-fifth, to late August or early September, a period in which there was little musical activity in the Italian opera houses, made it a particularly attractive opportunity to work the full season in both hemispheres. Toscanini accepted engagements at the Teatro de la Opera, Buenos Aires, in 1901, 1903, 1904, and 1906. In 1912 he returned, this time at the Teatro Colón. His next appearance in South America was twenty-eight years later with the National Broadcasting Company Symphony.

The spring symphonic programs at La Scala in 1902 contained the *Ninth Symphony* of Beethoven, which Toscanini conducted in full for the first time. (He did not prepare the *Missa Solemnis* until 1934, just before his sixty-seventh birthday.) The 1902-03 season began with a brilliant production of Berlioz's *Damnation of Faust* as an opera. There had been growing tension between Toscanini and segments of the La Scala audience, particularly with respect to encores during a performance. The 1901-02 season had ended with Toscanini storming out of the theater in the middle of an opera because of such an outbreak, but when his passion subsided he had returned to complete the performance. On the final evening of the 1902-03 season there was another such demonstration, and this time Toscanini did not return. He sailed for Argentina.

The autumn of 1903 found him without a post in Italy. La Scala had engaged Cleofonte Campanini for three years, and he was suffering (as others were to do) the exquisite misery of being a man of lesser powers following in the footsteps of a Toscanini. Moreover, La Scala wanted Toscanini to come back. He accepted only two offers that season, appearing in symphony concerts in Rome and leading two operas at Bologna. In May he returned to Buenos Aires. In the autumn of 1904 the same procedure was repeated. Toscanini remained at home in Milan, and La Scala went its own way. The following April he conducted in Turin, and in June (he did not go to South America that summer) he brought the Turin Orchestra to La Scala for a pair of symphony concerts. It was a pointed lesson to the Milan audience that was no doubt understood. He even rewarded its good behavior by playing an encore.

Early in the 1905-06 season Campanini departed from La Scala after a culminating battle with the orchestra. Toscanini was conspicuously active near by in Bologna and Turin, and at the close of the opera season he took the Turin Orchestra on another short tour of nothern Italy, after which he again sailed to Argentina.

La Scala had had enough punishment. He was invited to return, and henceforth the program carried a notice that encores were forbidden. Toscanini found that everything had gone slack in his absence, and he went to work restoring order and discipline. The Milan audience, still not entirely pleased with the manner in which he had treated them, was none the less eager to have him back, and all went well. Among the works of the 1906-07 season was the first Italian production of Richard Strauss's *Salome*.

This period at La Scala lasted only two seasons. In the second, 1907-08, he again offered an important Italian première, Debussy's *Pelléas et Mélisande,* and a revival of

Charpentier's *Louise,* in addition to staples of the national repertory and *Die Götterdämmerung.* One would think that a conductor who could offer such fare would have his public behind him, but the limitations and boorishness of much of the audience must be reckoned with. *Pelléas* nearly provoked a riot, and many of the finest passages were lost in the din created by Yahoos who understood nothing more subtle than *La donna è mobile.* When the opportunity for Gatti-Casazza and himself to go to the Metropolitan Opera House in New York arose, it was natural that Toscanini should accept it, just as it was natural that the chauvinistic elements of the public (which had never forgotten that he had been able to walk out on his adversaries and go to South America) should make his departure uncomfortable. He led two symphonic concerts at the end of the season, and split violently with the management of La Scala when they ordered him to include two specific works in his third program. Another conductor complied with their wishes, and Toscanini took his leave. This time he was not to return to La Scala for twelve years.

Toscanini arrived on the North American scene in the autumn of 1908. He was a man of forty-one who had been a conductor for twenty-two years. His great reputation in his own country was known, but he was by no means the conductor of universal renown he was to become in later years: indeed, his appearances had been limited virtually to northern Italy and three South American countries. His career in the United States fell into four sections, each of which ended with a full close: that is, the expectation that he would return to Italy and not be heard again in the United States for some time—if at all. The Metropolitan period was of seven years, 1908-15. There was then a gap of six years until Toscanini returned briefly to tour the United States with the La Scala Orchestra in 1920-21. Five years passed, and Toscanini came back to be guest conductor of the New York Philharmonic, became its principal conductor in 1928, and appeared with that orchestra during eleven seasons, until 1936. Nineteen months later he was back to assume direction of N.B.C. Symphony, which he led for seventeen seasons, until his retirement in 1954.

Toscanini faced a New York audience for the first time on November 16, 1908. Five years before, when he had first turned his back on La Scala, the Metropolitan had been interested, but he had not wished to enter an unknown situation in an unknown city. When Gatti-Casazza, whom he trusted, also was approached, the situation became attractive to him, and, to the degree he had been indifferent before, he now became enthusiastic. The presence of Gustav Mahler among the other conductors at the Metropolitan convinced Toscanini of the high standards of the house.

Reading the review of his American debut, one can easily imagine the performance that it describes: a performance no different from those which one later heard from the Old Man. It is doubtful that Toscanini was ever an immature musician, stylistically at a loss and unable to control his men. If I were told that his *Aïda* in 1886 was equal to the one I heard in 1949 I should be tempted to believe it. In any case, because the performances of his youth and middle life were experienced by few Americans, let us not suppose that they were any less miraculous than those of his later years.

Writing of that 1908 *Aïda* that opened the Metropolitan season and introduced Toscanini to New York, Richard Aldrich says:

"He is a strenuous force, a dominating power, a man of potent authority, a musician of infinite resource. He had the performance at every point firmly and directly under his hand. . . . He is a man that insists on a clear-cut outline, on abundant detail, on the strongest contrasts, on vivid color. In fortissimos the brasses could not blow loudly enough for him, nor could the crescendos be brought to climaxes fulminating enough. But there were other and finer points that could not have escaped the attention of the close observer; the fine modeling of phrases, the symmetry of musical outline in many places where mere brute force was not in question. And the pulsating, dramatic blood he sent coursing through the score was never allowed to stagnate. . . . This prevailing spirit influenced every member of the cast. . . . Caruso . . . sang with probably more power, with more insistent dwelling on the highest tones, with a more prodigal expenditure of his resources, than ever he has achieved before. . . ."[2]

This was probably the finest *Aïda* New York had ever heard, and it typified what was to come. He gave them Italian repertory, including *Falstaff*, and the first performance in the United States of *Le Villi*, Puccini's first opera—a work in one act that he paired with *Cavalleria Rusticana*—and, in remembrance of Catalani, *La Wally*. There was an abridged version of *Die Götterdämmerung*, a memorable *Carmen*, and a special concert program of the Verdi *Requiem* and the prelude to Boito's *Mefistofele* which he led four times. On his return to Italy he prepared a concert in Naples to honor the memory of his friend Martucci, who had died earlier that year.

In the 1909-10 season he offered the Verdi *Requiem* twice and prepared both *Tristan und Isolde* and *Die Meistersinger* in addition to Italian operas and a revival of Gluck's *Orfeo*. In the spring the company went to Paris, and Toscanini found himself assigned to show Europeans the excellence of an American musical organization. (Twenty years later he was to repeat the demonstration with the New York Philharmonic.) He did his job well.

Toscanini's third New York season contained the world première of an opera on "an American subject"—Puccini's *The Girl of the Golden West*, a work that is musically completely Italian in idiom and American only in its setting and its absurd, melodramatic plot. None the less, it was taken as a compliment and was a success. A more important American première was Paul Dukas' opera *Ariane et Barbe-Bleu*, which received no comparable acclaim. For the rest, there were Toscanini performances of *Die Meistersinger*, *Tristan*, *Otello*, Gluck's *Armide*, in its first Metropolitan production (which held the stage for a single season), and

2 *Concert Life in New York* [New York: G. P. Putnam's Sons, 1941], pp. 234-35.

a number of standard Italian scores. Much the same fare was offered in the 1911-12 season. Toscanini was working hard, but he was satisfied with his audience and his results. That summer in Buenos Aires he repeated the Dukas without great public recognition and led a demanding schedule of German and Italian works.

It was not until the 1912-13 season, his fifth at the Metropolitan, that New York heard him conduct a symphony concert. The high light of the opera that year had been the American première in March of Mussorgsky's *Boris Godunov*, which was sung in Italian. Toscanini did not approve of opera being sung in several languages from the same stage at the same time. He never gave *Boris* in Russian. Chaliapin, who had been given rough and unjustified treatment by the New York critics during the 1907-08 season, declined the offer to return, in spite of his admiration of Toscanini which resulted from their work together at La Scala. (He did not sing the role at the Metropolitan until 1921, long after Toscanini had left its pit.) On April 13 (and again on the eighteenth), 1913, Toscanini led the "somewhat augmented" Metropolitan Opera Orchestra in Wagner's *A Faust Overture,* Strauss's *Till Eulenspiegel* and the Beethoven *Ninth Symphony,* in which Frieda Hempel, Louise Homer, Karl Jörn, Putnam Griswold, and the chorus of the opera house were heard in the vocal parts.

Richard Aldrich wrote of the concert:

"The orchestra in the years that it has been under the control of Mr. Toscanini has gained greatly in suppleness and plasticity as well as in precision and perfection of ensemble. . . . He revealed in the fullest measure the qualities of the great symphonic conductor. In [the *Ninth Symphony*] Mr. Toscanini met in an unusual degree Wagner's criterion of the *melos,* of keeping unbroken the essentially melodic line that underlies it. The orchestra sang throughout, and in all the nuances of the performance the melodic line was not interrupted; nor in all the plastic shaping of the phrase was the symmetry of the larger proportion of the organic unit of the whole lost sight of. It was

rhythmically of extraordinary vitality. It was a conservative reading without exaggerations or excesses. There
were subtle and significant modulations of tempo, but
never of a disturbing sort. It was devoted to the exposition
of Beethoven and not of Mr. Toscanini, and it rose to
heights of eloquence without the intrusion of the conductor's personality."[3]

The description matches what we heard later, and there
is no question that the *Ninth* given to New York in 1913 was
equal in every way to the fine performances of 1927-52
with which we are more familiar.

During the 1913-14 season he worked harder than ever.
Montemezzi's *L'Amore dei Tre Re* was given its American
première, and he continued to offer *Boris, Tristan, Meistersinger,* and Italian reportory.

One might ask again why a man of these powers should
not receive the full co-operation of management and sympathetic understanding from the public, but friction was
developing again. During the 1914-15 season the situation
built up to the threatening explosion. Although the company
was not operating with a deficit, Otto H. Kahn, the most
powerful member of the Metropolitan Opera Board, wanted
to reduce costs and introduced a number of petty economies
which served only to infuriate Toscanini, who was beginning
to look upon the star system, the socialite boors in the
audience, and some of the other aspects of the situation
with increasing aversion.

He managed to hold out until April, leading Wagner and
Weber, his Italian reportory, and even preparing special con-
fections like Giordano's *Madame Sans-Gêne* for Farrar. Then
the pressure mounted as high as it could go; there was a scene
with Gatti-Casazza, and Giorgio Polacco, a *routinier* for
whom Toscanini had only contempt, took over his scheduled
performances while the management announced Toscanini's
indisposition. Ill-disposition would have been better; so intense was his anger that he had no qualms about appearing
in public in New York while Polacco filled in at the opera

[3] *Ibid.,* pp. 395-97.

house for poor, sick Maestro Toscanini. Although he led concerts in the Metropolitan Opera House in later years, he never again appeared under the auspices of the Opera Board, and New York did not hear him conduct an operatic performance again for twenty-nine years, until he prepared *Fidelio* with the N.B.C. Symphony in 1944.[4]

At the end of the season he returned to an Italy which was on the verge of war. He had appeared in his homeland on only three occasions since his departure from La Scala in 1908; giving symphony concerts in Milan and Naples in 1909 and 1912 and preparing *Falstaff* and *La Traviata* at Busseto in 1913 to commemorate the hundredth anniversary of the birth of Verdi. Again he rejected offers and voluntarily entered into a period of inactivity. He was now forty-eight and had been a conductor for nearly thirty years. He led a few benefits, for which he accepted no fee, spent his savings, sold his house, and played with the idea of returning to the orchestra as a 'cellist, sparing himself the strain, the responsibility, and the frustrations of directing opera under the prevailing conditions.

After the tragic debacle which led to the internment of Karl Muck (a German national) as an alleged enemy agent (and real victim of wartime demagoguery), the Boston Symphony Orchestra approached Toscanini, offering him the musical direction of the orchestra for the 1918-1919 season. Referring to the Muck episode, Frederick P. Cabot, president of the orchestra, wrote that "a conductor such as you whose loyalty to the Allied cause is beyond possibility of question" could have "sole artistic responsibility" in all matters. The Italian government urged Toscanini to take the post, but for reasons that have never been clear he refused. The salary offered was less than he had received at the Metropolitan, but the duties were also less demanding. Perhaps Toscanini didn't like the idea of being given only a one year contract, or perhaps it was simply (as he remarked later) that he felt Boston was a dull city. In any case, he stayed

---

[4] He offered the third act of *Rigoletto* in a concert performance in Madison Square Garden in May, 1944, but I do not regard this as, properly speaking, an operatic production.

in Italy and continued to give benefits, even though super-patriots were continually harassing him because of his insistence upon playing music by Beethoven and Wagner. No sensible person could have questioned Toscanini's devotion to his country. His son, Walter, was an artillery officer in the Italian army, and the Maestro himself, although too old for active service, was decorated after he led a military band under fire at the battle of Monte Santo.

In 1920, his fifty-third year behind him, he resumed professional employment leading symphony concerts in Rome and Padua. La Scala had been closed by the war, and its doors were still shut. The problem was to secure a financial basis for the operations of the house. Toscanini was interested only in artistic quality: impresarios with their eyes on the till, rich patrons with tendencies to give orders, these he had seen and wished to see no more. This time he got his way. The new organization of the house provided public funds to pay the bills and put artistic supervision in the hands of the musical director. There had to be a new orchestra, and after it had been engaged, it had to be given something to do until the house was ready. During the summer and autumn of 1920 Toscanini selected and rehearsed his men, and two tours were arranged, one in the United States and Canada and another in Italy.

A "tumult of welcome" awaited him in New York. The orchestra landed on the thirteenth of December, and on the eighteenth began a historic series of acoustical recordings for the Victor Talking Machine Company in a church in Camden, New Jersey, where they were to hold eight further recording sessions prior to their return to Italy in March. On the twenty-eighth this initial battle with sound reproduction was forgotten and Toscanini returned to the stage of the Metropolitan Opera House to play to the Italian ambassador and an auditorium packed with persons who, as Richard Aldrich pointed out, hardly knew him as a symphony conductor. The program began with the national anthems of the United States and Italy and went on to the Vivaldi *Concerto No. 8 in A Minor* for strings, the Beethoven *Fifth,* Debussy's *Ibéria,* Respighi's *The Fountains of Rome,* and the *Prelude and*

Liebestod from *Tristan,* a typical Toscanini concert which he might have offered at any time between 1926 and 1954 without anyone remarking on the program. The opera auditorium did not do the orchestra justice, and the clean, transparent lines of sound which must have been produced in the Debussy and Respighi were not projected well. When he played his second concert, moving to Carnegie Hall (apparently his first appearance in the auditorium in which he was to lead so many triumphant performances) on January 3, 1921, the acoustics served him better. All in all he gave seven concerts in New York, five in the first series and a final pair in March. In a special concert at the New York Hippodrome on the sixteenth of January he played Dvořák's *New World Symphony.* The Beethoven *Seventh,* Brahms *Second,* Wagnerian excerpts, and contemporary Italian works were heard at other times.

The tour took him to twenty-five cities. He faced this circuit of North America with limited English and a defective geographic sense. The public was dazzled, he was presented with a golden baton, Italian neighborhoods turned out in droves, he missed trains, tangled with well-wishers, and all was a most infuriating hubbub at times. Even with the family records at one's disposal, it is impossible to tell where all he went. (Some thirty years later when he made his second tour of the United States one of the running jokes was that often the Maestro could not recall whether he was visiting a place for the first or second time.)

Chicago heard him twice, February thirteenth and twenty-seventh. It was his first appearance there as a symphony conductor, although Chicagoans had heard him lead opera with the Metropolitan in a tour some years before. On February thirteenth, he played the same program as he had at his opening concert in New York, and on his return offered the Brahms *Second, Don Juan,* the *William Tell Overture,* and Respighi's *Suite of Ancient Airs and Dances.* The drive to the west included stops in Des Moines, Omaha and Topeka where a Toscanini concert offered a musical experience that only the more widely traveled of the citizens could have encountered previously. On February twentieth Kansas City heard a program that included the *New World Symphony,* and *Juventus* by Victor de Sabata (better known today as a conductor), the *Tristan Prelude and Liebestod*, *The Star-Spangled Banner*, and *Garibaldi's War Hymn*. Convention Hall was packed, as well it might have been for such a program. There has probably not been a concert to equal it in Kansas City since!

The De Sabata orchestration of *The Star-Spangled Banner* stunned the critic in Columbus, Ohio, who wrote that the national anthem was "played as no American orchestra has ever played it." His reaction to the program as a whole was one common among those who write about Toscanini: "never in a thousand years could we describe this. . . ." The St. Louis critic ventured that "such speed was never witnessed or heard" before. A loop through upper New York and New England brought the same praise, and Boston listeners had grounds for mingling with their enjoyment a sense of regret that he had not been persuaded to become director of their own orchestra. Having made a circuit that included Portland, Maine, and the Canadian cities of Montreal and Toronto in the north, Tulsa in the west, Richmond in the south, and all major points in the center, Toscanini and his orchestra sailed home in April. In one respect they had made a miscalculation: several of the best players remained behind to lend their virtuosity to American orchestras, just as an earlier tour of the band of the French Garde Républicaine provided the Boston Symphony with some brilliant instrumentalists. Italy greeted the returning orchestra like a conquering Roman legion, and its tour of its homeland was, if anything, an ever greater series of triumphs.

La Scala reopened in December, 1921 with *Falstaff*, and the repertory for the first season contained *Meistersinger* and *Boris* as well as Italian works. The following year Toscanini prepared a revival of *The Magic Flute*, which the public accepted coolly (Mozart was not especially popular in Italy), and his symphonic series at the close of the season included the *Ninth Symphony* of Beethoven and the Verdi *Requiem*. The 1923-24 season contained new productions of *Tristan* and *Orfeo*, another work from Toscanini's Metropolitan repertory which he transferred to La Scala. All was going well; it was too good to last, and it didn't.

Mussolini was now in power and out to assert himself. Particularly he wanted the Fascist anthem *Giovinezza* played at La Scala on Empire Day, April twenty-first. In 1924 Toscanini refused, saying that such music was not played in a theater of the caliber of La Scala and the orchestral material was not available. For a short time he could get away with such an artistic defense, winning support among Mussolini's own inner circle, but it was obvious that the Fascist dictator could not be held at bay permanently. Trouble was coming, and Toscanini was preparing to meet it. Early in 1925 he allowed it to be known that he would like to return to New York, and the management of the Philharmonic eagerly took him up. They were out to drive a hard bargain, and instructed their representative to keep Toscanini's fee as low as would satisfy him and avoid, if possible, a surcharge for his traveling expenses, indicating that Willem Mengelberg, the principal conductor of the orchestra, paid his own passage. At the close of the negotiations, Toscanini got the fee he had requested, plus an allowance to pay the United States income tax, plus an allowance for transportation.

The 1925-26 season was, therefore, the first of the eleven in which Toscanini appeared with the Philharmonic. The management had anticipated "a very extraordinary artistic success for Mr. Toscanini's concerts with the Philharmonic" and they lived up to expectations. He led the orchestra for the first time in a Carnegie Hall concert on January 14, 1926. The program was typical Toscanini fare: opening with Haydn's *Clock Symphony* and Respighi's *Pines of Rome*. *The Swan of Tuonela*, one of the few Sibelius works in his repertory, came after the interval and was followed by his concert version of *Siegfried's Death and Funeral Music* from *Götterdämmerung*, a Wagnerian excerpt that appeared frequently in his American programs, and the overture to Weber's opera *Euryanthe*. He was only a guest conductor that season, and at the completion of his series in February he returned to his duties at La Scala.

That year back at La Scala, he prepared the première of *Turandot*, which had been left unfinished at Puccini's death and was performed in the form in which the composer had left it. The first Italian performance of Debussy's *Martyrdom of Saint Sebastian* was another innovation. Again there was a performance of *Falstaff* at Busseto to commemorate an anniversary of Verdi: in this case the passing of twenty-five years since his death. Another such date loomed: the hundredth anniversary of the death of Beethoven. Toscanini began his 1926-27 season by giving the nine symphonies in both Milan and Turin and introducing *Fidelio* into the repertory at La Scala. His series with the Philharmonic was cut short by illness in February, but he gave the *First, Third, Fifth,* and *Ninth* of the Beethoven symphonies, with Elisabeth Rethberg, Louise Homer, Richard Crooks, and Fraser Gange as his soloists in the latter work. In spite of his short stay, he took the orchestra out of town, and one of his four concerts was in the Academy of Music at Philadelphia.

. The 1927-28 season marks his transition from a guest conductor to one of the principal conductors of the orchestra. The Philharmonic-Symphony Orchestra of New York, as it was called after its amalgamation with the New York Symphony, had too long and demanding a schedule for one conductor to lead, and the practice then, as today, was to rotate the concerts among a group of conductors, each being responsible for a portion of the season. The greater part of the season through this period was directed by Willem Mengelberg, who did not leave the Philharmonic until 1930. Toscanini began the season at La Scala and went to New York late in January, 1928. He led over forty concerts during the weeks remaining in the orchestral season, the largest number of appearances he had made with the Philharmonic up to that time. A short spring tour took the orchestra to Baltimore, Washington, Philadelphia, Buffalo and Pittsburgh.

The autumn of 1928 found him giving symphony concerts in Milan and preparing for the season at La Scala. On December 26, 1928 he celebrated the thirtieth anniversary of his first season as a regular conductor at the house with the same opera he had chosen in 1898—*Die Meistersinger*. It was a gloomy year, none the less. Mussolini was putting on pressure and it was a relief to get to New York in February. His series there was shorter than that of the previous year, twenty-five concerts, seven of them out of town. The spring tour this time included Philadelphia, Baltimore, Washington, Pittsburgh and Rochester.

On his return to La Scala he embarked on another tour in May, taking the company to Vienna and then to Berlin. There was a grim note underlying this triumphal procession, for Toscanini knew that it was the end of his association with the company. His third La Scala period, the one that had promised the fullest opportunities for the realization of opera in an atmosphere of artistic perfection, was about to close after eight seasons, the victim of Fascism. He showed the Vienna and Berlin audiences what Italian opera could be, and then he took his leave. He had been with La Scala a total of fifteen seasons, and although he was to conduct there again, in triumph, in 1946, he never again was to enter the house as its musical director.

By the autumn of 1929 he belonged to New York, and Clarence H. Mackay and the Philharmonic Board eagerly awaited the opportunity to display their prized possession before the musical world. There was no longer any question over who was principal conductor of the orchestra, and Mengelberg was about to disappear for good. In future seasons the podium would be shared with men who were *persona grata* to Toscanini, as Mengelberg had ceased to be for some time. Toscanini was now entering his fifth season with the orchestra. They had prepared enough music together so that his programs became more flexible; rather than repeat a work several times, he might pick up a composition that had been given the season before, polish it briefly in rehearsal, and include it in a concert. Again one saw Toscanini at work as an orchestra builder. In 1954 one had final proof of his skill when his N.B.C. Symphony played brilliantly in concert without a conductor, but the same thing was happening with the Philharmonic. After the Maestro taught them a piece, he could recreate the performance in short order.

Toscanini conducted eighty-three concerts with the Philharmonic between his appearance on the opening night of the season, October 3, 1929, and its triumphant close in London, June 4, 1930. The European tour began on the third of May at the Paris Opera, and in the month to follow there were twenty-three concerts drawing upon a huge repertory for a touring orchestra—thirty-four compositions. From Paris the orchestra moved on south, to Zurich, and then into Italy where Toscanini returned to the La Scala stage with his American musicians and showed the Milan audience what they could do. In Turin there was a clash with the Fascists. The Princess of Piedmont attended the concert. Protocol demanded that the "Royal March" be played for her, but Mussolini's decree specified that *Giovinezza* must follow. Toscanini had fought that battle once and was not giving in, even if it meant no Turin concert. A compromise was reached. A local band (Winthrop Sargeant, who was a member of the orchestra at the time, writes in his *Geniuses, Goddesses and People* that it looked like a group of street cleaners) marched in and played the offensive airs while Toscanini stood on the podium with an unmerciful look fixed upon them. The Philharmonic went on to Rome, Florence, Munich, Vienna, Budapest, Prague, Leipzig, Dresden, Berlin, Brussels, and finally to London. Everywhere the public and the press exhibited the familiar reaction: if one had not heard Toscanini one had never heard this music before. A Berlin critic wrote: "The Toscanini orchestra is a perfectly and thoroughly trained instrument that is absolutely mastered by one mind."

After fifteen cities and twenty-three concerts one would expect Toscanini to be tired. Not at all. He had given two concerts in Paris, Milan, Rome, Vienna and Berlin, but for his first appearance before the British public he decided upon four programs, beginning in the Albert Hall on June 1st and closing in Queen's Hall, after four strenuous evenings of music, on June 4th. The opening night was an occasion. George the Fifth and his queen attended; so did Bernard Shaw and several thousand others. In properly solid prose the *Times* had its say the next morning:

"English musicians have been awaiting the opportunity of hearing Signor Toscanini in London for many years, and hopes held out from time to time that he might accept an engagement to conduct an orchestra here have remained unfulfilled. . . . [The concert was] an experience worth waiting for and a rich reward for patience. . . . There was no question about the absolute finish and clarity of yesterday's performances, a clarity which even the Albert Hall could not obscure, at any rate for long at a time. . . ."

Toscanini introduced himself to London by playing *God Save the King, The Star-Spangled Banner,* and the overture to Rossini's *The Italian Woman in Algiers* (the *Times* thought it trivial) in that order. Later there was the Brahms *Second,* and the concerts on the following evenings included the Mussorgsky-Ravel *Pictures at an Exhibition,* Debussy's *La Mer,* and Elgar's *Enigma Variations,* which was a more pronounced success with a British audience than the breathtaking Toscanini performance of Debussy's great score. The critic of the *Times* was not immune to the general feeling, ". . . the virtuosity of the players," he wrote, "and their extraordinary adaptability to their conductor's highly individual conceptions of the music completely carried the audience away. . . ." Indeed, after hearing the imprecise, underrehearsed performances of many British orchestras, it must have been quite an experience. The Elgar was not thought to be wholly satisfactory, although the *Times* conceded that ". . . probably never has the 'Troyte' variation been played with a more electric energy, or 'Nimrod' attained such an overwhelming final climax," but it was clear that no Italian conductor with an American orchestra was to be allowed to beat the British in their own music on their home ground, and the discussion went on to claim that Toscanini's ideas were "too definite for a satisfying reading of Elgar" whose "elusive quality" was lost in "this highly organized interpretation." To find that "elusive quality" all one had to do, I feel, was satisfy chauvinism by presenting a British orchestra, furiously sightreading under a beknighted conductor. I doubt if Toscanini took such criticism seriously.

Clarence H. Mackay, who had been sent regular reports on the tour (the satisfaction that it gave him was all the return he had for the more than two hundred thousand dollars it cost the backers of the orchestra), cabled congratulations and advice: ". . . overjoyed and frankly relieved that tour is at an end, and hope that . . . you will kick up your heels in a non-prohibition country . . . hurrah for the Philharmonic Orchestra born in 1842."

The question arose: "Why not tour the United States at the close of the 1930-31 season?" But Mackay did not support the idea. Like many upper-class Easterners he was oriented toward Europe rather than the hinterland of his own country. He wanted to send the Philharmonic to show Paris, Berlin and Vienna what a great orchestra New York could claim, but he had no desire to impress Des Moines, Iowa. The American radio audience that listened to Toscanini's Sunday broadcasts were therefore obliged to travel to New York if they wanted to hear him in a hall. Mackay argued that such an undertaking would be too hard on Toscanini, and that he wished "to avoid overtaxing this great and unique machine" since "at the end of the season he is very tired and nervous and acts like an overtrained athlete. . . ." That was the end of the American tour.

If Toscanini needed a long rest, he didn't show it, or take it. He was off to Bayreuth to conduct at the sacred Festspielhaus for the first time. He whipped an indifferent pit orchestra into shape and produced *Tristan* and *Tannhäuser*. It was his second triumph of the year. Then he gave himself a vacation.

In the autumn he was back in Carnegie Hall for the 1930-31 season with the Philharmonic. Erich Kleiber and Bernardino Molinari were the other principal conductors, and for two weeks in late November and early December Leopold Stokowski conducted in New York while Toscanini led the Philadelphia Orchestra, his first guest appearance away from the Philharmonic in the six seasons he had been in New York. Everything considered, Toscanini's relations with Stokowski were good, and it was not until the 1943-44 season when they were both conducting the N.B.C. Symphony that the Maestro's regard for him declined. There were sixty-two Toscanini concerts, including the usual loops down to Washington in the winter and spring. During the months when the Philharmonic did not require him he divided his time between his home in Milan and a villa he rented for many years which, with its grounds, occupied the whole of the Isolino di San

Giovanni in Lago Maggiore in the foothills of the Alps.

On the fifteenth of January, 1931, Winifred Wagner had cabled Toscanini: *"Parsifal* is yours. May I ask you to conduct *Tannhäuser* too because this opera wants your protection most of all? . . ."* He agreed to return to Bayreuth. In May, after the close of the Philharmonic season, he went to Bologna to prepare a pair of concerts in memory of Martucci, but found that the Fascists were ready to put their maximum pressure upon him. A political gathering was scheduled for the same day as the first concert, followed by a banquet, and he was informed that when the officials took their places in the concert hall the *Royal March* should be played. Toscanini refused. The *Royal March* was for the king, Toscanini felt, and, if the king were to be present, he would play it. But he would not play it for a gang of Fascist politicians. On his arrival at the theater on May 14 Toscanini encountered a mob that was out for trouble, and as he left his car he and his wife and elder daughter were attacked. Fortunately he was equal to the occasion, and they made their escape, first to a hotel, where they were abused verbally from the street. During the night Toscanini and his family drove to Milan where he was held in house arrest for about three weeks before being permitted to leave the country. He did not attempt to conduct in Italy again until 1946, but even his efforts to live quietly in his homeland, avoiding political issues, were thwarted in later years by politically-inspired passport difficulties.

Bayreuth went well musically, but Toscanini found his health suddenly impaired by bursitis. He carried on in pain, leading *Tannhäuser* and *Parsifal* with his left arm at times, but the Philharmonic season was too much to face. He led fifteen concerts and returned to Italy to rest and recoup his health. In April he was feeling recovered somewhat and returned to New York for a post-season benefit which raised $26,000 for musicians unemployed because of the depression. In June he went up to Paris to lead a special concert in memory of Debussy.

Inactivity had its rewards. In October, 1932, he opened the Philharmonic season, and led sixty-five concerts before his return to Italy in the early summer. In the spring there was a

Beethoven cycle, the first of several he was to offer in New York, and later in the year he accepted short engagements in Paris, Vienna, Copenhagen, and Stockholm. Bayreuth was now in Nazi hands, and Toscanini refused to go near it, although Hitler had personally appealed to him to return. The Nazi treatment of Jewish musicians offended Toscanini as if it had been intended as a personal affront. During the seasons 1931-34 he shared the podium of the Philharmonic with Bruno Walter, an old and respected friend who had suffered from the Nazi persecution.

In 1933-34 he returned to the orchestra a man of sixty-six, past the normal age for retirement in many professions. He cut down his schedule. Again there was a Beethoven cycle in the spring, which included this time the first Toscanini performances of the *Missa Solemnis,* but in all there were only forty-four Toscanini concerts that season. He was active in the summer, appearing in Paris and participating for the first time in the Salzburg Festival. In 1934-35 he shared the Philharmonic with five other conductors, among them Otto Klemperer, and Artur Rodzinski. His own appearances were down to thirty-five concerts, seventeen of which were given to his first Brahms cycle with the orchestra.

Toscanini returned to London in June of 1935 to lead a series of four concerts in Queen's Hall with the British Broadcasting Corporation Symphony. His British public had been eager to hear him again since his visit five years before, and welcomed him with the warmth and friendship he had known for so long in America. His programs included the *Enigma Variations,* still played *his* way, the Brahams *Fourth,* the Beethoven *Seventh, La Mer,* and familiar works by Mozart, Rossini, Mendelssohn, and Wagner. The B.B.C. Symphony was somewhat augmented for this series, and he found it a well-trained and responsive ensemble.

The summer of 1935 was a brilliant one at Salzburg. Toscanini prepared *Falstaff* and *Fidelio,* the latter with Lotte Lehmann who was then at the height of her powers, as well as symphonic programs with the Vienna Philharmonic. All seemed tranquil, but when he was unable to return to New York in time for the opening of the Philharmonic season the management, without asking his consent, engaged Sir Thomas Beecham to fill in for him. An explosion followed.

Toscanini stood by his rights as artistic director of the orchestra and challenged the right of the Philharmonic management to engage another conductor without his approval. Otto Klemperer, who was also to direct the orchestra that year, was *persona grata* because it was Toscanini who had arranged for his invitation. Beecham was another matter. Toscanini regarded him as something of a dilettante and had consistently declined to conduct at Covent Garden, which was then under Beecham's direction, because by Toscanini's standards the British informality in the rehearsal and scenic preparation of opera was inimical to high artistic standards. In an angry mood Toscanini reviewed his various clashes with the orchestra management and cabled that he would not return for the season following—that of 1936-37—and in the spring of 1936, stubborn and tired, he stuck to his decision.

There were thirty-three Toscanini concerts that year, including a special pair in Symphony Hall, Boston, in March when the Philharmonic was sponsored by the Boston Symphony Orchestra. He played Beethoven, Brahms, Weber, Wagner, Verdi, Debussy: composers he knew and felt deeply in mind and heart. In all his years in America he was virtually the only conductor of great reputation who never appeared with the Boston Symphony, and the tension which existed between himself and Koussevitzky had been a factor which deterred him from visiting Boston with the Philharmonic, although he appeared regularly in nearby Hartford, Connecticut. Even in 1950, after Koussevitzky had retired, he did not include Boston in his tour with the N.B.C. Symphony.

In New York, in April, 1936, he ended his subscription series with the same program he had played on his first appearance with the Philharmonic more than a decade before, led a farewell concert, and took his leave. He was sixty-nine and had been a conductor for fifty years. When he left New York, few thought that they would ever see him there again.

In the summer he returned to Salzburg once more, where his principal offering was *Die Meistersinger*, and in December of 1936 he went to Palestine where he led the first concerts of the orchestra which Bronislaw Hubermann had formed from some of the many fine Jewish musicians displaced by Hitler's racial decrees. (Afterwards the orchestra became the Palestine Symphony.) Barnstorming around Europe appealed to him. He visited Paris again, where he lectured to one of the violinists in the orchestra for bowing his own way. The offender's name was Charles Munch. In 1937 Toscanini made a second appearance in Stockholm and celebrated his seventieth birthday with the Vienna Philharmonic. In late May he was back in London for his second series with the B.B.C. Symphony. There were six concerts and a trip up to Oxford, where he serenaded the university with the *Pastoral* and the Brahms *First* in a benefit concert for the University of Oxford endowment fund. When offered the D. Mus. degree, *honoris causa,* he declined, as he customarily declined honors of this type. Being Dr. Toscanini meant nothing to him.

Again summer drew him to Salzburg, but this time there was Nazi Kultur in the air, and his production of Mozart's *The Magic Flute,* which drew a mixed reception, could well be taken as an act of homage and farewell to that composer's native city. Furtwängler was there to conduct the Beethoven *Ninth*. Toscanini resented his apparent capitulation to the Nazis and treated him with scorn. "We do not need you in Salzburg" Toscanini told him. "We have Bruno Walter."

In November there was a Toscanini reading of the *Ninth* in London with the B.B.C., and in an earlier program he gave his British public the *German Requiem* of Brahms.

To the delight of his American audience, his next move was to return to New York, where those who had witnessed his departure, nineteen months before, with justifiable gloom were prepared to rejoice that he had changed his mind and decided to return and undertake further musical activity.

The idea of engaging Toscanini and creating a new symphony orchestra for his broadcast concerts apparently came from David Sarnoff, who was president of the Radio Corporation of America at that time, and early in 1937 Samuel Chotzinoff went to Europe to act as Sarnoff's emissary. Toscanini was in Italy, living in semi-retirement, and, although willing to discuss the matter, was hesitant about the labors involved. As he described the situation in his letter to Sarnoff in 1954 (when he indicated his intention to retire permanently), "You will remember how reluctant I was to accept your invitation because I felt at that time that I was too old to start a new venture. However, you persuaded me and all of my doubts were dispelled as soon as I began rehearsing for the first broadcast. . . ."

The offer was appealing. Artur Rodzinski, whom Toscanini had personally introduced to Salzburg in 1936 and 1937, accepted Toscanini's invitation to engage and train the ensemble and share it with him during the winter season. Taking a leave of absence from his own orchestra in Cleveland, Rodzinski spent two months auditioning players and put many hours into drilling them into shape before the Maestro began preparation for his opening concert. Indeed, he drew the indignant wrath of his Cleveland trustees by engaging for Toscanini some of the best players from his own orchestra.

Toscanini's seventeen seasons with the N.B.C. Symphony proved to be his longest period of association with any musical organization. He never felt that the Philharmonic belonged to him. Other conductors led it for much of the season, and the management was never out of sight. To make the break even stronger, he had not been consulted about the appointment of his successor, and the job had gone to John Barbirolli rather than his candidate—Rodzinski. It was six years before he relented and, in honor of the orchestra's one hundredth anniversary, went back to conduct it again.

The seasons with the N.B.C. Symphony began with Vivaldi, the Mozart *Symphony No. 40,* and the *First Symphony* of Brahms on Christmas night, 1937, at ten o'clock. The audience, on entering a concert room known by the graceless name of Studio 8-H, Radio City, Rockefeller Center, New York (and presently to be called names that were worse than graceless by the serious musical public), read on their programs: "Since the modern microphone is extremely sensitive, your co-operation in maintaining silence during the music is urgently requested."

Sensitive or not, the change from the Philharmonic and Carnegie Hall to a new orchestra and a broadcasting studio was not brought about without a loss. It took more than a season of hard work to get the N.B.C. as responsive to his desires as the Philharmonic or the B.B.C. Orchestra had been, and what one heard in those early concerts was a fine, professional orchestra with which Rodzinski could secure excellent results, but which had not become sensitized through long association to Toscanini's desires and highly individual rehearsal methods. The only orchestra Toscanini ever trained from the very beginning was the La Scala ensemble he brought to America in 1920. There, of course, no language barrier existed. In the early years with his American orchestras Toscanini did not talk a great deal. They simply played for many minutes at a time, going over works again and again until the Maestro was satisfied. Rodzinski, who not only talked a great deal but was able to analyze difficulties and tell the men in detail how to cope with them, got his results much faster. The divided command soon ended. Toscanini broke with Rodzinski before the end of the second season. Eventually the N.B.C. became an instrument reflecting Toscanini's musical ideas, but it was a prolonged and sometimes violent training period.

There were further losses. In theory, anyway, when the Philharmonic was playing in Carnegie Hall anyone who wanted to attend could buy a ticket and go. When Toscanini returned to lead the N.B.C. Symphony this came to an end. Studio 8-H, although ample as broadcasting studios go, was not a large hall, and since the tickets to the concerts were not for sale, only a few members of the public could count on getting in to hear the orchestra in a "live" performance. Even so, Studio 8-H was not a good place in which to listen to an orchestra because of the acoustical treatment which eliminated all resonance. For the same reason it was not an ideal place to record or to broadcast an orchestra, although heard from the air in the New York area the concerts were comparable with most commercial sound reproduction of the day. Chicago (say) was a different matter, for after the music had traveled through a thousand miles of telephone lines the limitations in frequency response and volume had turned it into a pale substitute for the original.

In the spring and summer following his first thirteen radio concerts he was again active in Europe. Again he gave a series of concerts in Palestine without fee as a gesture of friendship to the unfortunates who had been driven from their homes by Hitler and as a gesture of defiance to the dictator. It was a costly gesture. Mussolini, who was becoming anti-Semitic at Hitler's behest, denied Toscanini further right to enter or leave Italy. In May he was in London with the B.B.C. Symphony for a series of six concerts extending into the middle of June. The major work was the Verdi *Requiem* and the shorter *Te Deum,* which he offered twice. There was Vaughan Williams' *Fantasia on a Theme of Thomas Tallis*, the Sibelius *Second Symphony,* the *Second Brandenburg Concerto* of Bach, a composer whose music he rarely played, and a generous offering of Beethoven, Brahms, Mozart, Schubert, and Strauss. The Anschluss had taken place earlier in 1938, and "liberated" Salzburg was now intolerable to him. His second public concert with the N.B.C. Symphony in Carnegie Hall on March 4, 1938, had been intended as a benefit for the Salzburg Festival, but when he saw the way political currents were flowing, he directed that the proceeds should go to unemployed musicians in New York with a smaller portion to the Verdi Casa di Riposo in Milan, the great composer's home for retired musicians, a cause which had always been close to Toscanini's heart. He joined Adolf Busch, whose inability to stand Hitler was on a par with his own, and in the two summers remaining before war swept over the continent, they offered their own music festival in neutral Lucerne. The programs were distinguished, among them a special concert at near-by Triebschen where he played the *Siegfried Idyll* on the site of its original performance.

His 1938-39 season with the N.B.C. Symphony was somewhat longer, seventeen broadcasts and a short tour of six concerts as far west as Chicago, which had not seen Toscanini since 1921. London awaited him and a Beethoven festival of nine concerts, of which he led seven (playing the symphonies through in numerical order) and two programs made up largely of concerti which were conducted by Sir Adrian Boult. Both the *Ninth Symphony* and the *Missa*

Solemnis were prepared, the latter work (given twice) serving to close the series and standing as Toscanini's farewell to London for twelve years. As the last days of peace ran to a close he was back in Lucerne, where he repeated the *Siegfried Idyll* with the original small orchestral forces in a private concert at Triebschen and filled the Jesuit Church in Lucerne with a special performance of the Verdi *Requiem*.

There were eighteen concerts in his 1939-40 series with the N.B.C. Symphony, and a nineteenth was added when Toscanini appeared at a benefit in New York with a special small orchestra with Heifetz as its concertmaster to play Mozart's *Musical Joke* (*K. 522*) and a romantic interlude by Gillet.

This year a major tour was planned, to Brazil, Uruguay and Argentina. The orchestra appeared in Providence, Rhode Island, for a pair of concerts in January and February and said *au revoir* to the United States at a concert in Washington on the fourteenth of May. The tour opened in Rio de Janeiro on June 13, scarcely two weeks before the fifty-fourth anniversary of Toscanini's debut there. After a pair of concerts they moved on to São Paulo, and then, on June 19, arrived in Buenos Aires where a series of eight programs was played. It was, undoubtedly, a happy reunion with the South American public that had supported him during difficult years at La Scala. In July there were two concerts in Montevideo, a return visit to São Paulo, and a final pair of concerts in Rio. As a gesture of inter-American friendship and support for the prestige of the United States in critical times it was an unquestioned success; but many North American cities could well envy Buenos Aires those eight concerts and wonder if the Maestro would ever come to play for them.

The 1940-41 season found him, for the first time, restricted to the United States, and so, for only the second time since his return to the United States, he left his own men momentarily and accepted an offer to be guest conductor of another orchestra. In addition to thirteen broadcasts, he went to Chicago and led its symphony for the first (and last) time in a special concert for the musicians' pension fund.

The summer of 1941 nearly saw the end of the N.B.C.

Symphony for the same reason that Toscanini had left the Philharmonic. After questioning the competence of a guest conductor who had engaged, without his approval, for a summer program, Toscanini refused to lead the orchestra in the winter season, feeling that its quality had been impaired and, most of all, that it was no longer his but a property of the radio network. He returned to Argentina in July to give the Beethoven *Ninth* at the Teatro Colón, and it was with the Philadelphia Orchestra that he celebrated his seventy-fifth birthday. He appeared with them in November for a pair of concerts and returning in January and February for six more, which included out-of-town dates in Washington and New York. He had traded orchestras with Stokowski eleven years before, and he still found the Philadelphia a responsive instrument of great beauty. In spite of his feelings about N.B.C. he consented to return for five special broadcast programs in support of the war bond drive.

Mussolini had plunged Italy into the conflict, and the Japanese attack on Pearl Harbor had caused the United States to enter the war in the previous December. Technically the Maestro was an enemy alien, although everyone knew that the Italian Fascists had no more intense foe. In the midst of war Toscanini made peace, first with the Philharmonic and then with the N.B.C. He closed the hundredth season of the Philharmonic with a six-concert Beethoven festival of all nine symphonies and the *Missa Salemnis*. In the summer he was asked to prepare the Shostakovich *Seventh Symphony* for its American première. The score, written during the siege of Leningrad, appealed to him at the time. (Later he considered it bombastic and crude.) He studied the photographic prints of the pages with care (discovering in the process that the Russians had transmitted one of them upside down) and delivered a powerful reading.

In the spirit of the times, he wanted to have an orchestra with which he could hurl his own defiance at the Fascists, and he agreed to return to the N.B.C. for the 1942-43 season. He also consented to give an autumn series with the Philharmonic, repeating the Shostakovich three times in those concerts. His first program began, however, with *The Star-*

Spangled Banner arranged for chorus, soloists, and orchestra and the dramatic symphony *Romeo and Juliet* of Berlioz, which was also given three performances. Later there was an all-Wagner concert, Toscanini's affirmation that great music belonged to the world and that Wagner was the property of neither the German state nor the Nazi party. In November he led a pair of concerts in Philadelphia and brought their orchestra to New York to repeat the program. December found him preparing a benefit for the Red Cross with the Philharmonic. The following February he again led a pension fund concert for another orchestra, this time the Cincinnati Symphony, and went from there to Philadelphia where illness prevented him from giving his final two programs. He never led the Philadelphia Orchestra again. There were fourteen broadcasts in his winter series and three of lighter music in the following summer.

The war continued. In the 1943-44 season there were two special concerts of which the most astonishing was in Madison Square Garden. Leading the N.B.C. orchestra in a program given entirely to "enemy alien" composers, Wagner and Verdi, he raised a sizable amount for the Red Cross. He repeated on this program Verdi's *Hymn of the Nations,* which he had revived in the previous season. When Mussolini finally was overthrown later that year, Toscanini was ready to commemorate the liberation of his homeland. On the ninth of September, with the Beethoven *Fifth,* the *William Tell Overture* and both *The Star-Spangled Banner* and the *Garibaldi's War Hymn* he jubilantly announced to the world the victory of freedom over the dictator whom he had long regarded as a personal adversary. Apart from these great events there were fourteen concerts in his winter series and four summer programs.

During 1944-45 he appeared with the Philharmonic for what proved to be the last time, preparing for the pension fund concert in January the same program of Haydn, Respighi, Sibelius, Weber, and Wagner that had introduced him to them in 1926 and with which he had closed his final series of subscription concerts a decade later. In April of 1945 he traveled to Los Angeles to give the pension fund concert of the Los Angeles Philharmonic Orchestra which Alfred Wallenstein, an old friend from the days in which Wallenstein had been first 'cellist of the Philharmonic, had conducted for a number of seasons. He made his first appearance on the West Coast a memorable one with a program of Rossini, Beethoven, Brahms, Weber, and Wagner specialties.

His N.B.C. series for the 1944-45 season ran for sixteen weeks, and there were six special concerts and two summer appearances. Notable was his production of Beethoven's *Fidelio* with its message of victory over tyranny. As the armies moved across Germany, Toscanini prepared for the victory concert to come, and when in the spring the end of Nazi domination was announced, he and his men played as they had rarely played before. When Japan surrendered he was ready again. For those who heard those concerts, even with the limited fidelity of radio, the effect, the passion, the intensity were unforgettable.

With the war over he wanted to return to Italy. There were seventeen concerts with the N.B.C. in the 1945-46 season, and in April he was once more in his homeland. Somewhat to his surprise, he found himself a hero. Parma had named a street for him, and everywhere he went he was viewed as a symbol of the resistance to Fascism. For the second time he reopened La Scala after a world war. Bombed and bruised, but restored, the historic theater was the setting for a second series of victory concerts, which began the eleventh of May and ended June 24 and 26 with the Beethoven *Ninth*.

Returning to the United States in the autumn, Toscanini marked his eightieth birthday during the 1946-47 season with the N.B.C. He was cutting down his load now. There were only sixteen programs that winter and in the following seasons eighteen and seventeen respectively, but in October of 1947 he took a small ensemble from the N.B.C. Symphony and played a special benefit concert at Ridgefield, Connecticut, to show his friendly feeling for the community and repay the hospitality of the Chotzinoffs, who spent the summer there. Two years later he repeated the gesture. After 1948 he began to make an occasional appearance in Italy again, but he wanted no heavy commitments.

None the less, when it was suggested that he tour the United States at the close of the 1949-50 season, he consented. For years thousands of persons had heard his broadcasts and bought his recordings without ever having an opportunity to experience his performances in terms of living sound in a concert hall. Now, in his twenty-fourth season in the United States since his return in 1926, he would go to them. Again there were seventeen programs in the winter series, and at their close (a public concert in Carnegie Hall) the special train pulled out of New York, bound southward to Baltimore, which knew him from his Philharmonic days, and on to Richmond (where the Frank Black arrangement of *Dixie* as an encore nearly caused a riot since Italian passion and Southern enthusiasm formed an explosive mixture), Atlanta, New Orleans, Houston, Austin, Dallas, Pasadena (where he played two programs), San Francisco, Portland, Seattle, and then eastward again via Denver, St. Louis, Chicago, Detroit, Cleveland, Pittsburgh, Washington and ending on familiar ground in Philadelphia. Everywhere he went he met houses sold out weeks in advance. It is difficult to imagine anyone who could have created more of a furor or commanded greater attention from the press and public on such a tour. In every city the requests for tickets came to a large multiple of the seats available in the hall.

So, his public had seen him at last, had feted him, observed him visiting the sights of their native cities, and tried (without success) to secure comments, interviews, autographs and the rest of the tokens of possession of a celebrity. In the end, he was tired, pleased and ready for an Italian vacation.

Those who had been asking, "How long can he go on?" now began to fear that the answer was at hand. An injury to his kneecap the following season reduced his broadcasts to four, and when he returned in 1951-52 there were only twelve concerts, although his hand seemed to be as strong as ever. That season ended with the Beethoven *Ninth*. There was a pair of summer concerts, the final pair it later proved to be, and in the autumn of 1952, before going to New York, he conducted at La Scala for the last time and gave the four symphonies of Brahms, the *Haydn Variations,* and the *Tragic Overture* in the new Royal Festival Hall, London, with the Philharmonic Orchestra. Queen's Hall, like so many other things, had fallen to Hitler's offensive: but Toscanini took the new auditorium and new orchestra in stride, and the packed hall and thousands of radio listeners heard his brilliant and eloquent farewell to his British audience.

His N.B.C. season in 1952-53 came to fourteen programs, closing with the *Missa Solemnis.* He would have liked to stop, but his friends and family persuaded him to return once more. His powers seemed undiminished. The season 1953-54 got off to a bad start. He was ill and canceled the first two programs, but when he reappeared it was the same Toscanini as ever. In January he offered a concert production of Verdi's *Un Ballo in Maschera* that was brilliantly played and sung. Then, suddenly he seemed very tired. The *German Requiem* of Brahms, which had been planned for the final concert, was replaced by a Wagner program. He did not feel equal to preparing so large and demanding a work. Indeed, in his rehearsals and broadcasts there were moments when he was no longer able to sustain the intensity of earlier years, and the music would suddenly go slack, only to regain its former strength a moment later. He asked to be excused from one of the scheduled programs for a needed rest.

The events of April 3 and 4, when Toscanini made his final public appearances, have been narrated a number of times, yet it is astonishing the inconsistencies and inaccuracies which appear in the various printed accounts. I was present on April 3 for what was to be Toscanini's final rehearsal, and I have heard the stereophonic recording which Victor made of the concert on the 4th. (Earlier I heard this concert in the muddled form in which it came over the N.B.C. broadcast line.) There is no mystery at all what the facts are, which makes it all the more distressing that Mr. Vincent Sheean and Mr. Samuel Chotzinoff should publish narratives more akin to romantic fiction than reporting. Sheean's (in *First and Last Love,* 1956) is a mishmash of memory slips and faulty conjecture. Chotzinoff's method is to subordinate the facts to inventive license and create a dramatic scene, and in his *Toscanini: An Intimate Portrait* this technique is used with far greater frequency than one might first suppose.

When Toscanini celebrated his eighty-seventh birthday on March 25 of 1954 he faced at last the prospect of having retirement forced upon him. His memory was plaguing him. He had nearly canceled the production of *Ballo* in January for fear that he would be unable to retain the score in his mind, and only his reluctance to deprive the singers and orchestra of needed work had led him to surmount his anxiety and carry on. Yet the moments of terror which the opera had brought him were still fresh as he wrote: "Now the sad time has come when I must reluctantly lay aside my baton and say goodbye to my orchestra." It was hard to write the words and harder yet to do the deed. The letter remained unsigned and unmailed until April 2. The network did not release its contents until after the concert of April 4.

The rehearsals did not go well. Worried about himself, Toscanini carried a second burden of concern for his daughter-in-law who lay ill in his great house in Riverdale and, indeed, had just suffered a serious relapse. (Before the end of the summer he was to mourn her death.) He worried, too, for the future of his musicians and the magnificent orchestra he had built, fearing rightly that without him the network could not secure a sponsor for the concerts and would dismiss the orchestra without delay.

When the dress rehearsal was reached Saturday afternoon, April 3, the program was still only roughly prepared. Normally these sessions, to which a small audience was invited, could be treated as informal concerts in which the program was simply played through to make sure all was well. This Saturday there was work to be done. Things got off to a calm start in the *Lohengrin Prelude* and *Forest Murmurs* from *Siegfried*, but in the *Rhine Journey* from *Götterdämmerung* Toscanini became confused and charged the tympanist with anticipating his cue, taking a twelve bar rest when the music called for him to be silent thirteen measures. In fact Toscanini was wrong, although 'cellist Frank Miller urged the tympani player to humor the Old Man by counting an extra bar. By this point, however, nothing could satisfy the Maestro. One can sense the logic of his anger. He was terrified that he might fail his men, and yet he felt that they were failing him. Pouring out his wrath bitterly he left the stage, leaving the program imperfectly prepared.

Many assumed that he would not appear for the concert at all, and the network had a stand-by conductor ready to take his place. Yet as the Sunday hour for the performance drew near, Toscanini announced that he would be there. He had no heart for it. As in his debut, one heard the trooper flinging himself into a bad situation rather than disappoint his audience.

The *Lohengrin, Forest Murmurs,* and *Rhine Journey* went smoothly, and Toscanini then turned to the *Tannhäuser Overture and Bacchanale* which had not been played on Saturday. As Wagner's evocation of the Venusberg neared its close, something disturbed the Maestro. Perhaps, as his son Walter has suggested, it was a combination of overconcentration and unexpected pain as acid perspiration flowed into his sensitive eyes. In any case, the baton faltered, the line of the music went slack, and the performance suddenly became ragged and insecure. As seconds passed the audience prepared for the worst, yet suddenly, as unexpectedly as it had come, the crisis was over. The beat became firm, the ensemble slipped back into its customary precision, and the work closed. No one can know what was in Toscanini's mind at that moment, but we do know what he did. He brought down the stick and plunged into the *Meistersinger Prelude,* which was virtually unrehearsed. Angry at himself, tense, and handicapped by the orchestra's uncertainty of his wishes, he gave a rough performance, and Toscanini of all men knew it. With the closing chord he let the baton fall and left the stage oblivious of the applause. He did not return.

For the millions who were listening on the air, there was an incongruous note, for Guido Cantelli had insisted that the program be cut off at the moment the Maestro got into difficulties, and after the usual banal plea of technical failure the listener was plunged unprepared into the opening bars of the Toscanini recording of the Brahms *First,* a standby record which had been planned for such emergency use. It lasted only a moment, and then, just as suddenly, one was returned to the stage of Carnegie Hall and the final pages of the *Bacchanale.* Because of this many still think that the orchestra stopped playing. It did not. The men did not fail the Maestro this time. Whatever his private agony, they went on and, with their music, drew him back to them.

Less than a fortnight later, on April 13, the network disbanded the orchestra. Toscanini, who had never fired anyone in his life (so far as his son can recall), now felt as if he had fired all his old and loyal friends *en masse.* It was two months before he could bring himself to lead the final pair of recording sessions when, early in June, he made the necessary corrections for the *Aïda* and *Ballo* recordings. Chotzinoff does not mention this and would have us believe that Toscanini appeared punctual and pleasant to make the tapes the following Wednesday—i.e. April 7. The actual dates were June 3 and 5. Shortly afterwards, at the farewell party he gave the men before his departure for Europe, Toscanini was so saddened by the thought that they were almost universally facing unemployment for the following season that he kept to his room, unable to face them.

He returned to Italy, to his island in the Lago Maggiore, to his home in Milan. During the early summer he could find some pleasure in the way in which his men were successfully organizing themselves for existence independent of N.B.C., although when they cabled him in June, asking that he return to lead them again, he was obliged to send only his best wishes. With the memory of his final broadcast remaining to haunt him, he wrote: "my age and my present feeling do not allow me to make plans for the future." In the early autumn the reorganization was completed, and the orchestra, rechristened "The Symphony of the Air," played a Carnegie Hall concert on October 27, 1954, that would have been distinguished in any season, but was particularly noteworthy because the sounds produced were the unique sounds of a Toscanini performance and the conductor's stand was empty.

In December Toscanini appeared at La Scala in the unaccustomed role of a spectator, when he attended the opening performance of the season (Spontini's *La Vestale*) in the box of the artistic director, Victor de Sabata. Earlier he announced that in the spring he would prepare *Falstaff* for the opening of La Piccola Scala, a new, small theatre built in a former courtyard at La Scala, but the curse that seemed to hang over his relations with the house continued to pursue him. His presence at rehearsals inspired some of the personnel to unexpected heights, but there were other rehearsals which he would not attend. Herbert von Karajan, whom he continued to consider (together with the late Wilhelm Furtwängler) a Nazi, had been invited to do *Carmen,* while Leonard Bernstein, whom he had once regarded in a friendly light, after some success in the previous season, produced a *Bohème* that the Italian critics panned without mercy. The score had been given its first performance under Toscanini more than fifty years before and was sacred to him. In previous seasons, viewing La Scala from the distant vantage point of New York, he could retain his affection for it and for the artistic goals he had hoped to achieve there. Seeing it at close hand he realized that, as he is reported to have said, "It is just another Metropolitan." Finally he could contain himself in Milan no longer. He canceled the *Falstaff* and fled to New York in February, 1955.

His friends and musicians welcomed him, and the house in Riverdale became alive again. There were evenings of chamber music, when former players from the N.B.C. came to serenade the Maestro, and there was a new task, reviewing the tapes of his broadcasts and selecting those which might possibly be released on disks. There was live Toscanini music too, the sound of his piano and his hoarse voice as he sang sections of operas he had loved, many of them works which the world had forgotten for fifty years. His eyes bothered him, but his hearing was as acute as ever, and the morning chorus of his colony of canaries was a steady source of pleasure.

Amid all this there were moments of loneliness, of withdrawal into the past, of bitterness. Once when asked what he was doing with his time he replied forcefully that he was being "eighty-eight and hating it." On one such day he told his son, Walter, "I am as good as I ever was, yet here I am doing nothing." Yet the Toscanini fire was never missing too long. The chamber concerts could quickly take on the air of the rehearsals of former years if the playing did not meet his standards, and if he became despondent over the flaws in one of his broadcast recordings, it was only necessary to play another conductor's version of the same work to restore his interest in making his own concept of the music available to the public.

For those who loved the Maestro, his final weeks brought the greatest crisis of all. Early on the morning of November 24, 1956, the LAI plane bringing Guido Cantelli to New York crashed and burned in the suburbs of Paris after takeoff from Orly airport. Toscanini had been anticipating his protégé's return and the concerts he was to lead with the New York Philharmonic, but he accepted the plausible excuse that Cantelli had been delayed. In the weeks that followed the Maestro's friends and children were confronted with dread the moment when he would have to know the truth, but every conference ended with the same question, "Do you want to be the one to tell him?" Other events intervened, and in the end, Toscanini never was told of Cantelli's death.

The Maestro spent the holidays with his family in Riverdale. His vision was now quite bad, but he was apparently in good spirits as the world of music prepared to honor him on his ninetieth birthday in March. Then, on New Year's Day, he suffered a stroke. News of his illness was withheld from all but the immediate circle. The last thing Toscanini desired was morbid publicity. For two weeks his hold on life remained firm. When it weakened he received the final sacraments of the church, and early in the morning of January 16, 1957, he died quietly in sleep. Only then was the news of his final illness made public.

His native country and his adopted one—his two cities, Milan and New York—gave him the funeral rites appropriate to their most honored citizens. The orchestra that had known him at his greatest, the Philharmonic, played the funeral march from the *Eroica*. At La Scala the flag hung at half-mast and rehearsals stopped for a moment of silence. In Chicago an old friend, Bruno Walter, led a commemorative performance of Beethoven's *Coriolan Overture,* and there were many more such tributes.

In two and a half days a file of five thousand mourners passed through the chapel where Toscanini lay in state, his face and hands framed by the velvet facings of a black silk conductor's jacket. There were nearly four thousand more at St. Patrick's Cathedral where a double quartet and Francis Cardinal Spellman sang the Solemn Pontifical Requiem Mass. The setting of the liturgy was that of the Maestro's old friend, Don Lorenzo Perosi of the Sistine Chapel Choir.

For nearly four weeks the coffin lay in a vault in a New York suburb. Then, on February 17, Toscanini arrived back in Italy for the last time. Draped in the flag of the country he loved and had defended, the Maestro's body was transferred from the Rome airport to Milan where it lay in state in the foyer of La Scala. During the second requiem, sung in the Duomo, Milan's great cathedral, by the Archbishop, a quarter of a million Milanese stood bareheaded in the piazza and along the route to the Cimitero Monumentale. The *Eroica,* played in the empty auditorium at La Scala, was carried to them through pouring rain by loudspeakers.

It was, however, with music of Verdi that Toscanini was laid in the tomb he had built fifty years before to receive the body of his son, Giorgio. Four hundred voices rose in the *Requiem aeternam* from the great mass in memory of Alexander Manzoni and the lament, *Va, pensiero,* from *Nabucco,* the chorus Toscanini himself had conducted at Verdi's funeral in 1901. With that hymn to liberty, written one hundred fifteen years before when it was Italy that, symbolically, cried for freedom, Toscanini reached the end of his journey. The career was closed, but the legend lived and with it the principles he had defended fearlessly during his seventy years as a public figure. This Toscanini now belonged to all whose hearts were moved by music or the cause of human dignity and freedom.

Looking backyard over his career we can begin to see Toscanini with some perspective. In his performances one heard the highest order of musicianship operating at a level of dedicated intensity, but for all his commanding appeal, he resisted the lures of a society which would willingly have lionized him had he allowed it to do so. He succeeded because of his unique powers and because he was unsparing of himself in his labors. He had married well and made a handsome income, but he did not become an ostentatious socialite, and again and again he gave large sums to causes he felt to be worthy. On the whole he moved within the world of music, and his three children shared that life.[5] Toscanini's daughter-in-law was Cia Fornaroli, who had been prima ballerina of La Scala; his younger daughter married Vladimir Horowitz, and his other son-in-law was Count Castelbarco.

Any person who achieves a great reputation is thrust into a dual role in which his public life and private life tend, sometimes, to merge. Toscanini avoided this with unparalleled success. He lived as he pleased with his family and friends. In later years he rarely appeared at social functions and was almost never seen in public places. He provided no news for the gossip columnists, attracted no attention to himself except through his art. Nor did he preside over a green-room reception after his concerts. It was not that he disliked people, but he was tired, in no mood for the flattery and gush that such relations with the public promote, and inclined to be short-tempered with those who spoke foolishly.

Adulation bothered him. The preliminary burst of applause that greeted his entrance to the stage seemed unjustified by anything he had done, and the applause after a work, although welcome, was usually excessive. Walter Toscanini recalls, "any time my father took three bows it was because one of us pushed him through the door back onto the stage." When conducting opera he rarely appeared at all after the performance. In concert he did so reluctantly. "What is an

[5] It is increasingly obvious, however, that the Toscaninis are a remarkable family and that the "art in the blood" expresses itself strongly in each generation. (Walter Toscanini is a scholar with a considerable reputation as a historian of the dance, and Walter's son, Walfredo Toscanini, is a young architect with a growing reputation in the New York area.)

artist, a clown who must bow and scrape the floor and prostrate himself before the audience?" he asked. "What do they expect me to do?" he once inquired of a friend. Bayreuth with its concealed orchestra pit suited him. There he wore no formal dress, came and went unnoticed, and did not need to acknowledge the audience. It was pure music. He wished a symphony concert could go the same way. He never read reviews, articles about himself, or troubled with scrapbooks, saving programs, or anything of the sort. He wanted no biography composed and offered no aid or support to anyone wishing to write about him. What was important was that he tried to be an honest musician, that he did his best, and that he was not a genius but performed the works of other men. To create music was the primary thing, to play it another.

At heart he was always an Italian, just as he never ceased to be an Italian national. Had the situation in Italy been different in his lifetime, he might have made his career at La Scala and appeared only rarely in other countries, but he could not make his career in Italy, and the United States offered him an obvious place to make a new start. The American people were friendly and receptive, the financial rewards were great, and his democratic principles were shared on all sides. No one expected him to lose interest in his homeland, and to say that he never became an American or participated intensely in American life is to suggest no criticism. He gave fully of himself and supported his adopted country whenever required; no more can be expected.

The sheer length of his career is so extraordinary that one forgets that the United States knew him in only thirty-six of the sixty-eight seasons in which he appeared, since this period is itself the active life of most conductors. Koussevitzky made his debut in 1908 and led orchestras for forty-three seasons until his death in 1951. The United States knew him for twenty-seven years, a long time, certainly, but shorter than Toscanini's North American career by nearly a decade. Toscanini was a veteran conductor, entering middle life when he first came to New York, and this was eighteen years before the 1926 engagement with the Philharmonic which most young people tend to regard as the beginning of his career in the United States.

Actually when he first came to the Philharmonic he had been a conductor for nearly forty years. Our view of him is fore-shortened and dominated by his final decades; we have lost the young Toscanini and see only the Old Man. Toscanini was a mature conductor in the 'nineties, years before he came to the Metropolitan, and because few of us have heard those performances does not mean that when he recalled them and said they were good they were not so good as the ones we were able to hear. The world has been very fortunate: this miraculous phenomenon, Toscanini's music, was available for a long time.

Unfortunately it was a phenomenon that was known to only a small number of places. Toscanini always disliked touring, and in his entire career there really were only four long tours, which coincidence placed just a decade apart: U.S.A., 1920-21; Europe, 1930; South America, 1940; U.S.A., 1950. He had little interest in appearing as guest conductor; indeed, to hear him one must really have heard him with an orchestra that he had trained for a season or more and sensitized to his demands. Thus for years he was not known to the public in Northern Europe, and during his years in the United States his activities were virtually restricted to New York with occasional visits to near-by eastern cities.

Further, in the twenty-eight seasons in which Toscanini was active in the United States after 1926, he probably gave fewer concerts and was heard in person by less people than any other conductor with a regular orchestral position. Forty appearances a season (including the repetition of programs) would be a round average for the period with the Philharmonic and less than half that number would be correct as an average for his years with the N.B.C. Since the Philharmonic audience was in large part those who had subscribed to a series of concerts, it is fair to suppose that actually he was playing to a large number of persons that remained unchanged week after week, while his N.B.C. Symphony concerts were not open to the public by way of a box office.

Thus Koussevitzky's celebrated remark about Toscanini, "Dat poor old man, how hard dey make him vourk!" really applied better to himself. In the season in which he was seventy-five Koussevitzky played a heavy schedule of concerts with the Boston Symphony, toured as far west as Chicago, and appeared in a summer series at Tanglewood, where he also taught conducting and undertook further responsibilities for his Berkshire Music Center. In the 1941-42 season, in which he had celebrated his seventy-fifth birthday, it happened that Toscanini limited his appearances to six broadcasts of about one hour each, eight concerts with the Philadelphia Orchestra, and a six-program Beethoven cycle with the New York Philharmonic.

Koussevitzky was around giving concerts until a short time before his death. It required no great luck or ingenuity to get to hear him. In that sense, Toscanini never was around, and certainly a great deal of the frenzy that he produced whenever he appeared outside the East came from the fact that thousands of regular concert patrons had been supporting the musical life of their cities for years, had heard virtually every great musician of the day who was appearing in the United States, and yet had never seen or heard Toscanini. In a sense it was embarrassing to him. All one had to do to start the stampede was announce that he was coming at last and offer to sell tickets.

The tour in 1950 showed where Toscanini's great audience was to be found: in the thousands of persons who knew him from his broadcasts, who had followed his programs, season after season, in spite of the poor sound, in spite of the awkward hours, in spite of the intermission talks that caused the music to run overtime and be cut off, in spite of everything that American commercial broadcasting could do to make them uninviting. The New York public had the chance of hearing the real thing, the unique qualities of an orchestra under his baton. The unbelievable transparency of the lines of sound, the range of color and temperatures, from warm, dark hues to icy blue-white, the bite of the attack, the cutting power of the brass, the weight of the full ensemble, these things were merely suggested in the broadcasts. The limitations of the AM transmission, the losses on the long telephone lines between cities, the manipulations of the engineers, the low fidelity of most radio sets made it impossible to duplicate them in the ears of the listener. In spite of it all, one heard the things that made a Toscanini performance great. The engineer at the controls could upset the balance but not the tempo, flatten out the dynamics but not the accents. Toscanini educated his audience, showed them how music should be played, and when they turned on their sets and heard him they knew that this was the way it ought to go.

In later years there were FM transmissions in the New York area with good fidelity, and there were always the records. Even at their worst they were equal to the broadcasts, and as they improved they showed one the things that the radio did not reveal, so that one who had followed the Toscanini recordings would not find the sound of his living performances a new experience. (Similarly, after hearing him "live" for a time the records had more meaning.) If one considers the millions of persons who never had been to a concert hall to whom he brought symphonic music at the highest level of performance, weighing his contribution to the cultural life and artistic standards of people of the United States against the cost of the broadcasts, they seem to be the bargain of the century.

The private life of many artists is, in contrast to their public role, one of loneliness, of studied escape from bores and opportunists, of rejection of both trivial relationships with those who cannot understand their aims and inner compulsions and of more basic relationships which may be desired but cannot be achieved. The life of a celebrated artist may be one of severe discipline and great denial, and the achievement which the public applauds may be realized only through dedication and unceasing effort such as the public cannot share or understand. The great artist may, however, have many of the routine desires of ordinary men, and only through the greatest strength may he sacrifice them to goals which may be only dimly seen.

Toscanini seemingly lived the life of a successful professional man, enjoying a degree of privacy unusual for one in his position and the affection and regard of his family, colleagues, and public. In a society oversupplied with poseurs and pretentious mediocrities he exhibited toward his art a degree of consistency of dedication that revealed an achievement in character as impressive as his power as a musician.

If one could merely say that Toscanini was a conductor of unique capabilities, sparing ourselves invidious comparison, one would still be faced with the necessity of recording his relations with the professional critics. As it is, Toscanini's partisans and detractors have been so conspicuous as to make it difficult to deal with this question objectively. Toscanini stimulated the public as well as professional musicians and critics to form strong opinions; to respect him carried the implication of membership in the cult, to criticize him allied one with the opposite faction. Actually, Toscanini's place as one of the great musicians of history is assured, and no critic can add to or subtract from the height to which he carried himself.

A perennial theme in Toscanini criticism was stated in the *American Mercury* for November of 1930 by Edward Robinson. Toscanini, he maintained, "has the single, phenomenal capacity for maintaining a persistent tempo with the mechanical rigidity of a metronome . . ." This, the author held, was ruining the great orchestra created by Mengelberg, by forcing it into a strait jacket of precision in playing and eliminating all spontaneity and expression in performance, substituting for these desirable qualities only the demand ". . . the notes must be clear, in tune, and observant of any expression marks that happen to be present. Beyond that [Toscanini] asks for nothing—and, I may add, gets it."

These remarks must be taken in context, for they came at a time when Mengelberg's public was irate about his displacement by Toscanini. The two men were opposite types. In the ten years he had been in New York, Mengelberg had made himself many friends, for his fine qualities as a musician were matched with an expansive, social nature. He came from Holland each year on a diplomatic passport with a cargo of liquor that made his parties unparalleled events in prohibition-ridden New York. Toscanini, in contrast, was aloof, frigid, and without interest in social success. Their opposite natures were reflected in their performances: Mengelberg's being romantic, lush, and expressive in the German (and Stokowskian) manner, which was undeniably better suited to some music than Toscanini's leaner and more ascetic approach. There was no question but that rivalry would not be tolerated by Toscanini, but similarly there seems to be no basis for holding that Toscanini ruined the orchestra, since the 1929 and 1936 Philharmonic recordings preserve the sound of a great ensemble.

Throughout Toscanini's American career there was always an element of criticism which came from skeptics, Teutons, professional highbrows, and others, who insisted that Toscanini was really an Italian vulgarian who played everything too fast, sacrificed beauty of tone to coarse brilliance and needless clarity, and felt at ease only in Italian music, or in any case could not play German, Russian, French, English, American, or eighteenth century works (or whatever other type of music the speaker championed) with understanding. This is partly nationalism, partly cross-cultural conflict, partly fabrication, and partly truth. Most of these points are discussed elsewhere in this study.

It is possible that Toscanini suffered less from bad criticism than from the adulation he received from other quarters. Toscanini's admirers quickly assumed the status of a cult in which the only approved attitude was that of worship. In its most violent form, the creed demanded of one the view that there was but one conductor, Toscanini, and that it was better to hear him play the *Dance of the Hours* than listen to an imperfect musician performing the Mozart *Linz Symphony* (to name but one great score which was not in the Toscanini repertory).

When Sir Adrian Boult introduced Toscanini to the B.B.C. Symphony for the first time he started to make a few remarks of welcome and appreciation, only to be cut off by the Maestro's insistence that this was not needed, that he was "only an honest musician." Such an attitude reflects the greatness of Toscanini, but apparently from time to time it underwent a certain alteration, and "only an honest musician" became "the only honest musician," which counts as quite a different thing. The fact has to be admitted that, although on the whole Toscanini's conduct in public was in good taste, he in private conversation expressed opinions of himself not greatly different from the views of his most fanatical admirers.

His relations with other musicians have reflected this attitude. Toscanini brooked no peers or critics, particularly critics who lacked the practical knowledge of a performing musician or presumed to lecture to him on matters of taste. The only role he willingly accepted was a slightly paternalistic one in which there was no challenge to his dominant position. His statement that he did not want to be called a great conductor but, as Howard Taubman puts it, "as man and musician apart . . . in a class by himself" suggests his abhorrence of rivalry or any implication that there were other conductors who might be regarded as being of the same rank as himself. Artur Rodzinski told me of a day in which he found Toscanini brooding over a popular book about conductors which had recently been published. "Look at this!" Toscanini shouted, holding the volume open at the much-read and offensive passage. It was a statement that Weingartner was virtually unsurpassed as an interpreter of Beethoven, and no sooner had Rodzinski read it than Toscanini hurled the book across the room.

Needless to say, Toscanini's comments on his rivals, as repeated by friends, lacked charity. Koussevitzky's Boston Symphony, he is alleged to have said, "did not sound like an orchestra" because of the high pitch to which it tuned. Its excellence as an ensemble resulted from the high quality of the men who composed it—not because Koussevitzky had provided them with training and leadership of a high order. In fact, although Koussevitzky was quite prepared at all times to play the role of Tsar, he treated Toscanini with respect and refused to conduct at La Scala in 1931 when the Fascists would not apologize to Toscanini for the Bologna episode.

As for Beecham, Toscanini appears to have regarded him with mild contempt as no more than a rich man's son playing with orchestras and opera companies the way that other rich young men amuse themselves with chorus girls and horses. Only grudgingly would he concede that Beecham had achieved distinction on the basis of some purely musical accomplishments. In this case the dislike was mutual. Although Beecham and Toscanini were both unique figures, their differences in temperament apparently were so great as to make it impossible for them to understand each other.

Wilfred Pelletier was a friend to the end of Toscanini's days. A number of young conductors were able, under certain conditions, to make friends with the Maestro and enjoy a pleasant relationship with him so long as he was permitted a dominant role. Thus in the 'thirties Toscanini favored Artur Rodzinski, whom he introduced to Salzburg in 1936 and 1937 and asked to engage and train the N.B.C. Symphony in 1937 and serve, with him, as its conductor. Rodzinski undertook the heavy duties of training the new orchestra (which came in addition to his responsibilities to the Cleveland Orchestra, which he then directed), without payment, out of affection and respect for the Maestro. During the initial season Rodzinski led the N.B.C. Symphony for a public concert at Carnegie Hall and in ten broadcasts, but in the 1938-39 season his appearances were reduced to four programs. The final one precipitated a breach with Toscanini which was never healed.

Although to Rodzinski it was a matter of jealousy pure and simple, it does not seem that clear-cut. He had programmed the Scriabin *Third Symphony* (*The Divine Poem*). Visiting the rehearsal Toscanini found that Rodzinski was using fewer musicians than the score called for and made an issue of this. Rodzinski protested that these were all the players N.B.C. would allow him to engage. Toscanini immediately went storming in defense of his colleague, only to be shown a letter from Rodzinski that stated the normal complement of ninety-two men would be adequate. For the Maestro this was a double sin. The wishes of Scriabin were not being followed, and Rodzinski had tried to conceal this by dishonesty. The result was that Toscanini never spoke to Rodzinski again and demanded that Rodzinski receive no further invitations to appear with the orchestra. One would have thought that time might heal the estrangement, but in this case Toscanini was unrelenting. Even when he sent his letter of resignation to General David Sarnoff on his retirement in 1954, Toscanini pointedly ignored Rodzinski's services to him (which were, after all, a matter of public record) and referred to the orchestra as "the group of fine musicians whom you had chosen." General Sarnoff deserves much credit for the greatness of the N.B.C. Symphony, but the injustice of that remark must have been clear to him.

In his enthusiasm for the Palestine Orchestra, in its early years Toscanini adopted one of its conductors, William Steinberg, and for several years held him in regard, although this friendship also cooled in time. In 1941 Toscanini launched George Szell in his American career, but there was little contact between them in later years.

Toscanini was friendly toward Charles Munch, but when the French conductor first appeared with the Philharmonic-Symphony Orchestra of New York, Toscanini managed, somehow, to have a recording made of a part of Munch's performance of the *Fantastic Symphony* and subjected it to withering critical analysis before friends. Although he invited Ernest Ansermet to be his guest with the N.B.C., he was also a friendly critic of his work with the orchestra.

Erich Leinsdorf was for a time a close friend. Among young American conductors, Milton Katims who played the viola in the N.B.C. Symphony under the Maestro, Walter Hendl, and Leonard Bernstein, all enjoyed Toscanini's favor. Several of the members of the Philharmonic of Toscanini's day have become conductors, one or two of them with the blessing of the Old Man. Alfred Wallenstein was Toscanini's first 'cello with the Philharmonic, and Leon Barzin was a violist in the orchestra at that time.

Many of the N.B.C. players justified the rigors of life with Maestro by the training they were receiving for their own future careers on the podium, yet of all the N.B.C. players only Katims has achieved a distinguished reputation in his own right. Samuel Antek, an alumnus of the violin section, was about to be appointed associate conductor of the Chicago Symphony when he met his premature death. Emanuel Vardi, a remarkable violist, has not achieved the recognition he deserves as a conductor. Frank Miller, who in later years was associate conductor of the Minneapolis Symphony, is currently back in the first stand of the 'cellos—this time with the Chicago Symphony. The truth seems to be that years of yielding one's will to Toscanini tended to destroy the capacity to command in one's own right. Katims can play Toscanini repertory and bring to it expressive qualities which grow out of his own personality, while Antek, unfortunately, could offer only copies of the obvious elements of Toscanini performances.

Every musician is human and, being human, has preferences.

In his later years Toscanini reserved most of his praise for a young Italian conductor, Guido Cantelli. "He is the only one who plays music as I do," the Maestro was once reported to to have announced, although Toscanini seems to have been more impressed by Cantelli's artistic dedication than his musicianship *per se*. Cantelli was, indeed, a musician of unusual promise, although it can be questioned whether the effect of being named as heir-apparent to Toscanini was entirely to the good. Cantelli's gift was essentially lyric, and he appeared at his best, in his first American appearances, when drawing a clean, expressive singing line from the orchestra. In the seasons immediately after Toscanini's retirement his style appeared to change, together with his personality, and in attempting to combine with his melodic sensitivity the overpowering motor energy of Toscanini he seemed to be making an effort to play works on a larger scale than his understanding of them permitted without pretension and distortion. However, there is no doubt about his death ranking among the most calamitous losses music has suffered in recent years. Cantelli probably had the capacity to achieve greatness, had he been given the years necessary to reach artistic maturity.

The music produced by the major composers of even the past century in Europe involves a number of distinct styles and no musician can be expected to have equal degrees of sensitivity for all these varied media of expression in musical terms. The things Toscanini best understood were the music of his own country, Beethoven, the early romantics, Brahms,

Wagner, and a group of romantic and post-romantic scores, especially the French impressionists. In these areas he was strong and secure and gave performances which surpassed those of any other musician of his day. Similarly he was, on the whole, not partial to Slavic and Scandinavian music, had no great interest in English or American composers, and had no proper feeling for much Central European music, such as the Bohemian, the Viennese waltz, or the highly personal vocabulary of Mahler. Old music and modern music left him cold.

We do not condemn a pianist because he cannot play the *Goldberg Variations,* the *Hammerklavier Sonata,* the Chopin *Études,* and Debussy's *Estampes* with equal skill and understanding. The uncritical adoration of Toscanini has tended to suggest that he could do no wrong, and that any way he chose to play a work was not *a* right way but *THE* right way. The more obvious truth was that Toscanini had special gifts in relation to music of certain types, that his performances of this music were exceptional, and that when he has played music for which he had no comparable degree of feeling his performances were, on occasion, indifferent or even downright bad. This subtracts nothing from his great achievements; it merely takes away the blindness of idolatry and sets the record straight.

The opinion that Toscanini was "really" the only conductor worth hearing was made absurd by the fact that even during Toscanini's most brilliant period other musicians played works deserving of one's most serious attention which Toscanini either never programmed or could not play as well as they. Indeed, since the living work of music is the thing to which Toscanini remained dedicated, and since his own changing manner of performance demonstrated that he did not regard even his own conception of many works to be taken as final, balanced musical intelligence would appear to demand that one regard with respectful attention any conductor who appeared to be able to give effective and justifiable statements of important scores. It is not a sign of intelligence to wish to escape from the complexity of a situation by offering a set of simplified and imperfectly qualified answers and then closing one's mind to the inadequacies of such a conceptual scheme. There is no one performance which reveals all the inherent characteristics of a great work of music, although certain Toscanini performances (such as that of *La Mer*) appear to have come as close as humanly possible to doing this. The size and scope of the true masterpiece is always larger than a single, consistent interpretation of it can convey. In many instances the Toscanini performances of a given score were clearly among the finest and best conceived one had ever experienced, but only a person with the outlook of an ignorant dogmatist could suggest that one should not listen to other statements of these same works, realizing that the music is greater than the musician.

Toscanini first came to America in 1908, in an era when the United States still looked to Europe as the source of the arts and sciences and could be aptly characterized as a rich, powerful, and productive nation that sought to buy and enjoy the culture which application to other than materialistic ends had produced in older and poorer countries. Toscanini saw the native arts in the United States when they were still, on the whole, second-rate imitations of European models, when few Americans made efforts to compete with the imported European artist (and practically no American artists were to be found in Europe), and the fashionable attitude, well preserved in the autobiographical writings of Santayana and Van Wyck Brooks, was one of unconcealed disparagement of American culture (an aggressive compensation for any feeling of inferiority) and a certain masochistic delight in being put in one's place by the culturally secure European. This has all changed. American artists have made world reputations in nearly every field, and with the growing power of the United States in the international scene, American cultural imperialism, which has met with universal success on the mass level, has made itself felt in more elevated forms as well. In this process Toscanini stood apart. His attitude toward American music was patronizing and hostile at first, mildly curious later, but never strong or enthusiastic. Toward the fine American musicians with whom he worked in his orchestras he was warm and even affectionate. He appreciated their skills and did much to develop them. But Toscanini himself was always the visitor, the representative of nineteenth century European musical culture. In the long run his greatest influence will probably come from the standards he gave us rather than the music he played.

Chapter 2

Toscanini's Musicianship

To EXPLAIN THE WAYS in which Toscanini was superior to other conductors of his time we must appreciate the fundamental qualities of his mind and character, qualities which produced performances which were not merely those of a musician of extraordinary technical accomplishment, but which seemed at times to reflect a perfection of concept and execution which might exist in the mind of the composer but which almost never is realized in a concert hall.

One of his most quoted statements was his insistence that it is the composer who is great, not the performer. "I am no genius. I have created nothing. I play the music of other men. I am just a musician." The achievements of Beethoven and Verdi (for example) as performing artists are now matters of merely historic interest, and the many triumphs before the public of Gustav Mahler and Richard Strauss, who knew extraordinary success as conductors, were, in Toscanini's eyes, minor when compared to their achievements as composers. In fact, Toscanini attempted composition. A *Scherzo in G minor*, written when Toscanini was seventeen, is filled with echos of Mendelssohn and suggests that at the least he might have found success writing light opera. Other youthful efforts use the familiar materials of Italian operatic style, just as Koussevitzky's somewhat later essays at writing music drew upon the conventions of the nineteenth century Russian school, and Furtwängler's scores reflect neo-Wagnerian romanticism. These men were not creative in this sense. The power to draw a great work of music from their inner resources was not there, but present in its place was the power to re-create, from printed notes, the original concept (or something very close to it) of composers with whom they were in special rapport. On an absolute scale this is a secondary talent, but in terms of the distribution of gifts in the population as a whole, it is a capacity almost as rare as the highest levels of artistic genius.

Many efforts have been made to explain Toscanini's unique capabilities, and many of them, I feel, have failed through superficiality in analysis. Explanation of a phenomenon as distinct as Toscanini's music is certain to be difficult, and excessively simple, misleading answers are easier to give than complex, accurate ones. If we are to avoid being naïve or incorrect, we must look deeper into this matter than has commonly been done.

Toscanini was a fanatic. In a work of fiction only an author with the powers of Dostoyevsky could create him or make him convincing. His concentration while conducting has to be considered in the same terms as the behavior of a mystic in contemplation or a poet in the throes of inspired creativity. Richard Mohr, who made all of the Maestro's high fidelity recordings, described it briefly with: "He gets transfixed. A look comes over his face." The distinguished English critic W. J. Turner said of the same phenomenon that he was sure Toscanini suffered, in the literal sense, as he conducted. In a memorable rehearsal recording, he admits to this himself. The difference between Toscanini giving himself to the music with intensity of this order and a *routinier* beating time in a relaxed and indifferent manner is the difference between St. Francis in ecstasy and a sleepy vicar stumbling through the order of morning prayer.

For Toscanini the ideal musical experience probably came when he read a score and heard it in his mind, for there seems no doubt that he could "hear" printed music with the sense of immediacy that ordinary men and women know only in actual performance. What he had to do was match this ideal experience with the playing of an imperfect and fallible group of men, and since Toscanini's concept of many works seemed to have been formed without any concern for human limitations, so long as string players must bow, brass and woodwind players breathe, and singers produce tones from a human larynx, Toscanini could never achieve exactly what he desired in every case. There are limits to virtuosity, and his concept of certain scores far exceeded them. He knew this. When the musicians with whom he was working shared his desire to achieve the best performance possible, and worked as hard, as conscientiously, and unstintingly as he, he could be patient, compassionate, even affectionate. Because of these qualities he accepted some poor playing and singing and allowed recordings containing flaws of this sort to be issued. The musicians who failed him were still, in his eyes, doing their best. Toscanini's rages were a response to the other aspect of the situation, that in which he felt he was giving his maximum in physical and nervous energy, concentration, and intensity of feeling, and others were being stupid or holding back and making things easy for themselves. The person who suggested he was unconcerned about whether or not he was operating at his highest level of skill could drive Toscanini into paroxysms of fury going far beyond the normal indignation of a conductor and approaching frenzy.

These tantrums were one of the few aspects of his personality which the popular press could exploit, although his rehearsals were always closed to reporters and the public (with the exception of close friends) and when his "dress rehearsals" with the N.B.C. Symphony were opened to a small, invited audience, Toscanini treated them as concerts, forbidding the spectators to applaud or make any sound, but never stopping the orchestra except for major errors and (with a few exceptions) controlling his outbursts with the same Stoic self-discipline he invariably displayed in public. During concerts he would restrain himself, even if a player made a catastrophic blunder. The tantrums, in other words, were for the orchestra, not publicity, and it was not Toscanini's intention that anyone should know of them, although no phenomenon in which so many persons were involved could be kept secret in an age of celebrity-worship. In the past, under provocation, he exchanged remarks with his Italian audiences, but in the United States and Britain, where Stokowski and Beecham had no inhibitions about lecturing concertgoers, Toscanini remained silent, feeling that it was inappropriate for him to step out of his role as a musician and speak.

Sir Adrian Boult, who was associated with Toscanini through several seasons of London concerts with the B.B.C. Symphony, has described Toscanini's rehearsals as models of economy and reasonableness, stressing that he never required the players to do more than was necessary for the preparation of the work, even if there was further time at his disposal. "Nothing that I have ever heard or seen of the Maestro and his work is out of line with a perfectly consistent pursuit of the ideal in music and an absolute horror of personal publicity and showmanship," he has written.[1]

B. H. Haggin has written that Toscanini's rages were a natural outgrowth of the internal state of "a man obsessed and possessed" rather than self-indulgence, "and such a man is not rational or reasonable—not in music nor in anything else."[2] Toscanini was primarily a creature of his emotions, and his emotions were unpredictable and likely to run to extremes. In the full eighteenth century sense he was governed by the passions of the soul. The proper attitude in relation to such a person, is not a patronizing air of superiority based upon one's sense of greater stability, but gratitude that the artist is willing to suffer in order to provide his audience with musical experiences which happy, well-adjusted musicians of lesser sensitivity cannot duplicate.

For Toscanini the music was all. To create the performance he conceived he would spare no one, least of all himself, from the utmost expenditure of every physical and emotional resource. To the hardened professional musician, out to earn his pay with as little work as possible, Toscanini was a horror—and the feeling was mutual. Toscanini used few psychological subtleties. His method was simple: to drive, assault, and flay his players until he broke their wills and forced them to yield the performance he demanded. Artur Rodzinski insisted on many occasions that the horrid aspect of conducting that takes it out of the realm of art and makes it in some ways analogous to lion taming comes from the fact that orchestras are made up largely of frustrated men who feel they can do a better job than the conductor and yearn unceasingly for a chance to assert their wills. To unify them into a well-integrated ensemble which co-operates with its leader and plays well together, as much psychology as musicianship is neces-

---

[1] *The Listener,* June 16, 1937, pp. 1177-78.
[2] *The Nation,* August 29, 1953, p. 179.

sary, together with an appreciation that orchestral playing is as boring an occupation as a musician can be asked to follow. Rodzinski's many successes in orchestra training and his good relations with his men (no demanding conductor is ever, strictly speaking, popular) supported this judgment. Toscanini's approach was more impersonal and reserved. He wanted obedience and veneration, and to get it he could be anything from the stern father to an avenging deity.

The relationship of conductor and ensemble here described is largely a product of the nineteenth century. There have been instrumental groups and virtuoso performers since the beginning of music, but the symphony orchestra under a conductor with a baton and absolute authority is a product of the mid-nineteenth century, and its development into the virtuoso orchestra is almost an event of our own times. Indeed, the emergence of the large, virtuoso orchestra, although anticipated in the music of Berlioz, can best be dated by the production of music scored for such a group, such as Strauss's *Don Juan* (1888). There is every reason to believe that the great orchestras of this century are the finest there have ever been.

The principles necessary for the creation and perpetuation of a virtuoso orchestra have never been particularly mysterious. Walter Legge stated them well when he founded the Philharmonia Orchestra of London in 1945. First, "all the best players must be in one orchestra," and, secondly, membership in that orchestra must be desirable enough to encourage competition for a place in its ranks. Thirdly, there must be no "passengers," in any section. Every player must pull his own weight. Fourth, there must be adequate rehearsals, and Fifth, "an orchestra which consists only of artists distinguished in their own right can give of its best only in co-operation with the most distinguished conductors."

The five principles cited here were printed in the special program issued for Toscanini's two concerts with the Philharmonia in 1952. I argue only with the sixth stricture on the Legge list: "No permanent conductor. A 'one man band' invariably bears the mark of its regular conductor's personality, his own particular range of sonority and his approach to music." It seems to me that this can be the most desirable of outcomes, assuming the one man is a great enough musician, and perhaps Mr. Legge has come to believe that as well, since he recently named Otto Klemperer conductor of the Philharmonia for life.

The conditions set forth here were, historically, realized in Central Europe and the United States before they became common in England, where the pioneer in creating permanent ensembles was Sir Thomas Beecham. From the 1890's onward the great American orchestras were able to play long seasons and give their personnel financial security, since the concerts were sold on a subscription basis. The present 'Big Five' in American music (in order of age, the orchestras of New York, Boston, Chicago, Philadelphia, and Cleveland) are still able to do this, with the fifty week season of the Boston Symphony the national paradigm of professional security. However, in the smaller American cities seasons are short and the need for extra-musical (or, or least, extra-orchestral work) creates the usual drawbacks of divided interest.

In the 'Big Five,' however, the conductor has at his disposal resources that are unequaled virtually anywhere else in the world. He also has a critical and demanding audience, and if he fails to maintain the standards American audiences have come to expect, he will probably not last beyond his first contract—although he may be able to pursue his career successfully in Europe.

The virtuoso orchestra is largely the product of the virtuoso conductor, who is both coach and teacher as well as musical director. The measure of his ensemble is a measure of what he has made of the orchestra. The first of the great virtuoso combinations in the United States was presumably the Boston Symphony Orchestra in its seasons under Karl Muck,[3] and next in order I would place the Philadelphia Orchestra as trained by Leopold Stokowski and the Boston Symphony as brilliantly transformed from a "German" to a "French" orchestra by Serge Koussevitzky. A peer of these great en-

[3] Perhaps the Boston Symphony reached this level at an earlier date under Arthur Nikisch, but there seems to be good reason to question it.

sembles were the New York Philharmonic Orchestra of the 'twenties under Willem Mengelberg, to which Toscanini came as guest conductor in 1926 and the season following. He had under him a fine orchestra, for Mengelberg was a strict disciplinarian and had trained it well, and although it always responded to Toscanini with sensitivity and fine playing, the Philharmonic apparently did not begin to take on all of the characteristics it was to exhibit under him in later seasons until 1927-28, when he led it for a longer period.

As the Boston and Philadelphia ensembles were polished to unbelievable brilliance they acquired a keen sense of pride, so that even under conductors of less ability than Koussevitzky and Stokowski they never fell below a high standard of excellence. The Philharmonic-Symphony of New York has never demonstrated this esprit, and even when Toscanini was its principal conductor was capable of wretched performances when led by musicians of lesser stature. In the hands of John Barbirolli, who could maintain neither the discipline nor the high standard Toscanini had established, the quality of playing quickly declined as incorrigible elements in the personnel (whom only Toscanini could control) were free to assert themselves. The cry was raised that Toscanini had ruined the orchestra—"burned it out" was a common phrase—when in fact it had not forgotten how to play as it had under his direction, but simply had been able to get by without doing so. When Toscanini returned at the end of the 1941-42 season it reverted to its former self within the first few minutes of his first rehearsal because it knew its man.[4]

The orchestral performances produced in Boston after Koussevitzky's arrival in 1924, in New York from the beginning of Mengelberg's tenure, and in Philadelphia as Stokowski perfected his distinctive style, together with contemporary performances (which I know less about) by Beecham, Furtwängler and so on, can be taken, not merely as the product of a golden age of orchestra conducting which is now drawing to a close, but as the historical fulfilment of a process of ensemble development which began in the eighteenth century.

[4] Or so Haggin maintains. *Music in the Nation,* New York, 1949, p. 253.

By 1939, of the three American orchestras named, only the Boston remained under the same direction it had had in the preceding decade; Stokowski was gone from Philadelphia and first Mengelberg and then Toscanini had left the Philharmonic, which was only to regain its former glory briefly in later seasons under Rodzinski. In Europe political troubles were providing serious obstacles to the arts, although the great orchestras of Amsterdam, Berlin, and Vienna survived the conflict and in Palestine an orchestra of distinctive qualities appeared to have been formed.

My own feeling is that the Boston Symphony as Koussevitzky had polished it in 1945 was the finest orchestra the world had ever heard, especially in French music. The Boston orchestra had the transparency which came from precision. The strings bowed in unison. (I remember him saying in rehearsal again and again, "Gentlemen, you are not together. It is no use if you are not together!") He had a variety of colors at his disposal, rich, glowing tones (that in Mozart were a little too gorgeous, although impressive none the less), richer hues (such as appeared in Russian scores), and weight of ensemble for German works.

At the peak of its development the Boston Symphony had carried the cultivation of refinement and virtuosity about as far as it could be expected to go, and the resultant orchestral sound was something which had to be heard to be believed, but might not be believed even when heard. If conductors were to be judged solely on the quality of the sound they could produce from an orchestra, Koussevitzky would be an almost unbeatable candidate for the title of greatest conductor of all time. There are, however, other factors, and the New York critic-composer Virgil Thomson correctly stated that after a number of years these beautiful performances had become over-refined and no longer were "about anything" except how beautifully the Boston Symphony could play. This came from long rehearsals, year after year, of the group of works which Koussevitzky had made the heart of the repertory, so when he remarked in one of his later seasons that he had worked seventeen years on a certain effect in *La Mer,* he was talking about a passage that he had played with the orchestra hundreds of times if the concerts and rehearsals were all counted.

Stokowski's orchestra was also capable of the highest level of virtuosity and produced sounds of spectacular beauty, but within a more limited range. The tonal qualities that Stokowski desired above all others were the darker, the more exotic, the openly voluptuous and erotic, and the flowing rhythmic inflection of music as he produced it, with brilliance mixed with Oriental languor and sensuality (particularly in his unconventional phrasing), could only be achieved in scores which permitted interpretation on these lines. Thus Stokowski was in his element with *Scheherazade* and at a loss in a Mozart symphony—with the result that he didn't play much Mozart. For a time he abolished the office of concertmaster (leader) and had the players bow as they pleased, so that instead of breaks he would have a smooth, viscous stream of tone moving through the string parts. The Stokowski approach was effective and musically justifiable only in a relatively small number of works. Indeed, Stokowski's tragedy was that he became tired of repeating the standard repertory and yet was confronted with a board of trustees which objected to his experimentation with advanced contemporary music. He therefore had to apply his experimental interest to the classics, although they did not need to be reworked in this fashion. If Stokowski had any serious failing, it was too much imagination and not enough self-discipline, but the future must forgive him that I think.

Toscanini's orchestra sacrificed some beauty to his demand for absolute clarity. His ideas of orchestral sound were based entirely on how the orchestra sounded to him, *on the stage*, thus his perverse affection for studio 8-H, which from his vantage point did not seem unsatisfactory. (One of the difficulties with Toscanini recordings is that people often do not realize that some of their faults are simply slightly imperfect reproduction of characteristics which Toscanini looked upon as virtues.) Toscanini's strings were transparent. Every line of the instrumentation stood out, because he wanted his men to play so that every strand had a little "edge" to it. He wanted the lines to stand apart, as if in relief, rather than blend. If one wanted a beautifully integrated section producing a magnificent sound of massed string tone one went to Boston. Toscanini did not regard this as "correct." Unlike the elegance and beauty of the Boston brass, Toscanini's ensemble had a decided "burr" and often he had his horns conspicuously "forward" in the over-all sound of the ensemble, blowing rather hard and producing a rather coarse, brassy tone that the French horn yields when blown hard. It was exactly what he wanted. (Heard on a recording of limited range the quality could be most disturbing.) His ideal was transparency to the point that one could listen with the score in one's lap and *hear* everything he saw in the printed music. Even modified, this made recording a nightmare. He was insensitive to the low fidelity and poor quality of the sound of many of his disks. He passed them because they were "correct," i.e., the playing was precise and the sound was reasonably transparent.

When one compares the Toscanini and Koussevitzky performances of such works as the *Italian* and *Classical* symphonies, *La Mer, Pictures at an Exhibition,* and the second *Daphnis and Chloe* suite, one finds that Toscanini offered more sensitive and controlled rhythm with an impressive feeling for the unity of the work and a spectacular level of transparency and virtuosity in the ensemble. In the Koussevitzky version the virtuosity was of equal, perhaps on occasion even greater degree, and the lines of sound were blended to provide a glowing whole. In the Koussevitzky performance one could not hear everything, because certain lines, regarded as accompaniments, had been made secondary, so as to focus attention on the principal themes. In a work such as *Daphnis* this always seemed to me to be more effective than Toscanini's method, which, in fact, was the more difficult, since keeping the many strands of the orchestration transparent and in balance was a task of titanic difficulty. Both performances were beautiful and both were right, if one means by that faithful replicas of the intentions of the composer as shown in the score. Which one preferred is a more subjective matter than most questions of criticism. Unfortunately, comparison today on the basis of recordings is difficult, because, both versions are to be heard only on old and defective disks.

The virtuoso orchestra emphasized and dramatized the role

of the conductor to an extraordinary degree, and it is natural that as attention was centered upon the eminent conductors of the day, composers and orchestral musicians might well come to feel that their contributions to the total performance had been slighted, particularly when one reads Koussevitzky's pronouncements, in which the "interpreter" appears to have a role only slightly inferior to that of the composer, or when one notes the many instances in which the conductor is given credit for the fine performance of an instrumentalist, who has every right to be regarded as a virtuoso in his own right. Chief of the conductor-hating composers has been Paul Hindemith, himself a conductor of not inconsiderable merit.

In *A Composer's World*[5] he writes with obvious feeling:

> "There was a time when leading an orchestra was the exclusive task of men with a universal musical wisdom, when outstanding musicianship and great musical and human idealism were the foremost requirements. Granted that today we have many conductors with these old-time qualities, we nevertheless cannot overlook the fact that with the many times greater number of orchestras and hence the multi-production and consumption of conductors, their musical wisdom is frequently anything but universal, their musicianship doubtful, and their idealism replaced by an insatiable vanity and a deadly fight against any other being who happens also to wield a baton."

The veneration in which conductors are held, Hindemith feels, is "disproportionate" to the actual skills they possess, but reflects a musical embodiment of a social-psychological phenomenon:

> "In an era that leaves little opportunity in the individual's life for the application and display of overt despotism, the demonstration of some defined and stylized form of oppression seems to be imperative. The listener in the audience who in his normal behavior has to suppress, thousands of times, his most natural human desire of governing, or-

[5] Cambridge [Mass.]: Harvard University Press, 1953. Pp. 137-38. Quoted with permission.

dering, dictating to, and even torturing his fellow men, projects himself into the conductor's personality. Here he sees a man who with the consent of human society exercises a power which we would look upon as cruelty if applied to dogs or horses. Identifying himself with these activities the listener enjoys the perfect abreaction of his own suppressed feelings: he now swings the teacher's cane, the dignitary's mace, the general's sword, the king's scepter, the sorcerer's wand, and the slave driver's whip over his subjects, and quite contrary to the effects such dictatorial manners have in real life, the result seems to be pleasant to all concerned."

I do not doubt that part of Toscanini's popular success was due to extra-musical factors, such as the legend of his autocratic mien and unyielding will. A London critic remarked of Toscanini's two concerts in 1952 that many of "the wrong people" were present for "the wrong reason"—curiosity better suited to the Roman arena, coupled, perhaps, with the hope that the Maestro might have a tantrum on the stage of the Royal Festival Hall. Anyone who knew anything of his character knew of his self-control in public, but this aspect of his life was not exploited by the popular press. It probably was true earlier that part of the incredible success of the 1950 Toscanini tour of the United States came from the purely theatrical desire to see the most celebrated martinet of our times.

Whatever extra-musical aspects Toscanini's reputation may have had, his career was based on his musicianship and the unique qualities which it exhibited. Certain obvious features of his musicianship were regularly advanced as the explanations of its excellence. We may well begin with having a look at these efforts, although most of them can quickly be seen to be incomplete or seriously at fault.

We are told, for example, that the impact of a Toscanini performance came from absolute fidelity to the score. This is an extremely ambiguous and misleading assertion. In the first place, there are many scores in which there is no possible standard of "absolute fidelity." The composer's markings permit alternative interpretations which, within certain vague limits, appear to be equally faithful to his intentions. Music, indeed, is a living art because no two performances are ever exactly the same, and yet it is possible for different perform- ances of a work to be "faithful," or "correct," or "effective and artistically justifiable," without being identical. Every time Toscanini stepped before his orchestra he felt, as a con- ductor must, that he knew what the composer had intended, but the more you study Toscanini performances the more obvious it becomes that the Maestro could play a given work in quite different ways on two consecutive days or, indeed, in two different portions of a single recording session.

Toscanini was particularly flexible in his reading of tempo markings. He would rush a work rather than run the risk of allowing it to go slack even for a moment, and in certain states of thought and intensity he seemed to fear this long before most of his listeners would sense any weakening in ten- sion. In general as he grew older he tended to take slow move- ments a little faster than marked and grow nervous when con- fronted with long stretches of music in a slow pulse pattern. Even here one cannot make a flat statement that Toscanini never played anything slowly. There are too many examples to the contrary.

Fidelity to the score is often taken as fidelity to the notes as they stand in print, and here again Toscanini's practices were personal and flexible. He was no musicologist in the usual sense of that term, and, further, he viewed most musical scholars with distrust. For one thing they lacked the practical, professional skills of a performing musician; for another their academic pretensions were alien to Toscanini's nature. None- theless, Toscanini did his best to secure reliable editions of the music he played. He insisted, for example, that Italian scores be given from material which was printed by Italian publish- ers, since he knew that the German houses liked to add extra brass parts. Moreover, he went to composers' manuscripts whenever he felt they might answer questions which remained after the examination of their music in published form.

Actually, Toscanini was a musical scholar of great percep- tion, but on an intuitive rather than a methodical basis. A good example is his performance of the Haydn *Symphony No. 98,* which he always played from corrupt material. He obviously did not know it was corrupt, or he would have corrected it, but he did know in various crucial passages that something was wrong, and generally, by means of tempo, or accent, he did something that fixed matters—although not, always, in the way that Haydn had intended. The best instance of this is in the finale where Haydn wrote out a harpsichord solo (for himself) which was not reproduced in the printed score. The result is a highly exposed passage in which the main instrument and main theme are missing, and here Toscanini retarded and accented the first violin part so that it sounded less like the accompaniment it was and more like the center of interest it had become.

Whenever Toscanini could solve a textual problem without touching the notes, he left them alone. Indeed, his performance practices eliminated some minor adjustments in instrumentation which nearly every well-known conductor followed. Such a case can be found in the first movement of the Tchaikovsky *Pathétique Symphony* where a slowly descending scale leads into a crashing chord (bar 160). Tchaikovsky begins the scale in the clarinet, takes it down to the bottom of its range, and then gives the rest of the scale to the bassoon. It is commonplace to replace the latter instrument with a bass clarinet, so that the tone color of the passage is not altered by the switch from a single reed to a double reed instrument, but Toscanini saw no need for the change.

However, in Tchaikovsky's *Manfred Symphony,* Toscanini's editorial pencil ran rampant, cutting a bar here and two bars there, tightening the bridge passages, eliminating instruments that coarsened the texture, or, conversely, adding instruments to strengthen a theme or build up an effect. The work is vastly stronger for what Toscanini did to it, but opening his score for the first time it is rather astonishing to see the full extent of the changes he made.

Toscanini, in short, was always faithful to what he took to be the spirit of the score, but not necessarily to the letter, nor did he stand for the literal duplication of a text in performance if he felt that the composer had made a miscalculation.

To Toscanini the conductor's responsibilities included correcting such mistakes so as to realize the composer's artistic aims. Any score that Toscanini used a great deal ended up full of the sort of markings one would expect to find in a scholar's books. If a composer wrote the same passage in an inconsistent style, Toscanini decided which of the alternatives was correct and made all the readings consistent. If a bad disposition of parts obscured a harmonic progression, buried a melodic line under the weight of the orchestration, or concealed an important feature of the counterpoint, Toscanini altered the voicing to make this detail clear. If Brahms gave the horn a low note that does not sound well, Toscanini reserved the right to cut it out. If Debussy wrote an important phrase which cannot be heard without doubling and reinforcing the part, Toscanini subtly supplied the extra tonal power needed to make it audible. In most instances it is impossible, even following with a score, to tell when changes have taken place, for they never alter the effect of the music. One simply knows, hearing flute tone standing out bold against the other sounds, for instance, that more than one instrument must be playing, even though the score reads, "First flute, solo."

Greatly as one respects Toscanini's insistence upon adhering to the intentions of the composer, this alone is not a sufficient explanation of his powers. His ability to grasp the dynamic levels in a score that the composer had only partly marked in this respect, or his editing of the score of *La Mer,* which provided a great performance with a solid foundation in a perfectly calculated text, reflect musicianship of a high order. Yet other conductors possess equal dedication to the composer and comparable editorial ability without being peers of Toscanini. These are only part of a complex of skills which made Toscanini unique.

In another example of incomplete explanation, we are told that Toscanini was a master of the orchestra, that he was familiar with the technique of all the instruments, and that as a result of years of experience he was able to use their resources to maximum effect. This was all true, but many conductors, some of them in no way comparable to Toscanini in their musicianship, can be said to have mastered the orchestra to this degree. Taking effects for their own sake, a considerable body of candidates could produce effects just as beautiful and striking in their own way as any effects Toscanini could command. One can agree, then, that Toscanini knew the orchestra forward and backward, but this was not the reason for his primacy among conductors.

The same must be said of his supposedly evocative power. He had no difficulty in projecting his intensity. Under his direction artists have repeatedly given themselves to the music without holding any emotional energy in reserve, offering performances which, by themselves, they could not achieve. This is a rare quality, but I do not think that Toscanini was the only conductor of our day to possess it, and it is not the thing which, of itself, sets him apart from his contemporaries.

Another explanation tells us that Toscanini was a master of styles, that he always played music in the manner best suited to it, thereby stating it in the most effective way. This is not even a partial truth. Toscanini was the master of only one style, his own. Music which was not well suited to this approach he played with a loss of effect or did not play at all. His own style, a purified and hyper-sensitized version of *bel canto* singing in orchestral terms, was well suited to a great deal of the finest music, but works which require a different sort of feeling, he could not transmit effectively except in unusual reinterpretations in *bel canto* terms. Such a score was *The Moldau,* which Toscanini played beautifully but appeared to transform into a piece of Italian music.

Certain other generalizations of a critical nature about Toscanini are not merely incomplete but faulty in a much more obvious manner. Some tell us that Toscanini's tempi for a given work were always faster than the norm set by other conductors. This is exaggerated. (It is nearly always absurd to say always, since the world is not such a clean-cut proposition.) For instance Toscanini's reading of *La Mer,* represented one of the slowest performances to be heard, while some of his readings of Wagner are slower than the "traditional" German versions recorded by Muck. Toscanini had a preference for tempi faster than those some regarded as conventional, but beyond this one cannot generalize.

Nor is there any basis for the contention that Toscanini's performances of a given work never changed—a thesis I shall contest in detail later in this chapter. Suffice it to say at this point that Toscanini's performances were continually in a process of change, but some changed more rapidly than others. In many cases the alterations were conspicuous; in others they were slight. Those who could follow him closely heard for themselves that he would play a Brahms symphony (say) one way in the spring and another way the following autumn. Produced from the heart and mind of an intense and perceptive musician, it was inevitable that—at different times and under different conditions—his performances should change.

Two skills contributing to Toscanini's success which have received less attention than they might are his ear and his baton technique. So called "absolute pitch" is often overestimated by conservatory professors. It is not a prerequisite for a brilliant musical career (Koussevitzky, for example, lacked it), or, of itself, evidence of particular musical gifts. Toscanini, however, had a remarkable sense of pitch (so acute, in fact, that the high 445 tuning of A in the Boston Symphony made him uncomfortable) and this has undoubtedly played an important role in his performances.

Whatever he may have had to do with the creation of the scoreless type of conductor, Toscanini was in no way responsible for the batonless species. He always used a stick. In later years these were made for him by his physician (as a hobby, rather than a professional service). Dr. Hubert Howe, working to the Maestro's specifications, produced a baton twenty inches long, four and three quarter inches of its length being a cylindrical cork and plastic grip about one half inch in diameter. Toscanini held his baton firmly with his three middle fingers (his little finger sticking out at right angles to the shaft). His beat was not of the textbook variety, although eloquent to an astonishing degree and (except for an occasional slip) completely unambiguous. He preferred circular motions (in common time he seemed to be stirring in a large, vertically positioned tub) in which the pattern of the beats flowed into a single, continuous rhythmic pulse. He never sat while conducting, never appeared to do anything showy, and never ceased giving the impression that he was aware of what each individual player was about. His degree of command, therefore, was phenomenal.

The truth of the matter, it seems to me, is that Toscanini's unique qualities came from a synthesis of the factors given above in combination with an unparalleled understanding of the nature of music and an ethic of honest musicianship in which it is not the great maestro but the great composer who speaks through the orchestra. For him the task of the conductor was to master the score and combine intelligence with musical skill in giving voice to what the composer has written. The gap between Toscanini and the "interpreter-conductor" who places himself above the composer and uses the music and the orchestra as vehicles for the assertion of his own will and the enlargement of his ego cannot be bridged; and because so many conductors have allowed themselves to be affected in this way the selfless musicianship of Toscanini was sufficient to place him in a very small and distinguished group of artists.

It is not straining an analogy to speak of music as a language. In a word-language used expressively, as in poetry, we have the elements of the meaning of words, accent, rhythm, and tempo; the combination of these things as we read a poem giving us our feeling of coherence, continuity, and form. A poem is an artistic unity. If we change words, drop out or rearrange lines, or read with accents other than those the poet expected the words to have, we destroy the integrity of the work and substitute an artless muddle.

In music the units are not words but combinations of sounds of short or extended duration, and just as words must have a certain order to make sense, so certain combinations of sounds when followed by certain other combinations of sounds have a significance they would not otherwise possess. It is this fundamental thing about tonality—that a given sound appears to lead naturally into only a limited number of other sounds—that gives us a basis for harmony and allows us to create feelings of tension and repose which, in a rhythmic pattern, constitute the fundamental elements of musical structure.

This combination of rhythmic stress, and suspension, the sustained alternation of strong beats and weak beats, with their ability to convey the sense of a rising and falling melodic line combined with the pattern of tension and repose, the "moving" unresolved tone and the "stationary" tone that offers momentary resolution, provides the basis for harmonic rhythm, that is, the integral union of the two basic elements of music, rhythm and tonality. In a Toscanini performance one heard what is surely the highest possible development of harmonic rhythm as a key to the exposition of music, since invariably he placed rhythmic stress on what is harmonically strong and made the unresolved harmony the weak beat.

It may be that it is the lack of these unities of rhythm and harmony which made contemporary music uncongenial to Toscanini, so that he could find some understanding for *Petrouchka,* which retains some of the conventions of tonic-dominant harmony (without adhering to it), but none for *Sacre du Printemps,* where rhythm is not clearly an outgrowth of harmonic patterns. It is to be noted that Toscanini appears to have played a certain amount of inferior modern music simply because it is comprehensible in terms of older harmonic-rhythmic unities. These facts constitute a reply to those who insist that "everyone" puts rhythmic stress on consonant harmonies. In many works one cannot escape from doing so, but this need not make harmonic rhythm as central to one's manner of performance as it appeared to be to Toscanini.

The foundation of a Toscanini performance was the rhythmic pattern he selected as best fitted to the expressive content of the music. His choice of tempi reflected two drives, first his emotional response to a given work, a response that apparently was heightened by fast tempi, and secondly, as was noted earlier, his desire to preserve continuity at all cost and avoid any strain upon the themes or the successions of intervals which compose and accompany them and, taken together in a time series, make up the musical structure. The rhythmic foundation did not change except when the composer indicated that it should. There is consequently a line to the performance, a steady propulsive force which is always felt and which is never sacrificed to a special effect, but remains and through its presence gives the work coherence and cumulative power. Toscanini's preference, even in rehearsals, for playing on to the end of a work, or the end of a part of a work, before stopping to go back and make such corrections as were necessary, reflects this insistence upon continuity. He must experience works as unfolding unities, not as bits and pieces strung together in a series. The wonderful plastic qualities of a Toscanini performance came from the fact that within the limits of the rhythmic pattern he could pass from the softest to the loudest dynamic levels and through a score of changes in expression or orchestral color without losing the integral drive of the harmonic rhythm. The nature of a work of music is such that it must be revealed as a sequence in time, but the composer and the performer must see it as a structural whole in which all parts are properly balanced in terms of the entire composition. The unique quality of Toscanini's performances came, essentially, from his awareness of form and his magnificent capacity to reveal it.

Toscanini's way of playing music, I have said, was an orchestral interpretation of song in the *bel canto* manner. Undoubtedly this was always a part of his artistry, since it is the ideal style for Italian music that lay in his heart and on his lips since childhood. It is not a traditional style for the performance of German music, nor was the Toscanini orchestral sound that of a German orchestra. The tone of a German ensemble rests upon a solid bass provided by the 'cello, contrabass, percussion, and the lower woodwind and brass instruments. If these registers are not well developed and forcefully present a German work will probably lack the body and strength of tone which is required. (In earlier years Toscanini often played German works with too little bass. As he grew older he appeared to have seen the need for firmer registration and strengthened these lines.) In a German orchestra violas and violins add to the bass strands of lighter substance and, especially in the case of the first violins, great brilliance in the upper octaves, but the parts falling in the higher voices never detach themselves from the unified sound of the whole ensemble and the firm bass it provides. Their brilliance is subordinated to the whole. Similarly the wind and brass (which may include somewhat coarser but more powerful instruments than the lighter B-flat trumpet and F horn—such monsters as the F trumpet, for example), although not without virtuosity, seemed to be in their element blowing chords that struck one like hammer blows and carried a weight that Koussevitzky's Boston Symphony, for example, could not duplicate. A well-integrated ensemble of the German type could have great beauty of tone, offering in place of the luminescence and overall brilliance of the Boston a mellow "old wine" quality such as I knew in the Chicago Symphony of my youth.

Toscanini never thought much of appeals to tradition, realizing that much of what was offered in this guise was due to the imposition of late ninteenth century emotional patterns upon music of another day. Style, for Toscanini, was implicit in the way the composer wrote and certain to be lost if every work was approached with the same aesthetic predilections. To play every type of music with the same lush ensemble sound destroyed individual characteristics of the great composers, just as the flavors of different foods would be lost if they always came to the table immersed in the same highly seasoned sauce. For Toscanini, the style appropriate to a work did not have to be sought in extra-musical inquiries. If you cleared your head of preconceptions, went to the music itself, and studied it with dedication and care, you would be able to discover the way it should be played. If you could not do this you were no musician, for what was the musician's art except to take the cold notes left us by the great composers and recreate them with the fullness and vitality of the creative imagination which had first conceived them?

Toscanini was not completely successful in realizing his own principles, but this is man's fate. What is of first importance is we realize the effect of those principles and the fact that, largely due to Toscanini's example, they are now dominant. Even thirty years ago the public quietly tolerated conductors rewriting music in a manner which would now lead to scandal. Frederick Stock, for nearly four decades the conductor of the Chicago Symphony, reorchestrated the Brahms symphonies in the manner of Richard Strauss and wrote a long organ solo into the final movement of the Chausson *Symphony in B-flat,* apparently for no better reason than to give the organist a workout. Stock was in good company. Mahler had reorchestrated Beethoven and Schumann, and Von Bülow had given poor old Ludwig a hand by introducing special effects for new instruments such as mechanical drums. Great music, in short, was something which could be up-dated and done over as the times changed.

German orchestral playing of the nineteenth century developed in an atmosphere of idealism and romanticism in which the overt expression of certain types of feeling was cultivated and approved, and warmth, spontaneity, and an almost improvisatory sense of flowing emotions was desired. This style of performance belongs to the past, and Toscanini deserves as much credit as any individual for killing it off. To achieve "expression" in the romantic style the tempo was adjusted at will (whether or not the composer had authorized such a departure), pauses were inserted before especially dramatic or impassioned outbursts, sighs, retardations, heaving and panting were slipped into passages *ad libitum,* rubato ceased to be an indulgence, and rhetorical emphasis, which made the most conventional series of cadential chords on a tonic-dominant pattern into a world-shaking *dah DUM dah,* became the staple elements of performance.

Some of these characteristics, qualified by genuine poetic feeling, are to be found in the conducting of the late Wilhelm Furtwängler. The Furtwängler method was to allow the music to fall into deceptively natural phrases (or groups of phrases) and a succession of simple, but carefully molded statements of this type, spun out in a series, made up the work. In the *Tristan Prelude,* where Furtwängler's feeling and understanding provided close affinity to the score, such a performance could be eloquent, moving, and beautiful, lacking the intensity, cohesion, and cumulative power of Toscanini, but in its place offering a degree of communication and a sense of shared emotion which the cool perfection of Toscanini never approached. It is difficult to find a Furtwängler performance that does not contain moments of great beauty and strength, however mannered the whole may be. Unfortunately, Furtwängler did not limit himself to music for which he had special feeling or which was best revealed in his type of performance, and in less congenial works one sensed a desire to create effects for their own sake, without any spontaneous feeling for them. Since these performances lacked firm rhythmic continuity, the obvious means of increasing tension was to increase speed, so that constant acceleration and retardation, together with the distention of phrases (often to the point at which they seemed to become parodies of themselves), were, together with other crude or insensitive manipulations, imposed upon a basic rhythmic pulse that rushed or dawdled. The effect of this was to destroy any sense of unity in the composition and reduce it to a series of episodes in sequence. Furtwängler's defects came from lapses in understanding and taste combined with an exhibitionist tendency that was insufficiently restrained.

The defects of Toscanini came from characteristics desirable in the mean being carried to excess. His rhythmic accuracy was splendid, but at times it became metronomic rather than musical thus giving the performance mere mechanical exactitude rather than a feeling of creativity and spontaneity. His intensity was magnificent, but on occasion it exceeded reasonable limits and the music was driven so hard that its power, eloquence, and natural melodic flow were impaired or diminished. The strength of his style was the way in which he allowed music to sing; the weakness came from his personal tension which often dominated and prevented this. Another of Toscanini's weaknesses was a tendency, like Koussevitzky's, to over-refine music played too frequently. As one works over a score season after season there is always the tendency for it to go stale, and the mechanism of "going stale" in Toscanini operated by the performance becoming fast, slick, mechanically perfect, and cool, a succession of beautiful, highly polished surfaces, none colored too deeply, and all practically without meaning. The musician must always balance himself between seemingly opposite poles: the achievement of near-perfection in polish and form at the cost of losing communicative and expressive power. With Toscanini the first extreme—near-perfection—was the reef on which lay the shattered hulks of several of his most-performed works and toward which, at the end of his career, much else of his repertory seemed to be moving in a steady breeze.

This much could have been heard simply from the commercial recordings which were available during Toscanini's lifetime, supplemented by a recollection of his broadcasts. There is always a danger, when confronted by a limited amount of data, to try to organize it. This is an occupational disorder of philosophers, although one from which I am gradually recovering. The truth is that the more one listens to the material available in Riverdale, the more apparent it becomes that any description of the metamorphosis of a Toscanini performance must be highly qualified. Certainly any schematization of the process must be offered in a tentative manner as a hypothesis that may be useful but should not, under any circumstances, be converted into law.

For one thing, there is not enough evidence even in Riverdale to support any suggestion that Toscanini's way of playing music changed in a uniform manner during his American years. There are tendencies evident, but they reverse themselves at times, alter direction suddenly, or halt without warning. I am convinced that Toscanini's performances in the Philharmonic years were, on the whole, somewhat broader, more rhetorical, and relaxed than those of the later recording sessions, but it has also become clear to me that Toscanini alone with musicians and microphones always tended to be more intense than Toscanini with an audience behind him.

Certainly, any valid description of Toscanini's changing tendencies would require a longer base than the N.B.C. Symphony seasons, and for this we would have to have more material from the 1920's and early 1930's than we actually seem to possess. Progress in recording techniques has been so rapid that we tend to forget that to record symphonic music from the air in the 'thirties one had to have two expensive disk cutters and keep switching back and forth as one changed recording blanks. None of the Toscanini air checks of this period that I have seen were made this way. Amateur jobs, they represent the efforts of men with a single cutter who were resigned to losing some of the music while switching blanks. They made use of the longest playing surface available at the time, 16-inch, .025-inch groove, 33⅓ rpm acetates. Most of these disks exist in the one copy, and that often is in poor condition. With a strong imagination, one can sense the original.

None the less, it is on the basis of what material exists that the question of Toscanini's changing manner of interpretation must be discussed. It seems clear that the least changes occurred in his performances of Italian music. There is a 1921 recording of the *Don Pasquale Overture*. We can put it on one turntable, place the 1951 version on another, and proceed right through the work, alternating passages between the two, without producing anything inconsistent or artistically disturbing. The *style* of both performances is the same, and thus they can be spliced into one another without violent injury to the music. The *detail*, however, differs somewhat, the earlier performance being somewhat more relaxed and containing some *tempo rubato* that the version of thirty years later lacks. (Such a composite recording was actually played during a talk I made on this subject for the B.B.C. Third Program.) There is variation *in detail*, but limits are imposed on the range of variation by the over-all consistency in *style*. The lesson seems obvious. The *bel canto* style which is correct for Italian music had been thoroughly ingrained in Toscanini from his earliest years, as I have noted earlier, and in the works in which it can be adopted he felt stylistically secure from the start of his musical life and, quite properly, saw no reason for altering his performances. I am therefore not at all surprised that the two *Don Pasquales* sound so much alike; what would shock me would be that they did not.

The surprises from the Philharmonic years are almost entirely in German music. A perfect example of speculative paths they open is an air check recording in Walter Toscanini's collection which preserves the Maestro's 1935 performance of the great slow movement of the Bruckner *Seventh Symphony*. So far as I know there is only the one copy of that disk in the world, and the reader may well curse me for whetting his appetite only to frustrate him, but those who heard the performance or have been lucky enough to hear the record, may recall that although the sound—imperfect as it is on the disk—is obviously that of a Toscanini ensemble, transparent and glowing. The tempi are those of German tradition, and the long phrases, in which the tensile strength of the line of sound seems enormous and the firm but slow rhythmic pulse allows amazing effects of spaciousness and splendor, follow one after another like a succession of miraculous invocations. I never heard anything of exactly this sort from the Old Man. What is preserved here in a fragile and incomplete form is a facet of his artistic character which appeared only momentarily later.

If the Toscanini of that Bruckner recording was the Toscanini of the Philharmonic days, a schematization of his artistic development is possible. As I set it down in 1954 Toscanini in his early years played Italian music in the *bel canto* manner which is correct and which, without significant deviation, he followed throughout his life. In German scores, however, he followed the practice of German conductors, and one heard the broader phrasing, slower tempi, and a certain number of the rhetorical inflections of the usual German style. It is clear that he adopted German practices to different degrees in different works, that whatever he adopted was absorbed within his own artistic personality and thus was never literally German but Toscanini-German. His concept of orchestral sound became richer and more robust in his later years, but always remained his own. Three "performances" could be distinguished. First, the "ancestral" performance, that is, the earliest Toscanini performance of a German work, based upon his assimilation of the reading of German conductors; secondly, the "transitional" performance, in which Toscanini's *bel canto* manner has replaced some of the German style and rhetorical devices have been subdued; third, the "singing" performance, in which German influences have disappeared and Toscanini has reconceived the work in terms of little or no rhetoric.

This is an explanation which holds up only if we agree there will be many exceptions to the rule. Its only alternative is to deny that there was any general tendency behind Toscanini's changing manner of performance. In short, we are in one of those awkward situations where there are enough regularities to suggest that a pattern of development can be found and enough irregularities that no pattern can be proposed that does not leave some glaring gaps. Most questions in the arts are questions of degree and most questions of degree have an inherent ambiguity. For example, when Toscanini was in the state of mind to give broader, more relaxed statements of German works we find he bestowed the same general approach upon Italian music, although not to the extent that one finds in the Bruckner cited above.

Moreover, the musical conviction of the "ancestral" performances we have shows that Toscanini had sincere feeling for this style at the time. It was later that he recognized that to follow the German approach required him to accept tempi and performance practices which were different from those he adopted in Italian works. The German manner became in time sufficiently different from his natural stylistic inclinations that he began to think there must be another, freer, way in which he might play this music, provided it was correct and faithful to the composer to do so. With more time he became convinced that it was German tradition that was wrong and his musical impulses that were correct. Toscanini was probably always convinced, at the moment of performance, that what he was doing was right. It was when the heat of battle was past that he turned to thought.

Toscanini's performances were based upon years of analytic study of scores with the determination to play them honestly and effectively. His style and tempi were thus the outgrowth of the application of a musical intelligence of extraordinary sensitivity to the music he had examined with attention to the slightest detail. His tempi, in particular, grew out of his sense of the plastic continuity of thematic material, from his feeling that a written melody actually contains its tempo inside itself, if one can only sense the pulse at which its intervals are linked with the greatest lyricism and freedom of movement.

Haggin's contention that ". . . any pace that Toscanini adopts is one in which he can make the music effective."[6] is true or false depending on how one takes the word "effective." Toscanini could make music thrilling at any pace, but often the effect was alien to the character of the music and violated the "natural" tempo of the material, suggested above. Toscanini's playing of the slow movement of the Mozart *Jupiter Symphony* may be effective, but it is not remotely what I can conceive as Mozart's intention, and I cannot regard it as other than a departure, through an excess of intensity, from Toscanini's normally great powers. In *La Mer*, on the other hand, I can accept his reading as a perfect statement of Debussy's concept of the work.

The elements of Toscanini's style were sufficiently predictable and consistent that it is possible to imagine the general outline of a Toscanini performance of works which, in fact, he never played. Winthrop Sargeant, one of Toscanini's musicians in the Philharmonic period, thus (involuntarily) gave his readers in *The New Yorker* a fine account of the Toscanini performance of the Tchaikovsky *Fifth*. I agree that the Toscanini reading of the score would be exactly as Sargeant described it. The fact that Toscanini never played the work is quite irrelevant, and Sargeant's graceful apology was not really necessary. If anyone desires I shall be happy to describe the Toscanini performance of the Berlioz *Fantastic Symphony*, the Toscanini account of the *Spring Symphony* of Schumann, and a number of other works which, for one reason or another, he never played. The only limitation on this exercise of musical imagination that I can see, is that sometimes when I have conceived Toscanini performances *a priori* I have been disturbed to find, not merely that the treatment of detail in the actual reading was different from that in my mental one (I was prepared for that) but that, inevitable human limitations being a factor, a particularly

[6] *Music in the Nation*, New York, 1949, p. 128.

grand Toscanini-effect I had heard in my mind failed to appear. A good example of this is the Brahms *Third Symphony*, for which I have conceived a Toscanini performance (based on what I have heard him achieve in the other three of that composer) far superior to any I actually heard him conduct. Others who followed his career for many years ought to have experienced a similar feeling at one time or another.

If we are to indicate Toscanini's influence upon orchestral playing and the standards of musical performance, omitting irrelevant matters such as Toscanini's memorization of scores, (necessitated by an eye defect which made it impossible to read music except at very short distances and producing— by accident—a crop of scoreless conductors) it centers about three points: (1) Toscanini was of primary influence in killing off the fashion of "expressive" performance, lingering from the nineteenth century, and substituting criteria based upon mastery of form, rhythmic and plastic continuity, and unity of concept. (2) Toscanini revealed new and hitherto unknown possibilities of virtuosity and clarity in orchestral playing, setting standards which no conductor has surpassed and which few have equaled in these areas. (3) Toscanini's continual attitude of honesty, dedication, and humility toward great music, the antithesis of the celebrated personage who sets himself above the works he plays, not only reaffirmed the highest standard of artistic morality, but resulted in the achievement of performances which exhibited an astonishing degree of penetration into the innermost and hitherto unrevealed aspects of many great works. Toscanini continued to show us new and unexpected things about great music which, in the hands of other conductors, we thought we knew fully in all respects. In his performances one enjoyed, again and again, unique musical experiences, and until there is another Toscanini, we shall never hear them again.

If at this point we turn to the Toscanini recordings, we can quickly find illustrations of change and development in the Maestro's performances. A natural starting point is the Beethoven *Eroica Symphony*, which Toscanini played more than any other, and which we have in three recordings documenting the years 1939, 1949, and 1953. They merit bar by bar comparison, score in hand, but since I cannot provide that sort of analysis here, it is easiest to say that these three performances are a perfect instance of the manner in which as Toscanini played a work over the years he achieved greater and greater degrees of plastic continuity so that, in the light of the artistic unity he finally achieved his first performance seemed almost crude and flung together.

Toscanini really never trusted the metronome. It was "only a machine." It did not breathe—had no heart. (His own metronome was an electric device, battered from being thrown across the room on numerous occasions, and wildly inaccurate. The latter part was perplexing until you realized that the Maestro wanted it to be so obviously untrustworthy that it could always be set aside for the direct musical impulse.) Unless you take a baton and beat out the bars with him you do not really appreciate the manner in which he kept the tempo thoroughly flexible without altering the sense of steady metrical progression. "Give every note its own room," was one of his precepts, but the room needed by a quarter note in common time was by no means a fixed thing. "Follow me—watch me—no two measures are alike," he would say, yet the difference between the two measures could be something so subtle that only he could explain it, the trace of an extra accent here, the slight prolongation of a held note there, a rhythmic emphasis too delicate to be ordinary rubato.

There is no better illustration of these things than the 1953 *Eroica*. To the end Toscanini was searching for the one right way to express every great thing in this music. The difficulty a conductor faces in the *Eroica* is finding a set of tempi which give unity and continuity to the score while still making clear the strikingly different ways in which Beethoven makes use of his thematic materials. The worst problems come from the passages in which Beethoven turns to contrapuntal development. Integrating these sections smoothly into the structure of the whole is a formidable task, with the transitional passages the worst of all.

It was probably always Toscanini's desire to respect Beethoven's marking by playing the entire first movement at one basic tempo. The score reads *Allegro con brio,* and Beethoven never indicates the need for a second such indication of pulse. In the 1939 performance, however, the basic pulse is subjected to a good deal of adjustment. The contrapuntal sections all involve an increase in speed, and the joints between them and the contrasting material are made overly obvious by the changes in the underlying pulse. In the 1949 version Toscanini was closer to his apparent aims. The joints are far less obvious, and the contrapuntal material is assimilated by a simple tightening up of the rhythmic pattern. Even so, a further degree of refinement was possible, for in 1953 the tempo accommodates both the polyphonic and homophonic writing without strain. We have reached the final development of Toscanini's searching for "how it goes," and his awareness of the structure and artistic logic of the movement seems equal to—and thus an ideal expression of—Beethoven's.

The most amazing thing about that *Eroica* of December 6, 1953, was the fact that the changes in its substance came out of the Maestro's mind and directly to his players via the baton. In the first rehearsal of the *Allegro con brio,* where the final performance took shape, he stopped the men only once, demanding more accent on the fortissimo chord at the beginning of the development. Otherwise there was not a word of speech. Except for a ragged moment the Maestro let pass the rehearsal sounds like the performance.

A few minutes later in that session when he turned to the *Marcia funebre,* Toscanini decided that the grace notes of the double basses should come before the beat rather than on the beat—where he had always placed them before. The difference is slight for the average listener, but it added a rhythmic strength which Toscanini wanted, even though it made things harder for the players who were now obliged to attack without a downbeat to cue them. Their first efforts were unclear, imprecise, and the Maestro patiently sang to them and tried again. It didn't go, "Encora!" Toscanini shouted again, and they tried once more. This time it went well, but when he returned to the passage some moments later, there was still trouble. In anticipating the beat, the strings had lost it entirely.

"Bassi," he said almost wistfully, "you are not together—and also too loud. And you 'cello. Nobody is with the stick. I am alone, poor man. Alone. I beat, nobody is with me." Again he sang the phrasing.

With this, seemingly, the difficulties ended. Perhaps the beat became clearer, or perhaps the player suddenly felt the pulse Toscanini wanted. There were no more pauses in that rehearsal.

The impressive thing about the 1953 statement of the movement, indeed, the rest of the entire performance as contrasted with its predecessors, is the way that it sings. The phrases flow one into another with the most miraculous fluid quality, yet never for a moment does the music stop being rhythmic and propulsive in the fullest sense. When a German conductor inserts a pause he generally does so in a fashion that you feel that the motion of the musical line has temporarily ceased, and there is even some of this in the *Eroicas* of 1939 and 1949. By 1953 even the rests move. It is all rhythm and song, even in silence, and a musician who can make the music of silence as eloquent as music in its full sonority has achieved full mastery of his art.

The superiority of the 1953 version continues in the final two movements, although less need be said of them. The problem of the earlier versions was the assimilation of the trio (and the horn solos in particular) into the total structure and the quick metrical pattern. This has now been fully achieved. In the finale the Maestro retained the flexibility in tempo of his previous versions, but there is now a sense of balance and repose which is noticably lacking in 1939. The opening passage in that performance sounds decidedly rushed. In 1953 it has all the same bravura, but it seems to flow effortlessly, and the change of mood in the bars that follow is more effective for this.

I doubt if I shall ever hear a finer *Eroica*.

The process by which a performance tightened up and lost musical force can be followed in the recordings of the *Dawn and Siegfried's Rhine Journey,* a Toscanini specialty that had every opportunity to reflect his changing approach to scores he gave frequently. If we play the 1936 version we hear the dawn arriving at an appropriate speed, and the first climax, beginning in the strings with the theme of "Brünnhilde as a mortal woman" and ending with that of "Siegfried as hero," although slightly quickened for effect, is followed by a return to a slower tempo and a gradual and powerful development of the material through the "Freedom" motif to the tremendous climax in the brass on "Siegfried as hero" at the close of the introductory pages. The *Rhine Journey* proper then begins, and this performance has changed relatively slightly since 1936, except to become faster and very lightly inflected indeed.

The 1936 recording we can imagine as part of an operatic performance in which, to quote Wagner's stage directions, "the red glow of dawn" gradually becomes brighter, and "full daylight" finally bursts upon us at the first climax, but as Toscanini played it in 1949 it is no longer related to dawn (unless it is the fastest sunrise in history) or to the opera house, but has become a concert work. The Brünnhilde material is therefore not merely given an increase in tempo for effect, but the fast tempo is retained after the climax, and the conclusion of the introduction with the big climax on "Siegfried as hero" becomes a frenzied outburst. No better contrast between the Toscanini of 1936 and the Toscanini of the last years can be found than that passage, which comes just at the start of the second side of the 1936 records. The early version is slower, more powerful, and musically justifiable; the second is a triumph of virtuosity, but unless this is enough to satisfy one, it must be added that in purely musical terms the effect has been diminished.

None the less, speed was what Toscanini wanted, and even at his final rehearsal when playing this score after preparation the day before and eleven past performances, the brass could not navigate the "Siegfried as hero" motif without errors (there are minor slips in the 1949 recording) and an outburst of hoarse shouts of *"Ignoranti!"* from the Maestro, and the strings, falling into a reasonable tempo in the Brünnhilde material, provoked another outburst with much pounding on the score and shouts of *"Subito! Subito!"* ("Hurry up! Hurry up!"), when in fact they were playing at a tempo which musicianship and intelligence would specify.

In his later seasons there must have been many times when the only thing that saved Toscanini from disaster in some performances was the phenomenal virtuosity of his orchestra, which could play anything at virtually any tempo, even though his demands required them at times to rush, simply to get all the notes in, without an opportunity to shape the phrases or accent them in the manner which one had previously expected to find in a Toscanini reading.

In the case of the *Haffner, Clock,* and Beethoven *Fourth* symphonies the newer Toscanini recordings give us performances that tightened up in a consistent manner, and the contrast is therefore the obvious one between a relaxed and naturally-flowing melodic line and one that is artificially hastened and intensified. There are also cases where the opposite effect has taken place, in the contrast between a tight 1929 *Sorcerer's Apprentice* and a relaxed 1950 version, or a poor Mozart *G Minor Symphony* from 1938-39 and a fine one, again, from 1950. (1950 was a good year for Toscanini; it is a pity he did not make more records then.) The two *Leonore No. 3*'s offer a more interesting contrast. In the 1939 version the opening pages are played with the breadth and nobility implied in Beethoven's specification that the tempo should be *Adagio.* The more rapid performance of 1945 does not capture this so well. With the second of the two famed trumpet calls the 1939 recording picks up speed and proceeds to the finish in a faster and more brilliant style. In spite of its quicker opening, after the second trumpet call the 1945 recording adopts a trifle slower tempo than that of 1939. In time the faster pace of the opening pages of the 1945 version compensates for a few seconds' difference in the final ones. The 1945 set covers the material of the first side of the 1939 recording in seventeen seconds less time, which is a fair difference in only thirty-six bars of music. The faster opening of 1945 is distinctly in keeping with the accustomed style of Toscanni's later years.

In the case of the Brahms *Third Symphony,* Toscanini apparently never found a performance which satisfied him as an adequate statement of the score. There were basically two approaches we heard from him, the first a tight, hard-driving version in which lyricism was sacrificed to intensity; the second, a slower, relaxed statement of the score that was even a little loose and slack on occasion. The second version, when held well in hand, always appeared to me to be the more enjoyable and Brahmsian, but when, before making the recording, Toscanini pieced together an "ideal" performance for himself it was of the former type. Ironically the recording is a mongrel. It certainly is not the "ideal" performance he had in mind, and it is an inferior statement of the relaxed version compared with those I have heard on other occasions. I find it a very interesting disk, largely because I look upon it as a failure, and in analyzing its weaknesses we learn something about Toscanini's customary strong points.

"The first movement of the *Third*," Rodzinski once told me, "contains more problems than all the rest of the four Brahms symphonies put together." The opening bars clearly are to be taken two beats to the measure and at a reasonably brisk pace which gives a firm rhythmic feeling to the phrases, but Toscanini's tempo is actually too slow to provide this. A problem arises over the semi-staccato notes which close bars 4, 6, 8, and 10. The proper feeling for them is of a lighter, i.e., "up" beat, but Toscanini gives the passages in question a choppy, irregular rhythmic quality by taking the semi-staccato notes lightly accented but at their full written value and allowing the first note of the bar following to be heavily accented in bar 5 by the supporting harmonies in the trombones and tympani. The question of scanning this figure is not made easier by Brahms' deviations in the notation. For example, in bar 10 these notes are marked staccato; but to give a most troublesome instance, in bar 129 the notes are written semi-staccato, although two bars later in bar 131 they are staccato once more. (References are to the Eulenberg edition of the score.) Koussevitzky's solution was to take these notes as if they were staccato in every case, thus the shorter, more accented playing of them in his performance. In bars 60-63 the first note of each phrase must be given the slightest accent and the final one the slightest prolongation beyond its written value if the interweaving of the voices is to be smooth and the sense of forward movement secure, but Toscanini's listless execution of the passage lacks these desired qualities. His response to the points at which Brahms asks for a slight retardation (such as bar 109) and his interpretation of the *Un poco sostenuto* marking in bar 112 involve excesses, which in the former case almost halt the forward progress of the music. Repeatedly he fails to set a strong, rhythmic pulse when it is required, and in bars 187-94 where the cross-rhythm demands an absolutely solid and reliable feeling for accent and scansion, Toscanini fails utterly, with the result that the playing is meaningless confusion. While the "ideal" version was forceful and consistent in style, this is insecure and tentative.

The second movement is easy and goes well, and the third, which gave Toscanini difficulty in the past, was here stated effectively, if one has no objection to the slow tempo. The final movement again calls for intensity and strength, and here Toscanini simply throws away his opportunities and fails to make the score yield up more than a fraction of its glories. The opening phrases are slack, although the same material is better stated later in the movement (perhaps a splice from another take?). It must not be thought that this was a recording from one of Toscanini's final concerts. Only a month before he had played the score brilliantly and within a week of this session he made his powerful and characteristic Beethoven *Eighth*. I suggest that he had over-prepared the score, like a schoolboy who studies too hard for an examination. The weaknesses exhibited here anticipate features of a few performances the year following, in his final season with the orchestra, in which old age was clearly responsible for a decline in his powers. Meanwhile, it would be a good thing if the "ideal" version were released for general circulation.

If the Brahms *Third* gave Toscanini troubles, the final passacaglia of the *Fourth,* which the majority of conductors do not play correctly, was perfectly grasped and achieved in a manner all but unequaled by any of his contemporaries. The basis of a passacaglia is an eight-bar phrase, usually in the bass (although Brahms does not always keep it there) which provides a vertebrate foundation for a series of variations in the upper voices. In the final movement there are exactly thirty variations after the statement of the theme, and it is on bar 249 that the final variation ends and the transition into the coda begins. The form, then, is a strict one, and it demands strict respect in the execution of the work. Specifically, since the eight-bar phrase is the link which holds the variations together, it must always be stated at the same tempo so that the cumulative effect of the thirty-one varied repetitions will come with the full weight the composer intended. It is therefore a great pleasure to hear the movement played with the careful attention to continuity which Toscanini provides, and especially to find that the fourth variation is not speeded up, nor the twelfth retarded beyond the indicated change in the time signature, and that the many other things (such as the surging power of variation 25, which are lost through the insensitivity of other conductors to the form of the work) Toscanini does exactly right. In this recording, therefore, we have from him a model for all others to follow in performing this great score.

Ironically two of Toscanini's finest performances have not been generally recognized as such and have provoked a considerable amount of criticism, usually from those whose opinions are based upon misplaced respect for faulty traditions of style, or whose judgments of music are based entirely on its emotional effect: in other words persons who fail to see that the critic is not simply an individual who for one reason or another is allowed to circulate his opinions and impressions in print, but rather one who (at least ideally) is competent to study a score, secure a justifiable, musicianlike concept of how it should be played, and appraise whether or not a given performance appears to be a satisfactory statement of the composer's intentions. This is particularly important in this case, since a musically honest version of some scores is emotionally less stimulating than a grossly exaggerated one, and if the degree of stimulation is, in fact, the criterion invoked, debased musical values are asserted.

The critiques of Toscanini's performance of the great *C*

Major Symphony of Schubert reflect a lack of study of the score and the instructions the composer clearly provided in the music. At the best one can concede that a slightly slower tempo might be appropriate for the *Andante,* but the most rudimentary comprehension of the score justifies Toscanini's practice and rebuts the standard of the insensitive "traditional" performance which is invoked against him. The Tchaikovsky *Pathétique Symphony* is another case of the same type, but worth fuller discussion. Here the criticisms are three in number: that Toscanini does not know the proper "Russian" style or Tchaikovsky style; that his performance is completely unsympathetic; that his performance diminishes the content and value of the music. Let us consider these in order.

Actually, Tchaikovsky was regarded by his hyper-nationalist contemporaries of the Mussorgsky—Borodin—Rimsky-Korsakov school as a German, that is, as a composer who rejected a distinctive Russian idiom in musical expression. Certainly the demand that as pure and universal a work as the *Pathétique* be played with heavy, overdone "Russian" style is an absurdity. Toscanini's approach is musically justifiable beyond any doubt.

The orchestral sound of the Toscanini performance is clear, bright and transparent, an unfamiliar effect in Tchaikovsky, where conductors tend to run the lines of instrumentation into a thicker, darker tone. None the less, Toscanini uses the same type of sound (it was his standard approach) in *Manfred, Romeo and Juliet,* the *Nutcracker,* etc., without any comparable chorus of discontent. The answer is, I suppose, that although scored with wonderful transparency, the *Pathétique* is *supposed* to sound dark and murky and suggest the limp, hooded figures Victor invariably placed on the album cover.

The *Pathétique* is apparently thought by some to be unadulterated purple passion from start to finish, and they want it played that way. The orchestral sound must not only be dark and mellow, but the phrasing, accents, tempi, etc., must depart from the composer's printed instructions and turn the work into a traumatic circus. The demand for such falsification is an insult to the emotionally mature listener.

To appreciate this performance one must follow it, at least

once, with the score, noting the splendid transparency and balance and the skill with which every detail is stated clearly and effectively, and yet as a part of a whole. The beginning is really the marked *Adagio,* but without excess. There is no fussing with the solos in the woodwind here, or anywhere else, the *ritenuto* in bar 17 is that, and no emotional upheaval, and the following *Allegro non troppo* is just that, with the figures clean and well defined, consistent, rhythmically accurate, and firm in their propulsive force.

When one has experienced such things as the middle section of the slow movement with the strings and woodwind blending in lovely, controlled motion as the composer intended, followed by the march as a thing of lightning and fire, moving forward with increasing brilliance, and heard the final pages of the score as the quiet chant of low voices, each singing clearly and well to the very end, one will, I think, appreciate that this is the way it ought to be, that this is a beautiful and effective performance of a magnificent score, and that anyone who tries to tell him different is talking nonsense.

Another such model is Toscanini's performance of *La Mer,* which, although played in fifty-three concerts during his American career, miraculously escaped over-refinement and remained fresh and brilliant, probably because it is not a German work and the style appropriate to it was based upon clarity and song, the two basic elements of his musicianship. Here again the appreciation of his performance demands that we hear it, at least once, with the score and discover for ourselves the manner in which he does, literally, give our ears everything which the printed music presents to our eyes.

Debussy's instructions are that the first part of *La Mer* (*From Dawn to Noon on the Sea*) should begin very slowly with the sustained low note of the contrabasses and tympani suggesting the darkness covering the water just before the first appearance of light. The rising theme in the 'cellos, which moves to the violas and finally the violins, suggests the gradually increasing luminosity as the dawn begins to break, and the sustained countertheme in the woodwind and trumpet conveys the sensation of air moving over the now visible water. Toscanini achieves these effects splendidly, and at number 2 in the score,[7] where Debussy asks for a gradual increase in the movement of the voices to prepare for the change in the time signature from 6/4 to 6/8 at 9 bars after 2, Toscanini produces the desired effect subtly and establishes the moderate and very supple rhythm requested with consummate understanding of the composer's desires.

As I have mentioned before, music is the one art in which the creator of the work cannot speak directly to the public but must employ the services of an intermediary. Were musical notation perfect, it might be possible for the composer to indicate exactly how he intends his music to be played; but musical notation is not perfect, and a good performance demands of the performer that he be able to read into the printed notes the elements of style and execution which lie beyond the limits of the notation itself.

The middle section of the first of these symphonic sketches is given to a series of vigorous passages which suggests the movement of the water as the sun gradually climbs higher in the sky and casts changing patterns of light on its surface through the clouds. This material comes to an end 5 bars after 8 in three massive chords for full orchestra, and a quieter mood follows. At 2 bars before 9 there is an unusually imaginative passage in which the strings depict a sudden upward swell in the waves and the tympani and horns in turn echo the sound. During the remaining pages of the movement the scene tends to be more subdued than before, until suddenly, from the peak of its arc, the noonday sun bursts through the overcast sky and casts a blazing shaft of light down upon the water.

The second part of *La Mer* (*The Play of the Waves*) is the most difficult work Debussy wrote for orchestra, since its climax depends on a faultless execution of one of the most demanding passages ever scored for strings. The tempo of the music is fast, but again Debussy insists upon a supple rhythm, and it is clear that he wants a flexible, sensitive beat rather than metronomic accuracy. In the very first bars we

[7] References are to the numbering of the sections in the copyright score published by Durand & Cie, Paris.

hear the rise and fall of the water, and, high, above, the graceful soaring flight of a bird. (It is a part of Debussy's genius that his pictures are always vivid but never crudely explicit.) This interplay of water and air continues for a few minutes, a violin solo suggesting the foam flying before the breeze, and out of this image a climactic passage for full orchestra is developed. At *33* the true climax of the movement begins, and if Toscanini has not produced marvels enough up to this point, he now surpasses himself in the manner in which he keeps his orchestra integrated and holds the groups of notes in a firm, singing line, so that no detail intrudes upon the complete form of the whole, ending with a breathtaking statement of the four supremely difficult bars before *38*. It is an amazing vision of air, water, and light in motion.

The Dialogue of the Wind and the Sea which concludes the three sketches is a somewhat grimmer picture than those which precede it. Over a hushed bass note we hear the splash of angry waves, to which the wind replies with a faraway call from vast spaces ruled by no man. This is developed, and at *46* we hear the song of this wilderness of air sung over the steady slap and fall of the earth-bound water, and out of this grows a climactic passage. Quiet follows, and then, over the unworldly sound of a sustained harmonic in the violins, the wind, soft and with great expression, sings once more. A short, climactic passage follows, full of moving water, and this leads to the final pages, a magnificent vision of swirling air and choppy water mounting to the intensity of the final blast of flying spray that breaks and brings the work to a close.

La Mer is a difficult and complicated score. When we realize that in 1860 *Tristan und Isolde* was regarded by presumably competent persons as being so difficult as to be impossible to produce, the mere fact that *La Mer* could be written in 1905 with the thought of a performance shows the great advances in the technique of orchestral playing in the final decades of the nineteenth century; and the fact that a Toscanini could achieve a performance of this level, not merely in 1950, but by all reports in 1926 when he first played the score in New York, and probably soon after he first played the work in Europe,[8] shows the level of mastery which he introduced into the art of orchestral conducting. Perfection in art is the rarest of all things, especially in an art with as many difficulties as conducting. Toscanini's *La Mer* is an example of such perfection. It is, to begin, one of the greatest pieces of music ever written. His conception of it shows complete understanding, sympathy, and mastery at every point, not merely in the things given in the written notation, but in the elements of style, color, texture, etc., which the notation can never give. Finally it is a performance polished to the highest limits of virtuosity by an orchestra completely familiar with his methods, demands, and artistic creed. The result is something which will stand indefinitely as a triumph of orchestral playing and which sets a standard for the performance of this work which few conductors will ever meet and none is likely to surpass: for here surely, one feels, is the very image that lay in the composer's mind.

[8] Toscanini first gave *La Mer* some time in the period 1905-18, since he prepared it during Debussy's lifetime, but the exact date cannot be determined.

Chapter 3

The Toscanini Recordings

ON DECEMBER 18, 1920, Toscanini gathered the La Scala Orchestra into a compact group before the horns of the acoustical recording apparatus in an ecclesiastical structure that, in this secular role, was known as the Trinity Church Studio of the Victor Talking Machine Company in Camden, New Jersey. In that setting he made his first records, a minuet from a Mozart symphony and a Respighi transcription of a work by the father of Galileo.

Toscanini was at the mid-point of his career. A man of fifty-three, he had been conducting for thirty-four years, and thirty-four more years were to pass before he retired from the direction of his last, and greatest orchestra. In the decades between 1920 and 1956 Toscanini made or approved for commercial release about two hundred and fifty recordings (in addition to taking part in a non-commercial series for the American armed forces). Thus preserved are Toscanini performances of some two hundred compositions, a substantial number of which have been recorded more than once, the champion being the *Scherzo* from Mendelssohn's *Incidental Music to "A Midsummer Night's Dream"* which was released in five versions: 1921, 1926, 1929, 1946, and 1947. By the year of his retirement over twenty million copies of Toscanini recordings had been sold for more than thirty-three million dollars. In every way it was a fabulous achievement. Few conductors remained active so long, recorded so much of their repertory, or were accepted so universally by the musical public.

This chapter contains a full chronological list of those records, but more than that, it is an appraisal of the documents in sound which Toscanini left for the generations who will never hear him in a concert hall and must rely (as many of his contemporaries were obliged to do) upon recordings for an understanding of his musicianship and an appreciation of his contribution to orchestral playing.

Recording is not a new thing, but faithful reproduction of anything as complex as the sound of a symphony orchestra is a recent phenomenon. The acoustical method was adequate for preserving human voices, and recordings of singers made even sixty years ago give an accurate impression of the artist. Pre-electrical recordings of symphony orchestras, on the other hand, are poor as a group, although some early electrical recordings have life in them in spite of limited fidelity. Really faithful reproduction of orchestral sound is less than twenty years old, with the work of the past dozen years greatly superior to that of the preceding fifteen and complete verisimilitude still to be fully achieved, at least with the sound equipment available in the average home. Because of this it is still possible to view recordings with a certain amount of patronizing indifference. The truth is, modern electroacoustical techniques are adding a new dimension to the history of music and making the re-creation of past experiences an actual possibility.

If one were to document the sixty-eight years of Toscanini's career with records, it would first be necessary to have adequate disks from his early period, and, secondly, widely spaced re-recordings of a number of works, so that important changes in his manner of performing them could be noted. The recordings necessary for such documentation do not exist, although acetate recordings of the N.B.C. Symphony broadcasts, recordings taken from the air of his broadcasts with the Philharmonic-Symphony Orchestra of New York, and similar materials extend the available recordings considerably beyond the list of commercially released disks given here. The greater part of this supplementary material is in the family archive at Riverdale under the supervision of the Maestro's son, Mr. Walter Toscanini. Unfortunately, technicalities currently prevent the circulation of recordings of broadcasts, rehearsals, and the like, even for study purposes. One hopes, however, that at some time the range of generally available Toscanini material will be extended (with permission of the American Federation of Musicians) to include some of the great broadcast performances that have up to now been neglected. My own feeling is that a Toscanini Society Series is in order to preserve, in limited editions for students and musicians, Toscanini performances that may be flawed in one way or another, but still contain miracles.

For half of his career Toscanini made no records. In middle life we have a brief acoustical series from 1920-21 followed by early electrical recordings from 1926 and 1929. As acoustical records go, the Toscanini disks are good, and the 1926 and 1929 records are technically adequate for their day. One would have thought that in eleven seasons with the Philharmonic-Symphony Orchestra of New York there would have been recording sessions at regular intervals, but in fact all that are documented are his first concerts with the orchestra as a guest conductor, the period in which he left La Scala to become the principal conductor of the Philharmonic, and his final season. (Victor's great 1936 series is the lasting demonstration of what the Philharmonic had become in his hands.) There were three good reasons for this apparent neglect of a unique opportunity: (1) The country was in a state of depression and the record business was supposedly finished because radio could provide limitless "free" music in the home. The natural reply to this was Victor's famous advertising slogan, "The music you want when you want it." (2) Toscanini didn't care whether he made any records or not, since he could not see how anyone could obtain musical satisfaction from listening to them. (3) An experiment at taking recordings from a broadcast during 1933 using optical sound recording (an early technique to get around the limitations of disks and secure some of the technical advantages later obtained with tape) had produced versions of the *Fifth* and *Pastoral* symphonies of Beethoven which were so unsatisfactory they were not even played to the Maestro. This meant the only way to get records was to invest money in an expensive recording session with the hope that something could be obtained which, when released, would pay for the job. The 1936 investment seems to have liquidated itself nicely.

The thing Toscanini particularly hated in recording was the

need to stop at the end of a four minute "take" and then try to begin a new one with the same tempo and rhythmic drive he had established previously. The whole point of a Toscanini performance is plastic continuity, and the way to secure this was by recording continuously, without pauses. Therefore in 1936 the engineers set up their recording machines so that they could switch from one to another at predetermined points in the score, without the orchestra stopping, and for this reason the sides do not always begin and end as neatly as they might. Often the cutters were running for several seconds before the break was made and the sound fed to them. None the less, the three days of recording that took place on February 8 and April 9 and 10, 1936, produced the finest series of disks then available in the Victor catalog and preserved a group of brilliant performances which Toscanini was never able to duplicate.

Toscanini went to Britain in October, 1937, and made two excellent sets for the His Master's Voice Company with the symphony orchestra of the British Broadcasting Corporation. Their first efforts to record him had been unsuccessful, but the 1937 series was an unqualified triumph. Returning to the United States in December, he made his first records with his new N.B.C. orchestra the following March. They marked the beginning of the seven lean and dreadful years of Toscanini's American recording. The orchestra was not at first as responsive an ensemble as the Philharmonic or the B.B.C. had been, and the recording was done in the notorious Studio 8-H.

It was in this studio that Toscanini played and recorded for about thirteen years, an appropriate interval of time, everything considered. The main thing wrong with 8-H was that it was heavily treated acoustically to eliminate the natural reverberation which, it was thought, would be bad for broadcasting, and the sound took on a dead, wooden quality even in the brief interval that it lived before being absorbed by the walls or ceiling. One had the sense of listening to an orchestra play in a soundproof box, and it was this distorted and unnatural sound, made worse by low fidelity reproduction, that one heard on a Toscanini broadcast and in many Toscanini recordings of the period. Indeed, in 1954 these disks were being used for research in the addition of resonance to music, since they were practically the only available recordings of an orchestra playing in an almost completely dead room. Unfortunately this quality was not what was wanted in records for home listening. A bad consequence of this is that it set up a form of conditioning in some people, a few of them critics, that Toscanini recordings could always be expected to be technically inferior to those of other conductors. The facts do not support this. Although unsatisfactory by present-day criteria of fidelity, Victor gave Toscanini excellent acoustical recording in 1920-21 and electrical recording in the 1929 and 1936 series. The sudden decline in quality was a departure from their previously high standards. In later years the level of excellence was restored.

In 1938 and 1939 Toscanini was alternately making superior recordings for HMV in England and technically poor ones for Victor in the United States. After the outbreak of war the British engineers had no further opportunities to work with him, and from 1940 to the beginning of the recording ban by the American Federation of Musicians in 1942 Victor could do their worst, without competition offering any basis for invidious comparison. After recording resumed in 1944 their work was uneven, with startling improvements followed by temporary relapses into earlier ways.

In 1940 Victor responded to the criticism of its Studio 8-H recordings by moving to Carnegie Hall for the Brahms *Piano Concerto No. 2,* producing a set that, on the good machines of the period, sounded full and beautiful, and conveyed a reasonable likeness of an exciting Toscanini-Horowitz performance. On the high fidelity equipment of today the set is severely limited, but this is not a fair test of the effect it produced when it first appeared.

Unfortunately Victor did not keep their work at this level. One of the big problems of the time was the rapid wear of the bass cut in shellac records, due mainly to the heavy pickups and "permanent" or "multiple play" steel needles that were then the standard equipment in home-type machines. Victor tried to reduce bass wear by emphasizing treble and reducing bass (in some records one could actually hear the volume being turned up for the passages with important low notes and turned down immediately after they had sounded), a practice which could only distort and coarsen the sound of Toscanini performances. Most of the 1941-42 recordings bear the scars of this, the worst one being the *Traviata Preludes,* made with the nearest thing to no bass at all.

For the two years following, due to the union edict, there were no recording sessions, but sixteen works were taken from broadcasts at that time and released on V-Disks for the American armed forces. When Victor resumed work, after an abortive start with still another broadcast recording, the quality of the sound had improved remarkably. Bass was back, the middle registers, supported now from below, had solidity, and the highs were not distorted by overemphasis. There was still a certain amount of coarseness, due mainly to limited frequency response that gave us the hard, fundamental tone of an instrument without the overtones which make the live performance brilliant and agreeable to the ear. At times the sound was confined or flattened out by excessive monitoring, but the greater part of the 1944-47 recordings can be played on high fidelity equipment and reveal themselves to be competent, medium fidelity, disks which can still be heard with satisfaction.

In the early 'forties Toscanini finally became somewhat more interested in making records. It was now possible for recorded sound to approximate the actual sound of an orchestra. Always before, the drastic reduction of the relative levels of volume, the lack of presence, and the loss of tonal values, together with the generally artificial quality of the sound, had prevented him from securing any pleasure from listening to records, and he found it difficult to understand how others could enjoy them. "That must be a flute," Walter Toscanini recalls his father remarking as something was being played, "because the violin cannot do that. But [pause for growing exasperation] it does not *sound* like a flute!"

At that time he was listening to his own recordings on a large and handsome RCA Victor machine, supplied him by the company. It was typical of the best home-type phonographs of the period. The public demanded record changers, and, indeed, with four-minute 78 rpm disks they were a great convenience, so the playing unit was a changer mechanism with a small motor driving a table that might carry the weight of a dozen records or that of a single disk, with the speed changing as the weight increased. The pick-up had to be heavy, since the record-changing cycle subjected it to a certain amount of abuse, and the needle was of the quasi-permanent metallic sort. A high-output crystal head fed into a low-gain amplifier with a functional top limit at about 3,800 cps, a weak middle range, and distortion up to fifty per cent in some frequencies at high volume settings. The speaker was a large, single cone type hung on the front of the cabinet without an adequate baffle. There is no question but that the sound produced by such machines was poor, but the public as a whole did not know that there was, in fact, much better sound on their records, and that with adequate re-producing equipment it could be heard.

The irony was that Toscanini never really heard his records and rejected a number of things that, played today, seem much better than those that were approved. Victor wanted a Beethoven *Ninth* from him very badly, and, judging from the test records, made a very tolerable one in 1938 at the close of his first season with the N.B.C. Symphony. It was not approved for release, although inferior recordings of the *Eroica Symphony, Egmont,* and two of the *Leonore Overtures* from his first Beethoven cycle with the orchestra during the season following were given his approval. In this case the issue was largely dynamics. A 1938 recording could not capture the climaxes of the Toscanini Beethoven *Ninth;* they had to be monitored in order to keep them on the record, just as the softest passages had to be raised in volume to keep the level of the sound above the surface noise of the shellac records. This did not suit the Maestro. "That is NOT my *fortissimo,*" he would shout as the record was played, just as a moment later he would insist, "That is NOT my *pianissimo.* That is not even *pianissimo.* That is *PIANO!*" Everything considered, it is probably miraculous that he gave his consent to the release of as many records as he did.

Recording was always something of an ordeal for Toscanini. Even if the disk was low in fidelity, it preserved something, and if it said Toscanini on it, it had to meet his criteria of perfection. From the very beginning he recorded only on the condition that he have the right to reject any disk which failed to meet his standards. In 1920-21 he lavished the greatest concentration of energy and skill on nine recording sessions from which emerged sixteen sides of acceptable music (six of them only ten inch) which, at best, could reproduce only a small part of the over-all effect of the performance. The 1926 and 1929 records, even the great 1936 series, left him unsatisfied.

Tension never vanished from his recording sessions. When cutting a 78 rpm master a single slip could ruin a take and four minutes of tense and otherwise perfect work. A series of minor slips could ruin an entire album and prevent its release. Stopping and starting were unwelcome requirements which persisted even after 1949 when Victor began using tape to replace wax master disks. For a time Victor wanted to record in seven-minute takes to fit 45 rpm surfaces. Tape did, however, make splicing and correction relatively easy. Improvements of this sort made it easier to convince the Maestro that his agonies were for a worthy cause.

The most celebrated instance of a long and expensive series of recording sessions producing nothing for commercial release is the Maestro's work with the Philadelphia Orchestra in 1942. Two symphonies, the *Pathétique* and the Schubert *Ninth, La Mer, Ibéria,* the *Midsummer Night's Dream* music, *Roman Festivals, Death and Transfiguration,* and Berlioz's *Queen Mab Scherzo* were recorded in brilliant performances, but the level was too low, there were occasional flaws (such as an oboe that could not be heard properly at the beginning of the second movement of *La Mer*) and in some instances no duplicate masters were cut, which means there was only one wax blank of the take. When the whole lot was damaged in the process of electroplating the wax blanks, there was no way of salvaging the recordings, since the level of the surface noise was as high as that of the quieter parts of the music. It once seemed none of these disks would ever be available to the public, splendid as the performances were, but there is now hope that at least a few can be issued.

Early in the 'forties Walter Toscanini had a high fidelity system built for his father's use. Twelve speakers were wired in parallel and mounted around a large room in groups of four, giving the sense of non-directional sound emerging from a wide source. With a high quality amplifier which could provide a great deal of volume without distortion, some feeling of orchestral presence could be secured, and at once the Maestro accepted the idea of making records and preserving his performances on disks. He was finally coming to think that the result was worth the effort it demanded. The Toscanini home began to contain a profusion of recording and playback equipment, and the dozen speakers gave way in time to a large, corner-type baffle with supplementary speakers located in near-by rooms. The principle of non-directional sound, low distortion, and volume levels equal to the concert hall original were maintained, however. The Maestro wanted a record to sound exactly as the music sounded to him on the podium.

Of all conductors, Toscanini most needed high fidelity. The brilliance of the sound he produced with an orchestra, the transparency of the texture, the clarity of the lines of the instrumentation, all required recording which gave the effect of the strings, brasses, winds, and percussion properly balanced, and placed in resonant space without any loss of definition and overtones. Anything less than this was not merely poor recording but a gross distortion of the sound of the original, since something which was blazing and beautiful in the hall might well, when cut down to 3,800 cps on top and confined by a low volume level, come out coarse, blatant, and wooden.

Starting in December, 1944, with a respectable Studio 8-H version of the Beethoven *Prometheus Overture*, Toscanini's records could be compared favorably with those being made by other conductors at the time. The following May, again in Studio 8-H, he recorded Gershwin's *An American in Paris*, and the sound was so good that when the record was released in the 'fifties (for some reason it never appeared on 78 disks) in a longplay transfer, most critics accepted it as recent work.

A part of this improvement could be laid to a "new technique" being used for recording in the studio. The orchestra was taken off the rather shallow stage and set up on the floor, which had been cleared of the seats normally occupied by the audience. In this way fuller use could be made of the natural resonance of what was, all in all, a reasonably large concert room. Unfortunately Victor moved Toscanini into another, smaller studio, 3-A, for three recording sessions in 1946 and one in 1947, and here they reached the low point of their work in the 1944-47 period.

Nonetheless, the majority of Toscanini recordings were then being made in Carnegie Hall, and although the uneven quality of the engineering of the period can be found in the contrast between the poor sound of the Carnegie Hall recording of the Mozart *Jupiter Symphony* and the excellence of *An American in Paris* or the Mozart *Divertimento K.287*, both made in Studio 8-H, on the whole the technical side was doing well by the Old Man. With a few elementary adjustments in equalization, filtering, and the like, nearly all of the records of 1944-47 can be heard on high fidelity equipment with pleasure. Fundamentally the sound that is there is an accurate replica of the playing of a great orchestra.

Medium fidelity gave way to high fidelity with the sudden upheaval of the American recording industry caused by the introduction by the Columbia company of the modern longplaying record in the early summer of 1948. Because of these disturbed conditions, Toscanini directed no recording sessions for fifteen months.

His first major work in the new period was a complete recording of *Aïda,* made during broadcasts in March and April of 1949. There were no formal recording sessions until November when somewhat disappointing versions of the Beethoven *Second Symphony, Daphnis and Chloe,* and the *Eroica* were done in Carnegie Hall on wax masters. After that, tape was used and improvement was rapid. A group of recordings made in Carnegie Hall in December, 1949, are all excellent, high fidelity disks, and two groups of recordings made in Carnegie Hall and Studio 8-H (the last, in fact, to be done in that inglorious place) in March and June, 1950, immediately before and after the Maestro's American tour with the N.B.C. Symphony, are highly acceptable. There is then a gap until January, when he made the first of the recordings which represent the 1950-51 season.

The seasons 1951-52 and 1952-53 were Toscanini's period of intense, high fidelity recording. More than forty compositions were recorded in the 1951-52 season and the summer following, and better than twenty were done in 1952-53. In his final season with the orchestra he canceled the recording sessions which had been arranged, as well as the Brahms *German Requiem* which he had been asked to prepare for his final concert of the spring series. A number of recordings were made during broadcasts, and in June he returned briefly to make a few corrections for insertion in his broadcast performances of *Aïda* and *Un Ballo in Maschera*. With that he stepped down.

As we survey the thirty-four years in which Toscanini made records, we must be thankful for the length of his career and the opportunity given us to preserve his unique powers on high fidelity disks. If, like Koussevitzky, he had retired at seventy-five, there would have been no Toscanini recordings later than 1942, and his position would be similar to that of Weingartner, whose excellence is still universally acknowledged but is suggested rather than retained in the recordings he left us. Of the distinguished conductors of the generation before (some of them Toscanini's contemporaries) very little remains for us to hear. Mahler—only seven years senior to Toscanini—would have remained active, in all probability, until the 'thirties, had he not died prematurely. He made no recordings. Nikisch, whose recording career was limited to a few, historic oddities, we have lost, while Muck's ancient-sounding disks offer only imperfect replicas of great playing. Toscanini we have in full blood.

In July of 1955, hardly a year after his retirement, Toscanini began the systematic appraisal of his broadcast recordings with the hope that all those appropriate for general circulation might be edited and reprocessed in accordance with his demands. This was the beginning of the Riverdale Project, so named from the Maestro's home in the northern reaches of New York City where a former billiard room had been converted into a professional sound laboratory. Walter Toscanini carried the burden of organization and administration, and the technical responsibilities went to two highly qualified engineers long associated with the Maestro, Messrs. Richard B. Gardner and John Corbett.

Toscanini was eager to help, and old friends from the orchestra often dropped in to listen as well. "I am just beginning to realize," he told one of them one day, "how much beautiful music we made together." During the first year of the project about a half dozen additional Toscanini recordings were released and about a dozen further items were edited to the Maestro's satisfaction. Then, early in 1957, Toscanini died.

Victor executives expected Toscanini's will to forbid the release of any recording he had not personally approved, but when his final decision was made known it was found that his son, Walter, had been given the right to issue posthumous recordings from the archive that now filled the basement. As the painful immediacy of the Maestro's death became less acute, the Riverdale Project went on with Walter Toscanini in charge and John Corbett as his resident engineer.

But now there was trouble ahead. The summer of 1958 brought the stereophonic record and the entire sales force of the recording industry was marshalled to sell the new product. The Riverdale records were not stereophonic, many of them didn't even qualify as high fidelity. Toscanini had ceased to be a public figure four years earlier. In short, there was little place for this material in a record market that was concentrating on current celebrities and the new sound of stereo rather than excellence in musicianship. The public, in fact, has yet to hear all the recordings which Toscanini approved in his lifetime.

The Riverdale Project went on, preparing tapes against the day when Toscanini performances would be recognized for musical qualities that compensated for any engineering drawbacks. That day is coming soon. The first impact of stereo is past, and the more serious record collector is thinking increasingly in terms of excellence in performance rather than opulence in recorded sound. Moreover, we are finally securing the needed perspective so that the merits of the finest Toscanini recordings stand out much more plainly. Perhaps as good an example of this was the autumn of 1961 when two companies (one of them RCA-Victor) issued new, lavishly cast, and gorgeously stereophonic editions of *Otello*. The critical consensus was that neither could rival the fourteen year old Toscanini version. This is not an isolated case. There are many instances in which a Toscanini recording is the finest musical realization ever given a particular score on discs. As a growing and maturing musical public comes to appreciate this, Toscanini will regain his audience and the Riverdale legacy will come into our hands.

CHRONOLOGY OF THE TOSCANINI RECORDINGS

In the Toscanini family archives at Riverdale there are some 1,200 hours of sound on tape—enough to keep one occupied for four months of concentrated listening. All the Maestro's commercial recordings are there, plus many (but by no means all) of his broadcasts. Moreover, there are a large number of more personal sound documents of his life and work, such as a steel rack of conversations with friends and a huge, seven by nine foot rack that is filled on both sides with tapes of rehearsals. The conversations have not been played since his death. The family is accustomed to hearing the Maestro's working voice in rehearsal tapes, but his off stage voice, the social and affectionate voice of their life together, might still be too strong a reminder of his loss. Since the family archive is a private collection, there is much there which the public will never, and need never, see or hear, but the essential elements for a documentation of Toscanini the musician, his working methods, and his achievements are all safely preserved. They are supplemented in the N.B.C. files by films of ten concerts which were telecast, films that show not only the finished result but also some of the rehearsals that went into its preparation. Among the programs so documented are the two parts of *Aïda* in 1949.

The list that follows is a compilation of the Toscanini recordings we have had available at one time or another, plus some of the obvious and better known extensions of that material. It is in no sense exhaustive, but it is complete in certain categories. I give by date all the Toscanini recordings released commercially, all the Toscanini V-Disks in the World War II series for the American armed forces, and all the material which Mr. Walter Toscanini has authorized or issued in private editions. (When such a private edition duplicates a commercial record, only the commercial disk is cited.) Also listed are the American tape editions of Toscanini recordings.

I indicate some fifty items which constitute prime Toscanini material, either for sheer enjoyment or for the study of his artistry, which have not appeared as commercial recordings. Some of these works may appear commercially in the future. Others are already in circulation through the medium of unauthorized (or pirated) copies taken from the air. Such air-check copies are generally of poor to mediocre quality, and the fact that certain of these performances can attract an audience even in this form would seem to demonstrate that there is a market for high quality editions from the Riverdale tapes. By making the public aware of the existence of this material I am, in effect, inviting you to speak up and say whether or not you want the opportunity to buy these works in authorized versions.

Except for one or two cases where a recording was never released in the United States, the numbers given here are exclusively those of the American editions. All records are to be taken as twelve inches in size unless otherwise noted. Those who wish to find a full account of the various numbers under which these recordings have been pressed in the United States and elsewhere are referred to Clough and Cuming's *The World's Encyclopedia of Recorded Music* of which there are at present three volumes (London, 1952/53/57).

A star * indicates that the recording was out of print in the United States early in 1962.

All 78 rpm. recordings are listed under the album number by which they were best known during their stay in the catalog, but any 78 rpm. set which was transferred to long-play disks is listed only in its $33\frac{1}{3}$ rpm. form. The same applies to material which was transferred to the 45 rpm. speed. I list no 45 rpm. records which are duplicated by long-play disks.

Mr. Robert Hupka is in the process of preparing a listing of the Toscanini recordings which will go into detail on such matters as the number of times a given work was played during a recording session, the timings of the various "takes," microphone placement, etc. Since he has open to him research facilities at RCA which are no longer available to me, it has been my decision in revising this list to make it as simple as possible and direct it to those whose interest in these recordings is essentially musical rather than technical.

It is, however, necessary to make note of one or two problems arising out of RCA engineering practices.

It is the normal RCA-Victor procedure from time to time to replace the stampers from which a record is made. All Victor disks have in their surface a stamper number, so on examination it is possible to tell which of the various stampers cut from the master tape were used in the pressing of a particular disk. Some of the stampers used in the pressing of the Toscanini recordings have been markedly superior to others. For example, Debussy's *Ibéria* is best heard from the stamper identified as 12S. The full number on the preferred disk is E2 RP 4036-12S.

Some seven years ago a number of Toscanini recordings were transferred to disk with artificial resonance added. A great many people (among them the Maestro) felt that this served to coarsen the sound, and over the years most of these recordings have been replaced with new versions without additional resonance. There are only a few instances where this has not been done, and in those cases your odds of getting an early edition are pretty slim. However, when early or late stampers are particularly desirable, I make mention of the fact.

In general, Victor's practice over the years has been to try and make the Toscanini recordings sound as modern as possible, and thus most contemporary pressings of the older recordings have more stress on the low bass and high treble than the original sets. How well this will sound to you depends on your playing equipment, the acoustics of the room in which you are listening, and your own sensitivity to various degrees of frequency emphasis. Any effort to set down blanket rules on how to play these records is absurd on the face of it.

It has been my experience, using high quality component type sound equipment, that every Toscanini record I possess can be made to sound good enough to be worth hearing, while the majority can be made to sound very good indeed. To get the best from most Toscanini disks you ought to have enough controls that you can set the bass and treble equalization separately and augment this setting with a good steep cutting filter and fairly efficient tone adjustment. I suggest a basic playback curve of 800 cps. in the bass (this is the so-called rollover point) and minus 16 db. in treble. (If you have to choose a single curve for equalizing both bass and treble, use that of the original Columbia longplay records.) Working from this you can find the position in which the record sounds best, cutting rollover back to 500 cps. if the disk is bass heavy or does not need frequency emphasis extended so far up the scale, or brightening the top by cutting the treble only -10 or -12 db. if the upper ranges are clean and clear. If you have good equipment, and it is in good working order, almost all these records can be made to sound agreeable, although some, naturally will always sound better than others.

When this book first appeared in 1956 the best of the Toscanini recordings were as fine technically as anything we possessed, and the differences between these disks and their immediate predecessors were therefore acutely clear. By the standards of 1962, however, all Toscanini recordings are products of an earlier phase in the development of the recording art. This gives us perspective. The differences between a 1949 Toscanini and a 1953 Toscanini are slight compared to those between the best Toscanini and some of the most recent productions we have been given by his old friend Bruno Walter. For Walter the delight of modern recording was that the imagination need no longer come to the assistance of the ear, the effect of a splendid recording being now so close to that of live music that the transition from one to the other is accomplished with ease. All Toscanini recordings need some assistance from the imagination, assistance which is most readily supplied by those who heard the Maestro in concert and know from recollections of the living music the mental adjustments which must be made in the electronically reproduced replica. This is a disadvantage, but it is not a very serious one. The best of the Toscanini recordings give us all that is needed to make the fact and reason of his greatness clear, and it is perhaps to the good that when we turn to Toscanini these days we do so exclusively for the sake of music rather than any preoccupation with sound as sound.

ACOUSTICAL RECORDINGS

Recordings with the La Scala Orchestra of Milan, made in the Trinity Church Studio of the Victor Talking Machine Company, Camden, New Jersey, U.S.A. Numbers are of the Victor acoustical series.

1920

GALILEI (*Orch.* RESPIGHI as *No. 2* of Respighi's *Suite No. 1 of Ancient Dances and Airs*)
Gagliarda
  Recorded December 18.
  *74672, later recoupled with *Fête Bohème* as *6301

MOZART

Symphony No. 39: Menuetto
  Recorded December 18.
  *74668, later recoupled with *Finale* as *6303

Symphony No. 39: Finale [Allegro]
  Recorded December 20.
  *74669, later recoupled with *Menuetto* as *6303

PIZZETTI

La Pisanella: Sul molo di Famagosta
  Recorded December 20.
  *64952, later recoupled with *Suzanne* as *840 (10")

BEETHOVEN

Symphony No. 5: Finale
  Recorded December 23.
  *74769/70, later recoupled as *6304

BERLIOZ

The Damnation of Faust: Scene 3, Rákóczy March
  Recorded December 24.
  *74695, later recoupled with Beethoven *Symphony No. 1: Finale* as *6300

1921

MENDELSSOHN

Incidental Music to "A Midsummer Night's Dream": No. 1 Scherzo
  Recorded March 9.
  *74779, later recoupled with *Wedding March* as *6302

WOLF-FERRARI

The Secret of Suzanne: Overture
  Recorded March 10.
  *66081, later recoupled with *Sul molo* as *840 (10")

BIZET

L'Arlésienne Suite No. 2: No. 4 Farandole
  Recorded March 11.
  *64986, later recoupled with *Carmen* as *839 (10")

MENDELSSOHN

Incidental Music to "A Midsummer Night's Dream": No. 10 Wedding March
  Recorded March 11.
  *74745, later recoupled with *Scherzo* as *6302

DONIZETTI

Don Pasquale: Overture
  The recording of part two, which was released, was made

March 29, but a successful recording of part one was not made until March 30.

*66030/31, later recoupled as *841 (10")

BEETHOVEN

Symphony No. 1: Finale [Adagio, Allegro molto e vivace]
Recorded March 30.
*74690, later recoupled with *Rákóczy March* as *6300

BIZET

Carmen: Prelude to Act IV [Aragonaise]
Recorded March 31.
*64999, later recoupled with *L'Arlésienne* as *839 (10")

MASSENET

Suite No. 4 [Scènes pittoresques]: No. 4 Fête Bohème
Recorded March 31.
*74725, later recoupled with *Gagliarda* as *6301

For acoustical recording of a symphony orchestra this series is really quite acceptable. The sound is, of course, greatly limited, distorted, and lacking in presence, but it has life and a great deal of vitality. There is no doubt that one is listening to a fine ensemble under a powerful musician. Given ample volume and the benefit of modern electronic filters to remove the surface noise, some really astonishing results can be obtained, not greatly inferior to those possible with early electrical disks.

The nine recording sessions listed here represent prolonged effort on the part of Toscanini and his orchestra and undoubtedly had much to do with forming his long-standing dislike of making records. The acoustical process was not sensitive enough to capture *p* or *pp* with accuracy, so dynamics had to be adjusted artificially, and what comes off the record as a soft passage had, in fact, gone into the apparatus as a fairly loud one. This was difficult for Toscanini, who demanded perfection then as much as later, and there were many retakes.

Originally sixteen single-faced disks were released, but in

the middle 'twenties Victor recoupled them as double-faced records. All of these items were withdrawn after the introduction of electrical recordings; most of them have been out of print for thirty years.

It is unfortunate that we have no complete recording of a major symphonic work in this series, but the feeling at the time was that the public wanted short pieces, indeed an average symphony on ten, single-faced records would have been quite expensive, so the aria, the instrumental solo, and the four-minute orchestral work dominated the catalogs.

Seven of the fourteen items in the series are available in new recordings of high fidelity standards. The *Don Pasquale* is virtually the same in the two versions, although separated by three decades. (Apparently Toscanini's performances of Italian music changed less through the years than his performances of works by German composers.) The Mendelssohn *Scherzo* is essentially the same as the 1929 and 1946 versions. The Beethoven *Fifth* is similar to the 1939 set, broader and more inflected than the 1951 recording, although the *First* is closer to the 1951 performance than the 1937 one. The *Menuetto* of the Mozart is a little slow, although the *Finale* is obviously the way the Maestro wants it to go, very fast indeed, and is quite similar to the 1948 broadcast performance, which, incidentally, is the only time Toscanini played this work in the United States or Britain between 1925 and 1954.

A society reissue of some of these things would provide a basis for further and wider comparisons. As things now stand the series is known merely to those who collect old records.

ELECTRICAL RECORDINGS

1926

MENDELSSOHN

Incidental Music to "A Midsummer Night's Dream": No. 1 Scherzo, No. 7 Nocturne
The New York Philharmonic Orchestra

Recorded in Carnegie Hall, New York, probably toward the end of January or early in February.
Brunswick *50074 [A second and somewhat more common form couples the *Scherzo* with the *Ride of the Valkyries* (under Mengelberg) as *50161].

Toscanini was guest conductor of the Philharmonic for the first time during the 1925-26 season, and this recording was made during those few weeks. The works appear in his programs for January 17 and February 1; presumably the recording was made close to one of those dates.·

The Maestro never liked this disk. The performance of the *Scherzo* seems slow and is inferior to other versions, such as that of 1929. I would classify it as a collector's item of no great interest.

1929

DUKAS

The Sorcerer's Apprentice
Recorded March 18.
* CAL-309

VERDI

La Traviata: Preludes to Acts I and III
Recorded March 18 and 29.
* CAL-309

HAYDN

Symphony No. 101 [*Clock*]
Recorded March 29 and 30.
* CAL-375

MENDELSSOHN

Incidental Music to "A Midsummer Night's Dream": No. 1 Scherzo
Recorded March 30.
* CAL-326

MOZART

Symphony No. 35 [Haffner]
  Recorded March 30 and April 4.
  * CAL-326

GLUCK

Orfeo: Dance of the Spirits
  Recorded April 5 and November 21.
  * 7138 (in * M-65)

ROSSINI

Barber of Seville: Overture
  Recorded November 21.
  * CAL-326
  The Philharmonic-Symphony Orchestra of New York
  Recorded in Carnegie Hall, New York.

As reprocessed on longplay records in the RCA-Camden series, these old disks had a pleasing, if greatly limited, sound which nevertheless reproduced the characteristic elements of a Toscanini performance. The Dukas is more relaxed and generally more enjoyable in the 1950 version, and the later recordings of the Gluck, Rossini, and Verdi are similarly preferable. Since all the Toscanini recordings of the Mendelssohn are out of print, this one is worth recalling, since it is among the best and probably easier to locate than the 1947 version.

Two items resist classification as uninteresting, antique duplications. The Haydn and Mozart are both played with a relaxed lyricism and beauty that is not found in the more intense versions of 1946 and 1947. Here the delicacy and effortless singing of the clock episode in the opening of Haydn's slow movement is breathtaking, and everything seems exactly right as the line of sound moves with just enough inflection to give it force and a sense of continuing motion. The *Haffner* sings with equal freedom, and the lovely melodic line flows without urgency. Toscanini is not afraid to pause for natural expression (as in the opening bars) and is under no demoniac compulsion to drive the music any faster than seems appropriate to its content. (The *Finale* of the *Haffner* is hardly retarded!) Perhaps the fast movements of the Haydn are better done in the 1947 version, but certainly the slow movement does not get the magnificent statement it received here.

1935

GEMINIANI

Concerto Grosso for Strings in G Minor, Op. 3, No. 2
   The British Broadcasting Corporation [B.B.C.] Symphony
   Orchestra
   Recorded during a broadcast, June 12, in Queen's Hall,
   London.
   Unreleased

Toscanini became fond of Geminiani briefly in 1933-35. The C Minor concerto, Op. 2, No. 2, was played at the Philharmonic concerts of April 1933, and this work was prepared a year later. The Maestro carried it to London with him for his initial series with the B.B.C. He gave it a beautiful, singing performance, classical in spirit, yet wonderfully sensitive to the sheer sensuous line of the melodic contours. The recording is comparable in quality to the other B.B.C. material.

1936

WAGNER

Die Götterdämmerung: Dawn and Siegfried's Rhine Journey
   [concert version by Toscanini]
   * CAL-375

Lohengrin: Preludes to Acts I and III
   * CAL-375

Siegfried Idyll
   * CAL-309
   The Philharmonic-Symphony Orchestra of New York
   Recorded February 8 and April 9 in Carnegie Hall.

The contents of this Wagner set became available briefly on Camden transfers, giving one a realistic choice between these performances and those of Toscanini's later years. In the case of the final two items, the Camden, for all its technical success, was no real competition for the superior sound of the more recent disks. The *Götterdämmerung* is a slightly different matter, since what is preserved here is a slower performance of the *Dawn* music than is heard on the later records. We can see here evidence for my argument in Chapter II that as Toscanini grew older he tended to speed up the performance of the works he played frequently. My feeling is that in 1936 he had the right tempo for the *Dawn* music, and that in later years his accelerated pace seriously diminished the dramatic impact of this passage. The 1936 recording thus must be regarded as the best documentation of his achievement with this score.

BEETHOVEN

Symphony No. 7
  The Philharmonic-Symphony Orchestra of New York
  Recorded April 9 and 10 in Carnegie Hall.
  *CAL-352

This symphony was one of the core works in the Maestro's repertory, and without any question he here gave it a reading that is breathtaking from beginning to end. The process of increasing tempi through the years has affected this work as well. The best statement of Toscanini's performance is this 1936 set *as originally issued,* that is, with the opening pages taken slowly and majestically. Unfortunately the master of the first side became worn, probably due to the process of making stampers, and a second master from the same recording session but with more rapid tempi was substituted with Toscanini's approval. It is in this form that the set was transferred to long play. I think the slower version was right, although the slightly faster one is tremendously effective as well.

Quite apart from this, in the 1936 performance Toscanini achieves a finer climax in the slow movement and better control of the movement of the lines of sound, particularly the tricky, sustained harmonies in the wind instruments during the final pages of the score. Toscanini at sixty-nine had a firmer hand on the performance than Toscanini at eighty-four, and although the 1951 version is fine, this is finer still.

BRAHMS

Variations on a Theme of Haydn
  The Philharmonic-Symphony Orchestra of New York
  Recorded April 10 in Carnegie Hall.
  *CAL-326

These variations were another basic item in Toscanini's repertory, and this performance is excellent. In this case the 1952 version is virtually identical except for a couple of expressive changes of pace which I find appropriate.

ROSSINI

The Italian Woman in Algiers: Overture
  *14161

Semiramide: Overture
  *CAL-309
  The Philharmonic-Symphony Orchestra of New York
  Recorded April 10 in Carnegie Hall.

Both of these recordings were outstanding in their day, and they still sound remarkably good. In the case of the *Italian Woman* (which through a mistranslation on the label became *The Italians in Algiers* for a great many people) this is something to be grateful for since there has never been another Toscanini recording in print. *Semiramide* was originally not even scheduled for the April 10 session, but things went well that day (all in all, it was probably the greatest recording session of the century!), so it was played with white-hot heat while the fires were still raging from the Beethoven and the Brahms. The 1951 version is not so delicate or quite so hair-raising as this. In both overtures the beauty of the Philharmonic's sound and the manner in which, in complete sympathy to Toscanini's wishes, it can build up and sustain a rhythmic line are marvels to hear.

1937

The Salzburg Operas

During his final summer at Salzburg Toscanini directed four operas: Beethoven's *Fidelio,* Mozart's *The Magic Flute,* Wagner's *Die Meistersinger,* and Verdi's *Falstaff.* All were recorded complete on the Selenophon, a precursor of the tape recorder. In this technique acetate film approximately a quarter inch in width was carried past a recording head which engraved a sound track vertically with a wide, shallow stylus. A reel was good for about a half hour of playing time. Because of the relatively fragile material of the film and the inherently delicate character of all vertical (or hill and dale) recording, these reels are not greatly superior to disks of the same vintage. Moreover the microphone placement appears to have been poor, giving undue prominence to the tympani and other bass instruments. As a final blow, the *Fidelio* reels have vanished completely, thus depriving us of what was said to be the greatest realization of that opera in its history.

Nonetheless, there is much on the positive side of the picture. Mr. Walter Toscanini made the restoration of the Selenophon recordings one of the first objectives of the Riverdale Project. A Selenophon machine was found and lovingly restored to working order, the reels were inspected, the film cleaned and repaired, and the sound carefully transferred to modern tape. When the Maestro thus heard again his *Meistersinger* he was reduced to tears and utterly insensitive to the technical limitations of the recording. I have heard it as well, and I understand why. The force of the music is so great in these performances that the imagination willingly compensates for any faults.

The documentary value of these recordings is incalculable, but it is still uncertain when or how they will reach the public. Presumably they cannot be issued on a regular commercial basis, but a limited edition seems feasible, and in time and with luck we shall have it.*

* *Falstaff* had Stabile in the title role, Somigli, Cravcenco, and Vasari as the merry wives. *Meistersinger* offered Nissen as Sachs with Noort and Reining as the lovers. *The Magic Flute* starred

BEETHOVEN

Symphony No. 6 [*Pastoral*]
  Recorded October 21 and 22.
  *LCT-1042

Symphony No. 1
  Recorded October 25.
  *LCT-1023
  The British Broadcasting Corporation [B.B.C.] Symphony
  Orchestra
  Recorded in Queen's Hall, London.

In 1935 and from 1937 to 1939 Toscanini appeared in London with the B.B.C. Symphony, which was increased to about ninety players for these concerts. The Maestro found it a sensitive and sympathetic ensemble. On these disks we hear performances that are clean, well-balanced, and entirely suave and agreeable in sound; in other words, highly civilized and very British. These are nearly perfect examples of the best pre-war recording. The range is limited and the presence is not too good, but as shellac technique goes, the HMV Company here gave Toscanini much better recording than he received from Victor in the six years following.

The *Pastoral* was a specialty of the Maestro, and for many years this was the definitive recording. The LCT version was made largely as a stop-gap measure until the 1952 edition could be put on the market, and since the later version is, if anything, a better performance and certainly is better recorded, this set can be put aside.

The *First* was recorded again 1951, and the new performance is tighter, more classical, and faster paced. One may well prefer the broader treatment given the score here.

BRAHMS

Tragic Overture
  The B.B.C. Symphony Orchestra

Novotna and Roswaegne with Kipnis as Sarastro and Domgraf-Fassbaender as Papageno. The Riverdale archive also contain from Selenophon rolls the Bruno Walter 1937 Salzburg productions of *Don Giovanni* and *Le Nozze di Figaro,* both with Pinza.

Recorded October 25 in Queen's Hall, London.
*15383/85 (in *M-507)

This is a spectacular Toscanini recording that has died an undeserved death. The work was on his first concert program in 1896, so he had been playing it forty-one years when he made this recording, which reveals a practiced hand thoroughly familiar with the score. The work is full of stumbling-blocks, as Tovey points out so well, and Toscanini is equal to them. All the points at which lesser musicians go bad (to begin with an obvious one, the tympani roll in the opening bars, which must be quiet, as marked, and on no account *f* or *ff*) are navigated with the greatest skill, and the final climactic passage for the brass is a magnificent example of how Toscanini could get an entire section to play as if it were a single musician of exceptional skill.

The work tends to be pretentious (under some conductors quite intolerably so) but for me Toscanini refines this away. One can hope for a new recording, say from the 1953 broadcast performance, but lacking that the restoration of this one would be welcome. There is plenty of good sound on the shellac records for an acceptable transfer.

1938

MOZART

Symphony No. 40
    The N.B.C. Symphony Orchestra
    Recording begun March 7, completed February 27, 1939, in Studio 8-H, Radio City, Rockefeller Center, New York.
    *M-631

In spite of his reputation as a performer of Mozart, few of Toscanini's Mozart recordings are satisfactory. This is one of the bad sets. The sound is poor and the performance is too intense. Toscanini wanted vital, powerful Mozart, with blood in it, but the more delicate parts of the works were scorched by such an impassioned approach. Happily, in this case we have a 1950 performance that is superior in every respect.

BEETHOVEN

Quartet No. 16 (Op. 135): Lento and Vivace
   *LCT-1041

HAYDN

Symphony No. 88
   *LCT-7
   The N.B.C. Symphony Orchestra
   Recorded March 8 in Studio 8-H.

The Haydn recorded here is not very pleasant in sound and, after being released in the LCT series, was withdrawn. It is a symphony of considerably lesser stature than those of the London period and had never been an important item in Toscanini's repertory. It is well played, but the orchestra does not have the beauty of sound revealed (say) in the 1953 recording of the *Surprise Symphony*. The Beethoven is beautifully played and preserves the feeling of a string quartet very well. It is unfortunate that this was never recorded again, and perhaps more unfortunate that Toscanini rarely ventured into the music of the late Beethoven quartets, although he regarded them as the greatest of the composer's works and was able to play them with a small string orchestra without destroying the texture, as commonly occurs when chamber music is played by larger groups than that for which it was intended. In the quartet the two movements come in the reverse of the order given here, and Toscanini has played them that way, but he felt that in concert it is better to close with the *Vivace* and thus provide some resolution for the slow movement.

MOZART

The Magic Flute: Overture
   The B.B.C. Symphony Orchestra
   Recorded June 2 in Queen's Hall, London.
   *49-0903

Having made three poor recordings in Studio 8-H, the Maestro took himself to an acoustically perfect hall (which was, unfortunately, to fall to Hitler's bombers within a short time) and made three fine recordings for the HMV Company. In contrast to the set above, it is one of the finest Mozart recordings, and the nobility of the music is deeply felt.

ROSSINI

The Silken Ladder: Overture
The B.B.C. Symphony Orchestra
Recorded June 13 in Queen's Hall, London.
*15191

One of Toscanini's finest Rossini performances, with very pleasant recording and unusually good woodwind sound. An enjoyable disk which ought not to have been allowed to disappear from the catalog.

WEBER (Orch. BERLIOZ)

Invitation to the Dance
The B.B.C. Symphony Orchestra
Recorded June 14 in Queen's Hall, London.
*15192

Another fine recording, although in this case there is a 1951 version in which virtually the same performance is heard in more splendid sound.

BACH

Brandenburg Concerto No. 2
The N.B.C. Symphony Orchestra
Recorded during a broadcast, October 29, in Studio 8-H.
To be released in 1962 as a 12" 45 rpm. Private Limited Edition for Walter Toscanini and His Friends

All that the world had left of this remarkable performance was a single acetate transcription with a deep scratch across its face. Painstakingly "de-ticked" and "de-coughed," it preserved the Maestro's last presentation of this music. (The reason he stopped playing it, incidentally, was that his principal trumpet no longer felt happy doing coloratura passages on a tiny, baroque-register instrument.)

The first hearing comes as a shock. The music is strongly

accented, vibrantly rhythmic with lots of bounce, and points up the link between Bach's serious writing and the dance forms of his day. The quality of sound is now agreeable, and the only signs of all the editing which has taken place are an occasional note or two that appear to have had a close shave. This is undoubtedly the best example we have of what Toscanini could achieve with Bach, and for that reason it is a very important part of the Toscanini legacy.

1939

STRAUSS

Salome: Salome's Dance
   The N.B.C. Symphony Orchestra
   Recorded during a broadcast, January 14, in Studio 8-H.
   Unreleased

A slow, sensual performance in which the Maestro was obviously greatly involved (he sang practically every phrase), this is more of a personal than a musical document. The Riverdale tapes come from acetates which preserve a high frequency squeal and add to the music a certain amount of grit and swish. There are two particularly bad bars where the surface noise dominates the music. Even so, as our only example of Toscanini conducting operatic music by Richard Strauss, this recording is of historic value.

BEETHOVEN

Symphony No. 5
   The N.B.C. Symphony Orchestra
   Recorded February 27, March 1 and 29 in Studio 8-H.
   *LCT-1041

Technically this is dreadful, although the original performances must have been excellent. A notorious set in its shellac form, this was improved in the process of transfer to longplay, although much of the sound remained coarse and wooden. Toscanini worked unusually hard to get this set the way he wanted it. An earlier attempt to do the symphony with the Philharmonic had failed to produce anything he would approve, and his broadcast performance in October, 1938, earlier in the same season, was quite different from the recording. The LCT disk actually did not duplicate the shellac album, since some of the transfer was made from second masters which had not been used in the eight sides of the original issue. The fact that three recording sessions are involved indicates there was probably a great deal of alternative material.

This performance is fundamentally the same one heard on the 1920 records. The 1951 set is faster by over two minutes (one of which reflects a quicker pace in the "slow" movement) and represents the symphony as Toscanini has speeded it up in his old age. If both approaches to the score could be heard with the advantages of good recording it would be quite clear that the slower tempi are the right ones.

ROSSINI

William Tell: Overture
  The N.B.C. Symphony Orchestra
  Recorded March 1 and 29 in Studio 8-H.
  *LM-14 (10")

An old clinker which can be given short shrift. The performance is wonderful, but the recording is cramped and wheezy without being in any way venerable. The same marvelous statement of the score is available in the excellent 1953 version.

BEETHOVEN

Symphony No. 8
  Recorded April 17 in Studio 8-H.
  *M-908

The best thing about this set when it was released was that it offered the first movement with the repeat marked by Beethoven and necessary for the form of the work to be properly revealed. Apparently recording was continuous with engineer-made breaks between the 78 rpm surfaces. There is now a 1952 version of this symphony that is better in every respect.

PAGANINI

Moto Perpetuo
   The N.B.C. Symphony Orchestra
   Recorded April 17 in Studio 8-H.
   *15547 (in *M-590)

An attractive piece of no particular weight, expertly played, and given a mediocre recording typical of the period.

BEETHOVEN

Leonore Overture No. 1
   *LCT-1041

Symphony No. 4
   *M-676
   The B.B.C. Symphony Orchestra
   Recorded June 1 in Queen's Hall, London.

June opened in London with one of the great days of Toscanini's recording career. Both of these performances are foundation stones for the documentation of his unique powers as a Beethoven conductor, which makes it all the more surprising that—despite the generally high quality of their sound —they have been out of the catalog so long. His achievement with the *Leonore No. 1* certainly makes one wonder why so few conductors play it these days, while relaxed lyricism, plastic continuity, and superb coloring of this Beethoven *Fourth* remain a standard for all others who attempt this music. Not even Toscanini could do it quite this way twice, and the 1951 version is thus no substitute for this greater achievement. Apparently continuous recording was used, since the seventh side ends in a spectacular cliff-hanging harmony. However, this flaw need not survive careful tape editing in the transfer process.

Symphony No. 3 [*Eroica*]
   Recorded during a broadcast, October 28.
   *M-765

Leonore Overture No. 3
   Recorded during a broadcast, November 4.
   H.M.V. *DA-1753/54 (10″) [No American edition.]

Egmont Overture

> Recorded during a broadcast, November 18.
> H.M.V. *DB-5705 [No American edition.]

Leonore Overture No. 2

> Recorded during a broadcast, November 25.
> H.M.V. *DA-1754/54 (10″) [No American edition.]
> The N.B.C. Symphony Orchestra
> Recorded in Studio 8-H.

Victor drew this series from Toscanini's first Beethoven cycle with the N.B.C. Symphony. Quite apart from the qualities of the studio, mentioned previously, and the introduction of a great many unpleasant audience noises (such as coughs between the opening chords of the *Eroica*), the sound has a rough and limited upper range, a coarse and poorly defined middle, and below that a grumbly and emaciated bass. It is the absolute low point of Victor's work with Toscanini, and one wonders how he could approve an *Eroica*, for example, in which the first note of the famous horn passage announcing the recapitulation (bar 394) is detached from the rest of the phrase in the infamous break between sides two and three, so that the effect of the E opposed to the B flat of the violins is totally destroyed. This type of technical failure is typical of the series.

In spite of the poor sound and discontinuities of the recording, these are musical statements of great power which ought to be preserved for no other reason than to provide a reference point in the study of his changing manner of performance. Happily, by going back to the sources and making fresh transfers with contemporary equipment, Mr. Walter Toscanini has produced tapes of these broadcasts which are considerably better than the original 78's. It will be noted that in this instance only one item of the series was released in the United States.

RECORDINGS WITH THE N.B.C. SYMPHONY ORCHESTRA
1940-54

BEETHOVEN
Violin Concerto (Op. 61)

1940

Jascha Heifetz, violin
Recorded March 11 in Studio 8-H.
*LCT-1010

Those who remember the cover of the Victor album may well think of this as the old diamond in the rough. Time has not made it any better. One wonders why no attempt was made to do it over, rather than transfer the old records to longplay. Again we hear the harsh, dry sound of the studio, and unless volume is boosted one loses *pp* and hears *ff* as wooden grunts. On the whole the recording is so dead and artificial that at times the thin line of violin sound is more reminiscent of something from the golden age of Thomas Edison's tinfoil cylinder than 1940. Even so, this is an historic album which had a considerable effect upon a whole generation of record collectors. Let it be entombed in peace.

BRAHMS

Piano Concerto No. 2
Vladimir Horowitz, piano
Recorded May 9 in Carnegie Hall.
LCT-1025

With the death of Toscanini and the present retirement of Horowitz from concert life, their collaborations assume a legendary character. The Brahms *Second Piano Concerto* is now the most popular in the repertory, and hearing it continually from artists of widely divergent degrees of capability, the excellence of the Toscanini-Horowitz performance becomes more apparent. In commenting upon it for the first edition of this book I expressed my preference for that of Artur Schnabel, and I stand by that. But of the pianists who take an intense, dramatic view of this music, who stress virtuosity (even for its own sake), and who are determined to impress, Horowitz managed not only to provide the most thrills, but to render the best service to Brahms. Moreover, the Toscanini accompaniment is something you are not likely to hear again for a long time.

In spite of a trip to Carnegie Hall the sound is disappointingly antique by contemporary standards, but there is enough on the records that those with good imaginations can reconstruct the power of the original. This, therefore, must be reappraised as one of the important legacies of two enormously influential musicians.

SIBELIUS

Lemminkäinen's Homecoming
Pohjola's Daughter
The Swan of Tuonela
Symphony No. 2
> Recorded during a broadcast, December 7, in Studio 8-H.
> Unreleased

This concert was all but Toscanini's farewell to Sibelius, a composer for whom he obviously had great sympathy despite the cultural differences between a son of the North and one of the Mediterranean. It was probably Sibelius' gift for drama which accounts for this, and it is the vigor of the dramatic element that makes these Toscanini performances so wonderful. When he heard the symphony again at Riverdale in his last years he was completely enthusiastic about it and eager to have it released (especially when played a current recording by another well-known Maestro of the Atlantic seaboard). I was familiar with the 1938 B.B.C. performance, but this one is even more powerful. We certainly ought to have it.

GLINKA

Kamarinskaya
> Recorded during a broadcast, December 21, in Studio 8-H.
> In LM-6026

The most interesting thing about this is the recording, which has been reprocessed from sixteen-year-old broadcast acetates and thus shows us what can be expected from this type of laboratory work. What Victor has done is to up-date the sound to the "medium-fidelity" period of the late 'forties. The over-all effect is good: one simply lacks deep base, brilliant highs, and the definition and presence that a wider range provides.

The performance itself is splendid, satisfactory both in "Russian" feeling and delicacy. The rhythmic and lyric charm are undeniable.

1941/48—V-Disks by Toscanini

The V-Disk project was carried on by the American armed forces 1944-49. The records were twelve-inch 78 rpm disks pressed on vinylite for distribution in service installations in this country and abroad. The Toscanini series was taken from acetates of N.B.C. Symphony broadcasts. The recorded sound is generally equal or superior to his commercial recordings of the period. Because of union regulations, contractual obligations of the artists, etc., these records were never available commercially, and when the project ended the masters were destroyed. None the less, there are a dozen Toscanini items in the series that cannot be had in another form, though the remaining twenty-four Toscanini V-Disks duplicate other records. I offer the list so that collectors may take a morose interest in its contents. The date of the broadcast which supplied the source recording is given in each instance; also the numbers of the V-Disks.

WAGNER: *Die Götterdämmerung: Orchestral Finale* [incorrectly labeled *Immolation Scene*], February 24, 1941 (Victor recording)—361

SMETANA: *The Moldau,* December 13, 1941—121 [an exceptionally fast performance]

STRAUSS, JOHANN, JR.: *On the Beautiful Blue Danube,* March 19, 1942 (Victor recording)—151

WAGNER: *Tristan und Isolde: Liebestod,* March 19, 1942 (Victor recording)—361

BRAHMS (*Orch.* DVOŘÁK): *Hungarian Dance No. 1,* January 10, 1943—593

BOCCHERINI: *Quintet, Op. 13, No. 5: Minuet,* April 4, 1943—226

HÉROLD: *Zampa-Overture,* April 4, 1943—95

PONCHIELLI: *La Gioconda: Dance of the Hours,* April 4, 1943—63

SOUSA: *The Stars and Stripes Forever,* April 4, 1943—31

ROSSINI: *William Tell: Passo a sei* [incorrectly labeled *Dance of the Soldiers*], April 4, 1943—226

VERDI: *Don Carlos: O Don Fatale* [with Nan Merriman] and *Rigoletto: Quartet* [with Ribla, Merriman, Peerce and Valentino], July 25, 1943—75

OLIVIERI: *Garibaldi's War Hymn,* September 9, 1943—31 [with spoken preface by Toscanini]

BIZET: *Carillon* from *L'Arlésienne Suite No. 1,* and *Carmen: Act IV, March of the Toreadors,* September 19, 1943—53

ROSSINI: *La Gazza Ladra: Overture,* June 25, 1944—461

TCHAIKOVSKY: *The Nutcracker Ballet: Suite No. 1,* June 25, 1944—261/62 also as 501/02

PROKOFIEV: *Symphony No. 1 (Classical),* June 25, 1944—481 [a very rapid performance]

SIBELIUS: *The Swan of Tuonela,* August 27, 1944—333

BEETHOVEN: *Leonore Overture No. 1,* October 29, 1944—392

KABALEVSKY: *Colas Breugnon: Overture,* January 21, 1945—675

DEBUSSY: *Prelude to the Afternoon of a Faun,* February 11, 1945—708

GROFÉ: *Grand Canyon Suite: On the Trail and Cloudburst,* September 2, 1945—561

GLINKA: *Jota Aragonesa,* November 4, 1945—593

ROSSINI: *Il Signor Bruschino: Overture,* November 11, 1945 —637

VAUGHAN WILLIAMS: *Fantasia for Double String Orchestra on a Theme of Thomas Tallis,* November 18, 1945—606/07

ELGAR: *Enigma Variations: No. 7 "Troyte,"* November 18, 1945—606

CASTELNUOVO-TEDESCO: *Overture to a Fairy Tale,* November 25, 1945—607

MOZART: *Symphony No. 40: First Movement,* January 27, 1946—638

VERDI: *La Forza del Destino: Overture,* January 27, 1946—638

PUCCINI: *La Bohème: O soave fanciulla* (Finale, Act I) [with Albanese and Peerce] and *Quando m'en vo* (Musetta's Waltz Song and Finale, Act II) [with Anne McKnight, other principals, chorus, etc.], February 3, 1946—654

DUKAS: Excerpts from *Ariane et Barbe-Bleu*, March 2, 1947 —836/37

GILLIS: *Symphony 5½*, September 21, 1947—826

VERDI: *Otello: Willow Song* and *Ave Maria* [with Herva Nelli], December 13, 1947—847

MARTUCCI: *Noveletta*, March 13, 1948—848

1941

MOZART, Leopold (Arranged Haydn)
Toy Symphony

SCHUBERT (Orch. JOACHIM)
Symphony in C Major [*Gastein*]
Recorded during a broadcast, February 15, in Carnegie Hall.
Unreleased

Generally Toscanini was wary of arrangements (other than his own). He played the *Toy Symphony* with the feeling that it was genuine Haydn, bestowing upon it all the felicity and charm of an affectionate grandfather presenting a gift to his grandchildren. The results are wholly beguiling. All the toys are played by virtuosos, and never again will you hear a bobwhite with the lilt of the Toscanini beat.

Schubert's *Grand Duo, Op. 140,* may be defended as an arrangement by the composer of the symphony he is reported to have written at Gastein in 1825. It is surely no ordinary piece of music for piano four hands. Joachim felt that it deserved instrumental form, and Brahms gave him a hand in reconstructing the presumably lost orchestral text. There is no doubt that the music is greatly improved by orchestration, and Toscanini gives it quite the finest statement I have ever heard. This is one of his great Schubert recordings, and it has come to us in sound which admirably conveys its unique qualities.

WAGNER

Die Walküre: Act I, Scene 3
Die Götterdämmerung: Excerpts from the Prologue
  Helen Traubel, soprano; Lauritz Melchior, tenor
  Recorded during a broadcast, February 22, in Studio 8-H.
  LM-2452

This is our only opportunity so far to hear Toscanini directing music of Wagner in a theatrical setting with voices, but perhaps we may be able to augment it in time with the Salzburg *Meistersinger*. As we hear this music it becomes clear that Wagner's main attraction for Toscanini was not his Teutonic heft but his inescapable genius as a composer for the stage. Toscanini could not fail to see that and be held by it, and you may wonder at the close of this record if any German conductor ever made this quality more evident.

The two scenes are sections of the *Ring* cycle for which the Maestro had long revealed his love. The *Walküre* episode begins with Siegmund alone by the fire in Hunding's house and continues to the close of the act. *Die Götterdämmerung* opens as the Norns have disappeared and proceeds through the *Rhine Journey*. The latter are pages which Toscanini gave us in concert many times and recorded on four occasions other than this. My feeling is that the best of the purely orchestral versions remains that of 1936, but obviously the best performance of all is this one, since it is closest to the opera as we would experience it in the theater. Both Traubel and Melchior were in excellent voice, and the set surely is as much a document of their great days (and the great Wagnerian era at the Metropolitan prior to World War II) as it is a testament to Toscanini. By any lights this is a monumental recording, but to hear it at its best you must increase the lower frequencies and give it more body.

Die Götterdämmerung: Immolation Scene
  Helen Traubel, soprano
  Recorded February 24 in Carnegie Hall.
  LVT-1004

During this period the musical director of Victor was Charles O'Connell, and there was tension between him and the Toscanini family much of the time. For one thing, O'Connell was himself a conductor, although apparently the Maestro could not take him seriously in this role. Something of a crisis followed Toscanini's rejection of this set on the grounds that trumpet passages were not well balanced with the voice. In his book, *The Other Side of the Record,* O'Connell says that it was Toscanini's own fault, but the Maestro stuck to his contractual rights, and the set could not be released. By this time the American Federation of Musicians' recording ban of 1942-44 was in force, and Victor went to James C. Petrillo, the chief of the union, who granted the dispensation necessary for Harry Glantz, first trumpet of the orchestra, to come before the microphone and record the passages again so that they could be dubbed into the original at the higher volume level Toscanini demanded. This re-recorded version was eventually released, and O'Connell claims that some of the freshness and impact of the sound was thus lost.

Since *Die Götterdämmerung* played an important role in Toscanini's career and this is our only recording from him of its climactic scene, we must accept this set primarily for its documentation of an exceptional performance.

WAGNER

Lohengrin: Prelude to Act I
Recorded February 24 and May 6.
*11-8807

VERDI

La Traviata: Preludes to Acts I and III
Recorded March 10.
*18080

STRAUSS, JOHANN, JR.

Tritsch-Tratsch Polka
Recorded May 6.
*49-1082
Recorded in Carnegie Hall.

Two of these were duplications of popular recordings from the two series with the Philharmonic. They are lacking in bass and limited and thin on top, so there is nothing to recommend them over the newer versions: the 1946 set of the whole of *Traviata*, and the 1951 *Lohengrin*. The Strauss can be forgotten.

BRAHMS

Symphony No. 1
Recorded March 10 in Carnegie Hall.
*M-875

Released to commemorate Toscanini's seventy-fifth birthday in 1942, this was welcome at the time, and I recall the pleasure I then secured from what seemed to be unusually good sound. There is now a 1951 version that duplicates and eliminates this set.

TCHAIKOVSKY

The Voyevoda: Overture
Recorded during a broadcast, April 19, in Carnegie Hall.
Unreleased

This is a prime example of Toscanini taking an unfamiliar Tchaikovsky score and showing you how effective it can be made when played well. Admittedly a minor work, *The Voyevoda* nonetheless is stirring enough here that you wonder why some other conductor has not revived it. The recorded sound is quite acceptable.

Piano Concerto No. 1
Vladimir Horowitz, piano
Recorded May 6 and 14 in Carnegie Hall.
LCT-1012

In 1941 a song called "Tonight We Love" transformed the opening episode of this work into the adolescent's dream of tonal ecstasy; overnight everyone from hillbilly virtuosi on the washboard and harmonica to Toscanini and Horowitz was taking this old war horse for a ride. Nobody who lived through those days will ever want to hear this concerto again, but there is always a new generation. For them RCA-Victor has given the quietus to this clangy old set (despite its tremendous sales figures) by issuing a new version from 1943.

WAGNER

Die Götterdämmerung: Dawn and Siegfried's Rhine Journey and *Siegfried's Death and Funeral Music* [concert versions by Toscanini]
Recorded May 14 in Carnegie Hall.
*M-853

The second of the three recorded versions of the *Rhine Journey*, given here, is nearly a minute faster than the 1936 recording, which is better paced and has a solidity and weight which compensate for the slightly brighter, but thinner sound of this version. This set can be forgotten.

1942

VERDI

I Vespri Siciliani: Overture
Recorded during a broadcast, January 24, in Studio 8-H.
In LM-6041

The Sicilian Vespers is today one of the most popular Verdi operas in the Soviet Union for the precise reason that it was one of the most unpopular operas with the Italian censors of the last century: it deals with a revolution. The overture is a rousing work in the early Verdi manner and Toscanini plays it with all the necessary fire. The recording captures this, but also the polish and dignity he gives the music.

Some history is required at this point. During the summer of 1941 Toscanini had a falling out with N.B.C., and when he recorded in February, 1942, it was with the Philadelphia Orchestra. This Philadelphia series was the final showdown between Toscanini and O'Connell, who left Victor shortly afterward.

The wax master disks of the Philadelphia recordings were damaged in the electroplating process, with the result that the surface noise was unusually high. Toscanini listened to some of the test pressings and gave his artistic approval to part of the series, only to have his decision countermanded by

Victor's quality control department. "It was never a pleasure for my father to listen to his records," Walter Toscanini recalls, and when Victor's decision was told the Maestro, he turned away from the series before he had heard all of the disks.

Strauss's *Death and Transfiguration* and the Schubert *Ninth Symphony*, both of which were approved by Toscanini, have now been reprocessed at Riverdale and are suitable for release. Respighi's *Roman Festivals*, Debussy's *La Mer*, and the Tchaikovsky *Pathétique Symphony* can probably be refurbished to a comparable level of quality, but Mendelssohn's *Midsummer Night's Dream* music, Debussy's *Iberia*, and the Berlioz *Queen Mab Scherzo* contain too many low level passages to be wholly freed from noise. With a union ban on recording looming ahead, and the damaged Philadelphia masters confronting them, Victor persuaded Toscanini to direct a recording session with the N.B.C. Symphony, which he had been leading only in War Bond Concerts. Seven twelve-inch sides were cut and approved from the March nineteenth session and these, with the sets listed above, constituted all the Toscanini material Victor had to release during the two years following, when, in the midst of war, tragedy, and crisis, music of adequate proportions was required.

With this Toscanini's recording sessions ended for thirty-one months, and the Great Petrillo Interdiction began.

BARBER

Quartet (Op. 11): Adagio for Strings
Recorded March 19 in Carnegie Hall.
*11-8287

Toscanini gave the world première of this score, which is the only really serious American work he ever recorded. The performance is a fine one, the sound adequate.

STRAUSS, JOHANN, JR.

On the Beautiful Blue Danube
*11-8580

THOMAS

Mignon: Overture
  *11-8545

WAGNER

Tristan und Isolde: Liebestod
  *11-8666 (in *M-978)
  Recorded March 19 in Carnegie Hall.

The opening pages of the *Mignon* are of great beauty, but lovely as they are, this is not enough to compensate for the light weight of the music. In any case, the 1952 version is even finer. The Strauss and Wagner both document Toscanini's tendency toward fast, metronomic, inexpressive performances in 1941-42. The waltz is completely out of style, and ruined by the bloodless, mechanical execution of the figures. (Note especially the ludicrous effect produced by the rigid, expressionless playing of the passage that concludes the first side.) Some of the fine, clean attacks are admirable, but this is small compensation. The *Liebestod* was cut as a filler, and perhaps that accounts for the speed, since it had to come out as a single surface, but it, too, is ruthlessly inexpressive.

SHOSTAKOVICH

Symphony No. 7 [Leningrad]
  Recorded during a broadcast, July 19, in Studio 8-H.
  Unreleased

There are rehearsal recordings of this score, plus the tape edited from the broadcast acetates, and a documentary disk of this historic performance is entirely possible.

1943

VERDI

Nabucco: Va pensiero sull'ali dorate
  The Westminster Choir, John Finlay Williamson, director
I Lombardi: Qui, posa il fianco
  Vivian Della Chiesa, soprano; Jan Peerce, tenor; Nicola Moscona, bass

Recorded during a broadcast, January 31, in Studio 8-H. In LM-6041

Both these operas have close association with the cause of Italian liberty and thus in 1943 were particularly close to Toscanini's heart. The performances show it. The great chorus of Hebrew slaves here has an eloquence which comes from universality, and hearing it one recalls that it was Toscanini who directed this music at Verdi's funeral in 1901. (It was heard again at Toscanini's funeral in 1957.) In short, the personal and historic associations involved in these recordings make them very precious to me, but even without these associations they are impressive simply as music. The recorded sound is entirely adequate to convey their substance.

TCHAIKOVSKY

Piano Concerto No. 1
  Vladimir Horowitz, piano
  Recorded during a broadcast, April 25, in Carnegie Hall.
  LM-2319

This preserves the second and final time that Horowitz and Toscanini played this music together in public. The occasion was a War Bond Concert, and the artists appeared without fee. Whether it was the wartime atmosphere, the fact that $11,000,000 had been pledged by the audience, or the natural enthusiasm of two musicians for a good score, the effect was a performance of the sort that should have made all subsequent attempts at the work anti-climactic. I am certain I shall never hear its like, and in this case the recording is vivid enough that even the lunatic high fidelity hobbiest will forget about frequency response and listen. We are fortunate to have an example of Horowitz and Toscanini's work together that is so faithfully documented. You don't need to imagine much. You know that it was wonderful.

VON SUPPÉ

Poet and Peasant: Overture
  Recorded during a broadcast, July 18, in Studio 8-H.
  LM-6020

The fact that there was one Toscanini performance of this potboiler more or less insured that we would have a recording. The performance and sound are both quite pleasant, but putting Toscanini's ability to work on music such as this was rather like having Escoffier prepare the hot dogs. Let us try and forget it ever happened.

VERDI

Luisa Miller: Overture and *Quando le sere al placido*
Jan Peerce, tenor
Recorded during a broadcast, July 25, in Studio 8-H.
In LM-6041

Luisa Miller, Verdi's fourteenth opera, preceded *Rigoletto* by two years. Based on Schiller's *Kabale und Liebe*, it is a tragic drama of love, treachery, and jealousy set in the Tyrol. Verdi seldom wrote with greater delicacy and emotion, and the overture in particular is among his most eloquent and ingenious operatic prefaces. Toscanini plays it beautifully. The aria, *Quando le sere*, from the second act has been likened to the *O du mein holder Abendstern* from *Tannhäuser*. It is one of the truly neglected Verdi masterworks, and thus it is rewarding to have it in such a fine performance. The recorded sound is thoroughly acceptable.

HAYDN

Symphony No. 104 [London]
Recorded during a broadcast, October 31, in Studio 8-H.
Unreleased

In his last year Toscanini nearly approved this performance for release, his sole misgiving being the tempo of the *Menuetto* movement. When recordings by six other conductors were played for him, he became even more convinced of this, finally deciding that a faster performance by Edwin Fischer's Chamber Orchestra was correct. Even so, he relented later and nearly gave his consent to make this performance available. We deserve to have it. The sound is beautiful, while the breadth of phrasing and strength of line which made Toscanini's Haydn great are fully evident.

VERDI

Hymn of the Nations
> Jan Peerce, tenor; The Westminster Choir, John Finlay Williamson, director
> Recorded as the sound track to an Office of War Information film in several sessions early in December in Studio 8-H.
> In LM-6041

Although contemporary with *La Forza del Destino,* this work reflects the early Verdi more than it anticipates the later one, and, indeed, it is the crudest product to emerge from the composer's collaborations with Boito. For Toscanini, however, the point was not the music but the patriotic fervor it displayed, and the Maestro apparently had no qualms about doing some rewriting of his own. Thus, in this version you will hear "Italy, my country, oh my betrayed fatherland," which, of course, is not Boito but Toscanini. Verdi made use of only three national anthems, Britain, France, and Italy, and to this ending Toscanini appended his own setting for chorus and orchestra of *The Internationale* and his arrangement for tenor, orchestra, and chorus of *The Star Spangled Banner,* making the work representative of all the nations allied against Fascism and Nazi Germany. Because of these extra musical references it is a very moving performance, and the recording conveys it forcefully.

1944

HAYDN

Symphony No. 92 [Oxford]
> Recorded during a broadcast, March 19, in Studio 8-H.
> Unreleased

This is the earliest Haydn symphony we are likely to get from Toscanini, since the acetates of his single N.B.C. performance of No. 31 [*Hornsignal*] are in dreadful shape. The *Oxford* is here given a tight performance in rather dry sound. The tape copy has been "de-ticked" and is acceptable for all documentary purposes, but we have more impressive examples of Toscanini as a Haydn conductor.

VERDI

Rigoletto: Act IV
  Zinka Milanov, soprano; Nan Merriman, mezzo-soprano;
  Jan Peerce, tenor; Leonard Warren, baritone; Nicola Mos-
  cona, bass; chorus directed by Peter Wilhousky
  Recorded during a broadcast, May 25, in Madison Square
  Garden.
  In LM-6041

Toscanini could not tolerate the practice of casting a coloratura soprano as Gilda and on the two occasions when he
gave the final act of *Rigoletto* in concert form he demanded
a singer with a richer and more dramatic voice. Milanov was
ideal, and, indeed it is difficult to think of better casting than
Toscanini secured for this historic performance. It is one
of the few instances in his operatic recordings when, despite
world conditions, he secured the best singers that were to be
had—certainly the best to be had in the United States. The
recorded sound is really quite good. However, the label is
wrong; only the N.B.C. Symphony was used in this performance, not the combined N.B.C. and New York Philharmonic.

PUCCINI

Manon Lescaut: Intermezzo
  Recorded during a broadcast, July 2, in Studio 8-H.
  Unreleased

One of the most effective of the few practical concert
pieces by Puccini, this miniature tone poem was given a
performance deeply infused with Toscanini's sense of theater.
The recorded sound is good.

BEETHOVEN

Piano Concerto No. 3
  Artur Rubinstein, piano
  Recorded during a broadcast, October 29, in Studio 8-H.
  *LCT-1009

Technically this is among the poorest of the conductor's

recordings; its faults include serious instability in pitch. The performance is ruined for me by the conflict in style between Rubinstein's romanticism and Toscanini's reserved, classical approach. None the less, Toscanini suggested this collaboration and showed unusual interest in having a recording made. The sound is thin, distorted and unpleasant. Many details of the orchestra part are obscured or lost entirely.

Piano Concerto No. 4
Rudolf Serkin, piano
Recorded during a broadcast, November 26, in Studio 8-H. Unreleased

As contrast to the item above, this is a much more successful concerto performance. Its roots go back to the Philharmonic seasons, when Serkin and Toscanini gave the work together three times. As we have it preserved, the sound is dry and compressed, lacking in brilliance as well as resonance. The balance is in favor of the piano. Even so, this is an exceptional collaboration, and it deserves recognition as one of the best concerto recordings in which Toscanini participated.

Fidelio
Principals: Rose Bampton, soprano; Eleanor Steber, soprano; Jan Peerce, tenor; Nicola Moscona, bass; Herbert Janssen, bass; chorus directed by Peter Wilhousky
Recorded during broadcasts, December 10 and 17, in Studio 8-H, and incorporating a recording of *Abscheulicher!* (recitative) and *Komm, O Hoffnung* (aria) made December 19, in Carnegie Hall, and the *Leonore Overture No. 3* made June 1, 1945, in Studio 8-H.
LM-6025. The recitative and aria were released as *11-9110.

Released in the United States exactly ten years after it was made, this recording must be regarded as a *tour de force,* a musical souvenir of a great performance which represented Toscanini's first presentation of opera in New York since 1915 and, for all but a few of his audience, served as the first experience of his art as an operatic conductor. For all that, although not comparable to a modern tape, the sound is not at all bad, and despite limitations, is agreeable. Therefore, since one must accept this set on the basis that an imperfect transcription is better than none, the imperfections are not such as to destroy the musical pleasure which the spendid playing of the orchestral parts and the excellent to routine singing of the cast provides. It has the usual faults of recordings made under concert conditions, but it also has the dramatic impact of Toscanini working with an audience, and the music is of self-evident greatness. The insertions are both well advised. Bampton's singing of the recitative and aria was much better controlled on the nineteenth than it had been on the tenth, and the 1945 disks of the overture were superior to the concert acetates.

The Creatures of Promethus: Overture

Recorded December 18 in Studio 8-H.

*LCT-1041 may have been taken from a "second master" cut in the same session. My remarks apply to it, and not to the release as a 78 rpm.

Opus 43 is one of the early masterpieces of the composer and is filled with the sort of things that Toscanini did superlatively well. For example, the way in which the opening chords establish a feeling of tension and a sense of continuity and rhythm, so that in the course of six chords and a fanfare the tempo has been established. We do not lose that sense of tempo in the quiet introduction that follows, and we have the feeling that we are still in time during the fast section, where the Maestro's sweeping motor energy carries us along with authority and strength. Beethoven used a similar introduction in his *Consecration of the House Overture,* which Toscanini recorded two years later.

As if to show us that a new day had arrived, Victor here made a very decent recording in Studio 8-H, proving to all doubters that it *was* possible (just as it was equally possible to make poor records in Carnegie Hall).

1945

RAVEL

La Valse

Recorded February 19 in Carnegie Hall.
Unreleased

Made during a special concert, this recording is an imperfect replica of an exceptional performance. The opening bars are buried in the vast spaces of the auditorium, there are intrusions of audience noise, and the bad surfaces of the original disks are all too apparent. Toscanini here shows us the golden mean in this work, delivering an account of the score that is not so fast as to be frenzied, nor so slow as to be a dance piece, but is just right to say what Ravel had on his mind. For that reason, this tape ought to be heard, although it does not lend itself to normal commercial distribution. (Toscanini later decided, incidentally, that he preferred Ansermet's performance of this music to his own.)

GERSHWIN

An American in Paris
Recorded May 18 in Studio 8-H.
LM-9020

At the time it was made, this was technically the finest Toscanini recording in existence. The fact that this was done in Studio 8-H only adds to his glory: a victory on a field where many battles had been lost. The sound is spacious and well-balanced—a faithful likeness of the playing of a great orchestra. As I said earlier the new technique used for some of the later (and better) 8-H recordings was to take the orchestra off the stage and put it on the floor, thus making use of the full resonance of what was, in fact, a fairly ample concert room.

The performance has the fine plastic qualities one expects from the Maestro; its only questionable aspect is that of style. This is Gershwin's finest work for symphony orchestra. It employs devices of both French and American popular music, and the question is whether symphonic jazz should be played as jazz or symphonic music. Specifically, should the blues sections in this work be given the traditional expressive inflections of blues style or not? Toscanini's performance implies not, for either he had no feeling for the blues style (I wonder, in fact, if he had any feeling for American popular music) or he rejected it. This performance gives a "straight" reading of the French episodes, the blues section, the Charleston theme and the rest. Those who want to hear the work on purely musical terms will probably enjoy the freshness of Toscanini's approach. But is that what Gershwin intended?

In spite of the date, this recording never appeared on shellac. One had to wait until the 'fifties to find what could be done in 1945.

SOUSA

The Stars and Stripes Forever
  Recorded May 18 in Studio 8-H.
  *49-1082

The 1943 performance on V-Disk—31 was more relaxed, somewhat broader and more spontaneously expressive, particularly in the final section. The recording ban prevented a commercial disk being made at that time; when this one was cut, a little more than two years later, Toscanini's performance had tightened up.

HAYDN

Symphony No. 98
  Recorded May 25 in Studio 8-H.
  *M-1025

This set was in and out of the catalog with great rapidity and vanished, apparently without any hope for resurrection or revival. This is a tragic state of affairs, since the symphony is one of Haydn's greatest (even when played, as it was here, from corrupt orchestral material), while the performance remains one of Toscanini's supreme achievements in music of the eighteenth century. Considering the small amount of Haydn we have from the Maestro, a loss such as this is a serious matter.

WEBER

Der Freischütz: Overture
  Recorded May 25.
  *49-1228

BEETHOVEN

Coriolan Overture
   Recorded June 1.
   *ERA-91

MENDELSSOHN

Octet (Op. 20): Scherzo
   Recorded June 1.
   *11-8966 (in *M-1025)
   Recorded in Studio 8-H.

The 1952 version of the Weber is identical or possibly superior in performance to this and technically superb, so the sick and obscured horn tones at the opening of this disk are painful to hear in contrast. The *Scherzo* is all quicksilver and froth, and superior to that in the 1947 recording of the entire work. (Toscanini here made use of a fully orchestrated version of the piece with wind parts as well as strings.) The *Coriolan* is not distinguished, and the Maestro's intensity is a disadvantage, since there is insufficient contrast between the two main themes—both are agitated. The 1953 broadcast performance is far superior.

BEETHOVEN

Leonore Overture No. 3
   Recorded June 1 in Studio 8-H.
   *LVT-1025 and in LM-6025 (*Fidelio*)

Toscanini saw this overture as an entire opera in compressed form without voices, and he usually convinced you he was right. My own preference in matters of performance is the 1939 version, but this one is nearly as fine and, in its later pressings, considerably better engineered. In this case you want high stamper numbers, 15 S or above, and reduce the treble if your ear detects distortion.

ROSSINI

The Barber of Seville: Overture
La Cenerentola: Overture

La Gazza Ladra: Overture
The Siege of Corinth: Overture
Il Signor Bruschino: Overture
William Tell: Passo a sei
   Recorded June 8 and 28 in Carnegie Hall.
   The Siege of Corinth is unreleased. The *Passo* is in *LRM-7005. The rest of the material is now LM-2040.

Of all the lighter music Toscanini played, his unique performances of Rossini remain the most enjoyable, and although these overtures deal with matters of less weight than the symphonies of Beethoven, there is no ground for being patronizing about them. These versions are not likely to be matched by new performances within the next decade or so. The recorded sound is good, agreeably bright on top and full below, and well-balanced except for a tendency for the strings to dominate the loud passages. *The Siege of Corinth* was rejected by the Maestro because he felt its clarity was marred by excess reverberation, but its lively chord sequences and saucy woodwind commentary ought to be preserved.

MOZART

Symphony No. 41 [Jupiter]
   Recorded June 22 and March 11, 1946, in Carnegie Hall.
   LM-1030

Although Toscanini worked on this in two recording sessions, it is not a success and reveals what dismal results could be produced even in a Carnegie Hall recording. The quality is distorted and unpleasant, especially in passages for full orchestra, and with weak bass, coarse highs, and related evils, some passages of the final movement become a hopeless scramble of poorly defined sounds. Dubbed on to tape and reproduced at the proper pitch, but twenty-five per cent slower in tempo, by use of A. M. Springer's ingenious playback machine, the final movement shows up the frantic, insensitive quality of the performance. The men are obviously hard pressed just to get in all their notes, let alone shape their phrases with polish or beauty, and at the reduced tempo the faults in the ensemble are easily spotted.

In the first edition of this book I wound up these remarks by saying that this was "a set to forget," whereupon Mr. Spike Hughes accused me of giving "a pontifical brush-off" to an exceptional performance. On the other hand, his comments (in *The Toscanini Legacy,* London, 1959) begin with discussions of two live performances, and only on the basis of this background does he turn to the recording. I never heard a live *Jupiter* from the Maestro, and from the confusion of the present recording I was at a loss to imagine what the original might have been. It was possible, however, for me to inquire how Toscanini felt about this performance when he heard it in later years. The answer makes me feel a little less pontifical. "It is no good," the Maestro is said to have concluded. "Too fast."

VERDI

La Forza del Destino: Overture
  *49-1175

WALDTEUFEL

The Skaters Waltz [*Les Patineurs*]
  LM-1986
  Recorded June 28 in Carnegie Hall.

It is instructive to regard the fate of these disks. The Verdi is now just an uninteresting old recording, replaced by the 1952 version which offers the identical performance with better sound. The Waldteufel can be heard in a very spectacular "updated" transfer which one would almost imagine to be a recent tape. The result is a pleasant, old-fashioned waltz turned into a stunning concert piece by the apparently simple device of giving it an incisive performance, in contrast to the slack and rhythmically inexact run-throughs one is accustomed to hearing on Pop nights.

BEETHOVEN

Piano Concerto No. 1
  Ania Dorfmann, piano

Recorded August 9 in Carnegie Hall.
*LM-1039

In the opening bars the orchestra creates a lively, flowing musical line made expressive by changes in coloring and accent; into this framework the piano enters, blandly moving along without the qualities of color, accent and continuity which Toscanini is exhibiting and which one would expect a perceptive soloist to duplicate. What is exciting about this performance, then, is the manner in which the orchestral part is played. But if one rightfully expects a concerto to reveal a unity of feeling on the part of soloist and conductor, this will not do. Miss Dorfmann has to scramble in the final movement, since the relentlessly pursuing Maestro hardly gives her time to get in all her notes. (This is a typical feature of a Toscanini "accompaniment" and one reason why so few artists would play with him.) He is clearly too much for her, although she is stylistically closer to him than was Rubinstein.

The recording is of middling fidelity, pleasant, and unexceptional.

BERLIOZ

The Damnation of Faust: Scene 3 Rákóczy March
Recorded during a broadcast, September 2, in Studio 8-H.
LM-6026

A polished and expertly prepared version of a work that is all too frequently given a heavy, slipshod performance. In spite of the coarse and limited quality of some of the sound, the musical values are of the highest level.

GROFÉ

The Grand Canyon Suite
Recorded September 11 in Carnegie Hall.
LM-1004

It is natural to be offended that Toscanini should have given his time to preparing and recording music as inconsequential as this, but once those feelings of indignation are overcome, it is interesting to find what he did with the score. In his hands it becomes lesser growth Respighi, American vintage, and then you suddenly realize why Toscanini bothered with this music at all. It was full of pictures and tunes and could be played simply by following his natural bent— something he could not do in something more serious and complex such as Copland's *Appalachian Spring*. The Grofé set has been an all time best seller, and everyone from Grofé on certainly can claim to have received his money's worth.

GLINKA

Jota Aragonesa
Recorded during a broadcast, November 4, in Studio 8-H. Released as V-Disk 593

The ancestor of Tchaikovsky's Italian caprice and Rimsky-Korsakov's Spanish caprice, this is still the paradigm of the Latin piece by the Slavic composer. Toscanini played it with real verve, and the recorded sound is good.

1946

PUCCINI

La Bohème
Principals: Licia Albanese, soprano; Ann McKnight, soprano; Jan Peerce, tenor; Francesco Valentino, baritone; chorus directed by Peter Wilhousky
Recorded during broadcasts, February 3 and 10, in Studio 8-H.
LM-6006

This performance marked the fiftieth anniversary of the world première of the score which Toscanini conducted at Turin on February 1, 1896. Writing of this set in the first edition of this book I said, "seldom have the musical and dramatic qualities of this work been realized as well as they were in these broadcasts," but it has taken a few more years (and the necessity to review a number of additional recordings of *Bohème*) to become completely aware of the truth of that statement. In this era of opera conducting, to hear the score with the authority, taste, and dramatic sensitivity of this Toscanini performance is to become aware of the charm and pathos of the music with fresh perception. *La Bohème* has its failings. It is blatantly sentimental and makes its bid for popularity by the most obvious means, so that the tragic close is marred by the melodramatic overtones of the calculated tearjerker. Toscanini himself was aware of this. In *The Maestro* (New York, 1951) Howard Taubman reports a conversation in which Toscanini said: "Puccini was very clever, but only clever," and contrasted the "sugary" quality of Puccini's supposedly tragic pages with "the passion, the truthfulness" in Verdi's treatment of similar situations.

This critical attitude did not, however, prevent Toscanini from becoming deeply immersed in this performance, and his participation involves frequent outpourings of "the Toscanini tenor." It is really for this that I prize these records. It has great musical qualities (for once the first act ends with the tenor and soprano singing the notes the composer wrote for them), but more than this it is a warm and personal document of the Maestro. It calls for empathy and love, and it is certainly the only recording of *La Bohème* that I ever want to hear.

WAGNER

Die Meistersinger: Prelude
  LM-6020
Siegfried Idyll
  LVT-1004
Die Walküre: Prelude to Act III [*Ride of the Valkyries*]
  *WDM-1564
Recorded March 11 in Carnegie Hall.

When I prepared the first edition of this book I was under the impression that there were two Toscanini recordings of the *Meistersinger Prelude*. I had two seemingly sound reasons for this. First, Victor kept insisting there were two versions; and, secondly, my stopwatch kept insisting that the two performances were of different length, particularly if you started them both off at an adjusted speed in which A was 440 cps.

It was only after I learned from the most trustworthy sources that, in fact, there was only one recording that I managed to discover how the differences in timing had occurred. They, in turn, involve changes of playing speed and pitch, so that factually I was perfectly right in my statement that the 78 version is slower and more relaxed than the longplay transfer, but that the longplay disk has the more brilliant sound. My suggestion, therefore, is to take the LM-6020 set, and copy it on tape, adjusting for the change of pitch at bar 122. This restores the merits of the 78 record.

The *Meistersinger Prelude,* the *Eroica,* and *La Mer* were the most frequently played works of Toscanini's American career, so this counts as one of the most important documentations of his art. It is a superlative performance by any standard.

There are three versions of the *Siegfried Idyll.* Between that of 1936 and this successor of a decade later the choice is primarily based upon sound. The performance here is warm, beautifully paced, and deeply felt, and the recording, although lacking the lustre of the upper string tones, is thoroughly acceptable. Since the 1950 version offers brighter sound at the cost of substituting an over-refined, cool, and slick reading of the score, this is the recording to take as the best statement of his distinguished performance.

Those who enjoy the dreadful concert setting of the Valkyries in flight will prefer the 1952 recording.

ROUSSEL

The Spider's Feast
> Recorded during a broadcast April 7 in Studio 8-H.
> Unreleased

An evocative set of French musical pictures are well recorded here in a properly sensual and exotic performance. The work is one of the off-beat Toscanini specialties, and we ought to be able to hear it again.

TCHAIKOVSKY

Romeo and Juliet: Overture-Fantasia

Recorded April 8 in Carnegie Hall.
LM-1019

This is not a traditional Tchaikovsky performance, for
Toscanini eschews the excesses and distortions often heard in
this composer's music. This is surely the most powerful reading of the *Romeo and Juliet Overture* that I have ever heard,
and yet the lyric passages sing freely. However, it is still
necessary to do a fair amount of adjustment in order to
reduce the high frequency emphasis and secure a natural and
pleasing orchestral sound.

BACH

Suite No. 3: Air [Air on the G String]
*49-3301

KABALEVSKY

Colas Breugnon: Overture
*49-3156
Recorded April 8 in Carnegie Hall.

These were two fillers. The Bach has admirable clarity but
is taken too fast. The Kabalevsky is an ugly piece of synthetic
music in which clichés of romanticism are distorted to produce "modern" effects. Toscanini has feeling for the rhythmic
vitality of the work and shapes it accordingly. The recording
in both cases is satisfactory.

HAYDN

Symphony No. 101 [Clock]
Recorded October 9, November 6, and completed June 12,
1947 in Studio 3-A, Radio City, New York.
LM-1038

Like the Mozart *Haffner,* this constituted a re-recording of
a 1929 set, complete to the original filler. After playing the
old records (Victor M-57) one may debate whether the
spacious, relaxed quality of the 1929 performance is more or
less effective than the faster and more intense reading of 1947.
I am inclined to prefer the slow movement in the 1929

version and the fast movements as they are given here.

The recording is better than the *Haffner,* though still cold, hard, and shrill on top. A filter takes the shrillness out, fortunately, but leaves sound that lacks bass and warmth and is artificially resonant.

GLUCK

Orfeo: Dance of the Spirits
   *49-3301

MOZART

Symphony No. 35 [Haffner]
   LM-1038
   Recorded November 4 in Studio 3-A, Radio City, New York.

A re-recording of a set (M-65) made with the Philharmonic seventeen years before. The 1929 performance is more relaxed, and the intensity of this one, though not excessive, may be more than some feel is appropriate. (I prefer the older version myself.) The studio sound has been reinforced by a number of echo chambers, and the artificial resonance is very pronounced and, unpleasant. The Gluck lacks clean definition, the sound of the solo flute being particularly undistinguished. It is newly available in the beautiful 1952 recording of the whole of Act II.

MENDELSSOHN

Incidental Music to "A Midsummer Night's Dream": No. 1
   Scherzo
   Recorded November 6 in Studio 3-A, Radio City, New York.
   *49-3156

The fourth of the five Toscanini versions of this celebrated *Scherzo* is of interest primarily for the contrast it provides with the brilliant 1947 version to follow. Essentially it is the 1921 and 1929 performance, and while the 1947 recording is lightness itself, swiftly flowing, yet wonderfully delicate and expressive, this one is, in contrast, much slower and rather heavily inflected.

SCHUMANN

Manfred Overture
  Recorded November 11 in Carnegie Hall.
  LM-9022

WAGNER

A Faust Overture
  *LRM-7023

The *Faust Overture* is early Wagner and one of his few works which was intended for the concert room rather than the theater. (It was to have been part of a *Faust* symphony.) The performance is splendid and the recording satisfactory. It is unfortunate, therefore, that the disk is not available.

The Maestro shows a special sympathy for the early romantics, and he plays this fine work so that its power and beauty are fully realized without sentimentality and distortion. Moreover, he was the only conductor of my experience to escape defeat in the syncopated intricacies of this score. Avoid the pressings with added resonance and, if necessary, play the 78's (*M-1287) or *LM-6.

VERDI

La Traviata
  Principals: Licia Albanese, soprano; Jan Peerce, tenor; Robert Merrill, baritone; chorus directed by Peter Wilhousky
  Recorded during broadcasts, December 1 and 8, in Studio 8-H.
  LM-6003

Toscanini's *Traviata* has to be taken on a basis similar to his *Fidelio,* that an imperfect recording of a great performance is better than none at all. It *is* a great performance, even though Toscanini is too tense during the portion that represents the first broadcast (fearful, perhaps, that he would not finish on time). No one could possibly do *Traviata* at this pace in an opera house with stage action taking place, but listening to a record is not going to the opera, and the fault is not too serious.

In a recent copy, of this set some coughs have been expertly removed (although Toscanini is as noisy as ever) and the sound is very much better than in early editions, bright and clear, seriously flawed only by being rather hard and cold on top and short of overtones. The singing still is not always of the best, and Merrill is quite unpleasant in quality at times when his own shortcomings are increased by those of the recording.

Great performances of opera being as scarce as they are, the thing to do with this set is forget the defects and listen to the beautiful things which are preserved here. I find that it repays such consideration, since its merits outweigh its flaws.

Portions of the rehearsals of November 25 and 30 are reproduced on a special Toscanini commemorative record which can be secured from The Musicians Foundation, Inc., 131 Riverside Drive, New York 24, N.Y., for a contribution of $25 or more. The foundation is a charitable organization.

1947

BERLIOZ

Romeo and Juliet: Dramatic Symphony
> Gladys Swarthout, mezzo-soprano; John Garris, tenor; Nicola Moscona, bass; Chorus directed by Peter Wilhousky
> Recorded during broadcasts, February 9 and 16, in Studio 8-H.
> Unreleased

Of all the Riverdale material, this is probably the best known and most desired. (RCA-Victor does not want to release this performance because it has a new stereo version in the works which it feels will absorb the current demand for the score.) Interest in a complete Toscanini *Romeo and Juliet* can traced back to these broadcasts. However, Victor was cautious about the risk and expense of committing the whole to disks and arranged only for the recording of the usual concert excerpts.

Hearing the performance again after fifteen years you are astonished by the way it grasps and holds your interest. The sound is the familiar, close 8-H variety, cramped at times and momentarily unpleasant in the strings, but in general well recorded with beautiful clarity and presence. The way the woodwinds and brass are handled you are likely to be overcome by the strength and shape of the musical contours and forget about any imperfections in the engineering. The soloists and chorus are very well recorded, and the singing is of high quality.

Compared with the performance of the concert excerpts in the recording session, the broadcast versions are considerably more sensitive and relaxed. (Toscanini always was better playing to an audience than he was facing only microphones.)

The Damnation of Faust: Scene 7

Mack Harrell, baritone; chorus directed by Peter Wilhousky
Recorded during a broadcast, February 16, in Studio 8-H.
Unreleased

Intended primarily as a filler for the broadcast, this nonetheless gives us one of the most poetic moments of a score long associated with Toscanini. It is the scene where Faust dreaming under a spell set by Mephistopheles, sees the vision of Marguerite. The voice of Faust is here sung by an unidentified chorister; the scene closes with the ballet of the sylphs. The singing is good, the ballet exquisite. For release on disks the Maestro insisted that two prefatory bars heard in the broadcast be omitted.

Romeo and Juliet, Dramatic Symphony: Part II, Romeo Alone and Great Festivities at the House of Capulet; Love Scene
Recorded February 17 in Carnegie Hall.
LM-1019

At present, all we have of this brilliant and wonderful score are the two excerpts here and a 1951 broadcast recording of the *Queen Mab Scherzo*. Happily, these are three of the finest sections and a fair sample of one of the great triumphs of orchestral playing in our time, although I cannot hear them without recalling that the *Love Scene* opens with a delicious little choral nocturne which is omitted here.

SCHUBERT

Symphony No. 9 [sometimes called *No. 7*]
 Recorded February 25 in Carnegie Hall.
 *LM-1040

Although this is one of the great Toscanini performances, adequately recorded, the 1953 version is superior on all counts.

DUKAS

Ariane et Barbe-Bleue: Concert Suite [Arranged by Toscanini]
 Unidentified female voices are heard in the performance
 Recorded during a broadcast, March 2, in Studio 8-H.
 Released as V-Disks 836/37

Toscanini was always fond of this opera, which he introduced to the United States in the Metropolitan production of 1911, but he felt in later years that it was a dull stage work. In an effort to preserve the music, he prepared this concert version in which singers have all but been eliminated. It is marvelously effective, adding another useful Dukas score to our rather limited stock. The recording counts as a particularly precious document, and it deserves revival.

MENDELSSOHN

Octet for Strings (*Op. 20*)
 Recorded during a broadcast, March 30, in Studio 8-H.
 LM-1869

It is hard to tell just how big an orchestra Toscanini used for this. It is studio sound, cramped and artificially condensed at its best, but I would gather that the eight players Mendelssohn called for have been roughly tripled. In some places this is good, in others this factor—plus the recording—makes for heavy textures lacking the effect of chamber music. The 1945 version of the *Scherzo* alone was, I think, a lighter and more polished performance. It is the most enjoyable movement, the work as a whole being a pleasant but rather small-scaled example of youthful romanticism.

Incidental Music to "A Midsummer Night's Dream" "Complete": *Overture, No. 5 Intermezzo, No. 7 Nocturne, No. 1 Scherzo, No. 10 Wedding March, No. 12 Finale* [with Edna Phillips, soprano, and female chorus]
Recorded November 4 in Carnegie Hall.
*LM-1221

During his American career, Toscanini played the *Nocturne* and *Scherzo* from this set of pieces in twenty-four cities, making it his perennial choice for touring. Indeed, so magical a performance could hardly fail to please any audience that was even slightly fond of music, regardless of sophistication—or the lack of it. He never prepared the entire work, but in the literal sense it almost never *is* prepared, except when the music is actually used in connection with a production of the play, and the "complete" score indicated here comprises all of the numbers which are appropriate to the concert room and enjoyable as pure music.

It is fortunate that when Toscanini remade this set—an earlier version was among the items of the Philadelphia series—he was given the benefit of good recording and was prepared to relax and sing. What one hears, then, is incandescent tonal brilliance, and playing in which the beauty, the delicacy of inflection, and the plastic distinction of the moving line cause one to gasp as wonder follows wonder. The volume level is low; with adequate gain the recorded sound is excellent. It is extremely distressing that this set has been so long out of print. There is no performance in the current catalog to match it.

MOZART

Divertimento for Strings and Two Horns (K. 287) [*The second minuet is omitted.*]

Recorded November 18 in Studio 8-H.
LM-2001

Both Toscanini and Koussevitzky were particularly fond of this work. Toscanini's grasp of its form gave him the means to overcome what B. H. Haggin has identified as "the difficulty of knowing what to do between the mere *p* here and the *f* eight bars later." For Koussevitzky, as Haggin has pointed out, the thing to do with this or any doubtful situation was to submerge the music in a flowing gorgeousness of sound that dazzled the ear, hoping thereby to conceal the essential lack of intensity or continuity. That the sound was gorgeous, no one will deny, but if one asked for more than that Koussevitzky was often unable to provide it.

In his book, *The Maestro,* Howard Taubman tells us that Toscanini made this recording for other conductors as a demonstration of how Mozart should be played. Among other things it demonstrated that in the slow movement Mozart had clearly indicated a cadenza for the first violin by writing a six-four chord, a rest, and a trill leading back into the melodic line. Haggin reports that when Toscanini heard the Koussevitzky performance, in which the chord, the rest, and the trill were played through exactly as marked, he exclaimed, "This man is no musician. He is *ignorante!*"

What we have here is simple, clear line of sound, moving at a speed appropriate to its melodic flow and expanding to *f* and *ff* and contracting to *p* and *pp* without changing the tempo of that flow or its plastic continuity. Whatever reservations one may have about Toscanini's other Mozart recordings, this one is very beautiful and technically satisfactory.

An extract from the November 15, rehearsal for this performance is part of the record released by The Musicians Foundation. (See *La Traviata,* 1946.)

Bassoon Concerto No. 1 (K. 191)
  Leonard Sharrow, bassoon
  Recorded November 18 in Studio 8-H.
  LM-1030

Mozart's only bassoon concerto (*No. 2* being considered spurious) is a pleasant work of no great weight with a number of fine passages that are capably realized in this performance. The recording is good.

BACH

Suite No. 3

BACH (Orch. Respighi)
Passacaglia and Fugue in C Minor

VIVALDI

Concerto in B flat for Violin and Strings with Continuo
Mischa Mischakoff, violin
Recorded during a broadcast, November 22, in Studio 8-H.

The *Passacaglia and Fugue* will be released in 1962 as a 12" 45 rpm. Private Limited Edition for Walter Toscanini and His Friends. The other two items are unreleased.

The chief interest in the complete *Suite No. 3* is a somewhat more eloquent performance of the famed air than one finds in the version of the previous year. Elsewhere the Maestro's approach is fast, the rhythms are tight, and drive is quite intense. The recorded sound of the brass is quite unpleasant, and some further work will probably have to be done before this tape is ready for the general public. The *Passacaglia and Fugue,* on the other hand, is agreeably recorded. A friend once remarked that Toscanini played this work "as if he *wanted* to show how badly Respighi had orchestrate it." This is not true, at least in a literal sense, but Toscanini presents the score more in the Respighi style than any which can possibly be related to Bach, and we must either accept it on those terms or forget about it.

The Vivaldi was the first American performance of a newly discovered work. With Toscanini's faultless classicism and clarity it becomes a prime example of the Venetian master. The balances are wonderfully exact, the soloist stands in high relief, and the ensemble gleams. This is a recording we certainly ought to have.

TCHAIKOVSKY

Symphony No. 6 [Pathétique]
Recorded November 24 in Carnegie Hall.
LM-1036

Two reactions are engendered by this performance. The first, which I share, is that it is a definitive version of a much-abused score. The second is that Toscanini's approach to the music is unsympathetic to an extreme, that he forces upon it a style quite unsuited to it.

Toscanini gave the first Italian performance of this work over fifty years ago, and though it is true that he never played another Tchaikovsky symphony in either Britain or the United States (indeed, that he never even played the *Pathétique* while with the Philharmonic), I do not subscribe to the suggestion that Toscanini disliked the music and played it only in deference to popular taste. A part of his great honesty as a musician, reflected again and again in his programs, was that when he had no real feeling for a work he did not play it at all.

What one hears on this record is an effort to present the score with the same respect for the composer's markings that one normally gives, say, to a symphony by Beethoven. The traditional banalities, the excesses, the exaggerations, the departures from the spirit of the printed music heard in the performances of other conductors are not reproduced here. In their place is the disciplined intensity of Toscanini. If one is so accustomed to hearing this music "interpreted" that he cannot appreciate it in an honest, musician-like performance, then this is not for him.

The first movement is played with great power and beauty, the second (always an irresistible temptation to any flaw in a conductor's morals) is played with muted restraint, perhaps too much. The march is dazzling, and the final movement reveals its stature and tragic grandeur without falling to the level of tub-thumping bathos and glycerine tears. The recorded sound is good except for some unpleasantness in the strings in a few loud passages. The bass should be boosted.

KODÁLY

Háry János: Suite
Recorded during a broadcast, November 29, in Studio 8-H.
LM-1973

This recording won a *Grand Prix du Disque* the year of its release, but to hear the quality which merited this award you must adjust the tone controls to secure more bass and eliminate the excess high frequency emphasis of the Victor transfer. Toscanini always had an interest in Kodály's music, and I leave it to you to speculate why when other national styles gave him difficulties he managed to find the Hungarian idiom of this suite so congenial to him. The performance is a good one and the music is attractive (if lightweight). This is a facet of the Toscanini personality we are happier for having had illuminated in this manner.

VERDI

Otello
Principals: Herva Nelli, soprano; Nan Merriman, mezzo-soprano; Ramon Vinay, tenor; Giuseppe Valdengo, baritone; choruses, directed by Peter Wilhousky and Eduardo Petri
Recorded during broadcasts December 6 and 13 in Studio 8-H.
LM-6107

Not until we could match this set with the full forces of stereophonic high fidelity did we realize fully how good it is. It is tremendous.

I shall not pretend that *Otello* is one of my favorite operas. It is undoubtedly one of Verdi's supreme achievements, and I honor it as such, but as a drama it falls into the category of uninstructive tragedies, works in which one grieves without any true sense of moral profit. Bernard Shaw once remarked that in *Othello* Shakespeare was writing, unknowingly, an opera libretto, a tragedy based upon a farce plot in which the coincidences all work out and the structure stands just long enough to produce the eventual denouement. The Boito adaptation of the play is a masterpiece among opera texts, but it necessitates further compression of the material and heightens the effect of precarious construction.

Toscanini plays the music with clarity, force, a breathtaking sense of theater, and an emphasis on a singing line that is all the more remarkable when you hear how consistently and seemingly effortlessly it is achieved. The singers are equal to the Maestro's demands. This is one of the great documents of Vinay and Valdengo in their prime, Merriman is lovely, and if Nelli seems at times lacking in the maximum tragic force, she nonetheless moves the heart. In short, this is one of the greatest of the Toscanini recordings.

In the current pressings (high S-numbers) the sound is quite good. Henry W. Simon's parallel Boito-Shakespeare libretto is a model for an operatic study text.

BEETHOVEN

Overture for the Consecration of the House
  Recorded December 16 in Carnegie Hall.
  LM-9022

One of Beethoven's finest works, this deserves to be played much more frequently. One reason for its neglect is a degree of uncertainty about the proper style for the piece. The traditional German approach is shown in the fine old Weingartner recording, based upon the premise that even though the writing is not "Beethoven style" it must be given a properly solid, four-square performance. Toscanini appears to recognize that the acknowledged influence on the work is Handel (who is not too dull and solid an individual, once we rescue him from the nineteenth century school of oratorio conductors) and that "Rossini fever" had reached epidemic proportions in Vienna at the time Beethoven was putting this work on paper. The Maestro's performance is not in the German tradition at all, and both Handel and Rossini have their say without having to don false, solemn faces. Although, in general, I don't always find Toscanini's fast tempi in fugues congenial, in this instance I am convinced and find his reading stunning—although there are also beauties in a slower and more rhetorical approach to some of these passages.

The choice is between compressed, overly monitored sound in the original issues or inflated, artificially reverberant sound in the later pressings. I suggest you look for a copy of the 78's (*M-1287) or the original longplay version *LM-6.

1948

Mozart

Symphony No. 39
> Recorded during a broadcast, March 6, in Studio 8-H.
> LM-2001

This is the least successful of the Maestro's Mozart recordings, an overly intense, unsympathetic treatment of a score that requires gentleness and love. The recorded sound is tight and dry.

Haydn

Sinfonia Concertante in B flat Major
> Recorded during a broadcast, March 6, in Studio 8-H.
> Unreleased

If Toscanini was in a bad mood for Mozart on March 6, he was in fine shape for Haydn and gave one of his best performances of that composer. The *Sinfonia* dates from 1792 (the year of such triumphs as the Symphony No. 98) and thus has the substance to respond to a great performance. Relaxed and happy with a group of his first desk men in the solo roles, Toscanini was radiant. The recorded sound is quite a bit better than that of the Mozart, although obviously a studio product.

Verdi

Otello: Ballabili
> Recorded during a broadcast, March 13, in Studio 8-H.
> In LM-6041

Only the French would think that the third act of *Otello* needed a ballet in its middle, but Verdi obliged them with a group of dances that count as his most mature and masterful creation of this type. Toscanini loved them as music, but he wisely omitted them from his recording of the complete opera. With this release that decision was doubly justified, for we have gained everything (principally a stronger *Otello*) and yet lost nothing. The recording was artifically brightened to produce more of a hi-fi effect, but a healthy treble cut ought to be sufficient to restore a natural orchestral sound.

BRAHMS

Academic Festival Overture

Recorded during a broadcast, November 6, in Studio 8-H. Unreleased

Toscanini obviously had less feeling for this work than its companion piece, the *Tragic Overture,* so he played it less—and less well. This is about as dramatic an *Academic Festival* as you will ever hear. It is impressive, but the humor and charm of the music are largely missing. The sound, however, is quite respectable.

Concerto for Violin and Cello

Mischa Mischakoff, violin; Frank Miller, cello
Recorded during a broadcast, November 13, in Studio 8-H.
LM-2178

There is no explanation for the frequency with which Toscanini prepared this work except the obvious one. He liked it. Putting his first desk players on the solo roles, it became a sort of fifth Brahms symphony, and that is how he played it. You will never hear such total integration in any performance in which the normal pair of solo eminences participate, since they will not be required to play together the way Messrs. Mischakoff and Miller were obliged to play together. Since both these gentlemen are up to virtuoso standard, this is probably the most perfectly achieved statement of the work we are likely to get on records for a long time. The sound is good.

Song of Destiny
Robert Shaw Chorale
Recorded during a broadcast, November 27, in Studio 8-H.
Unreleased

Those who admire Brahms' writing for chorus and orchestra can take whatever satisfaction they may from the fact that we have this work in an admirable Toscanini performance, well recorded.

1949

HAYDN

Symphony No. 99
Recorded during a broadcast, March 12, in Studio 8-H.
Unreleased

The sound is fine; the tempos are always good; and the finale explodes into driving quicksilver, a Toscanini tour de force in which the lightness of the ensemble is hard to believe. Haydn wrote one of his trick endings here, and Toscanini made it a fancy fooler for sure.

VERDI

Aïda
Principals: Herva Nelli, soprano; Eva Gustafson, mezzosoprano; Richard Tucker, tenor; Giuseppe Valdengo, baritone; Norman Scott, bass; with the Robert Shaw Chorale
Recorded during broadcasts, March 26 and April 2, in Studio 8-H and corrected with recordings made in Carnegie Hall, June 3 and 5, 1954.
LM-6132

In his later years Toscanini was known to refer to the Metropolitan as The Casino and ask why critics who praised his music also praised things that went on behind the gold curtain of the Broadway house. Didn't they hear the difference? If you match the orchestral playing of this set with the *Aïda's* encountered anywhere in the world today you will get the Maestro's point. This type of operatic conducting is rapidly disappearing, and yet it is this type of thorough direction from the pit which is essential if opera is to realize its potential as a fusion of music and drama.

No one will pretend that Toscanini's cast is very strong by 1962 standards. Leontyne Price, for one, is a finer Aïda than Nelli, Gustafson's Amneris is no match for Simionato, and Tucker is not the ideal Radamès. We can hear better people in these roles by sampling the current catalog (or going to the Metropolitan), but we have to give up Toscanini to do so and I am in no mood to part with him. For if he did not assemble as fine a cast as one might engage today, he presented a conception of *Aïda* which is valid for 1949, or 1959, or as many years as anyone will be interested in the music which Verdi gave us. This is not a singer's performance but a conductor's performance. We go to it for Toscanini, and the quality of the recording gives us Toscanini with such a vivid image that I, for one, am content.

I was concerned, though, about one or two points in the music, especially the revised ending the Maestro supplied for *Celeste Aïda,* so I looked in the score which Toscanini had used in 1949. It was a new printing. There are annotations in it from engineers, singers, and tape editors, but not a mark from Toscanini. He had it all in his head.

BEETHOVEN

Symphony No. 2
　　Recording begun November 7 and completed October 5, 1951 in Carnegie Hall.
　　LM-1723 and LM-6901

No other conductor revealed the stature of this score as effectively as Toscanini did, and its present frequency of performance is due in large part to his efforts on its behalf. As Toscanini plays it, it is a work of considerable force, a logical phase in the development of the young genius who wrote the *First* and has the *Eroica* awaiting him. The recording was disappointing in the early issues, but more recent pressings are quite satisfactory replicas of Toscanini's achievement.

SCHUMANN

Symphony No. 3 [*Rhenish*]
    Recorded during a broadcast, November 12, in Studio 8-H.
    *LM-2048

This is the orchestral work of Schumann in which the influence of Brahms is most deeply felt, and it is perhaps for that reason that Toscanini played it more than any other of the composer's four symphonies. It is one of the great Toscanini performances, particularly in the first and third movements, and it was wonderful to have it in the catalog, even briefly. Unfortunately, efforts were made to make this sound like a high fidelity recording, and these had to be counteracted to secure the original sound and adequate weight in the ensemble. The degree of success possible in such transformation depends on the control provided by one's phonograph, but the basic approach is to fortify the lower and middle frequencies and then reduce the highs to balance them properly and provide a pleasing string tone. None of the unreleased Riverdale material provides any greater problems of equalization and balance than this disk, so if you can get a satisfactory sound when you play this record, you can assume that any of the other things I have mentioned will provide equal or superior results.

CIMAROSA

Il Matrimonio per Raggiro: Overture
    Recorded during a broadcast, November 12, in Studio 8-H.
    Unreleased

All the qualities which make Toscanini's Rossini a delight are present here as well. The playing is light, filled with fun, and well preserved on tape.

RAVEL

Daphis and Chloe: Suite No. 2
    Recorded November 21 in Carnegie Hall.
    *LVT-1025

Toscanini felt that everything in this music must be heard, and he achieved a performance in which this was the case. It would have taken stereophonic techniques to capture it fully; instead it was given only medium-fidelity recording. The final longplay editions were able to suggest the marvel of balance and ensemble virtuosity that was the original of this disk, but it is questionable what posterity will be able to make of it. This seems to be a great performance which has been largely lost.

BEETHOVEN

Symphony No. 3 [Eroica]
Recorded November 28 and December 5 in Carnegie Hall.
LM-1042 and LM-6901

The second of our three Toscanini *Eroicas*, this one was available in a variety of editions which provided the choice between not enough resonance or too much resonance. Whichever choice you made, the results were not satisfactory. Happily, we now have a much better performance in much better sound, from 1953.

CHERUBINI

Ali Baba: Overture
Recorded during a broadcast, December 3, in Studio 8-H.
Unreleased

Have you ever heard a musical question mark? Toscanini plays one here (a couple, in fact). The work is as amusing as it can be, and the performance is filled with laughter.

TCHAIKOVSKY

Manfred Symphony
Recorded December 5 in Carnegie Hall.
*LVT-1024

To Toscanini this was an opera without human voices, Taubman relates; and having seen the Maestro's own score, I understand this. It ought to be reproduced for students and other conductors, since it is a perfect example of how by editing (the largest cut deletes fifteen pages of the finale) and selective rescoring Toscanini made this a better work than Tchaikovsky left it. For one thing, everything that needs to sound clearly does sound clearly in this version, and for another, the redundant elements in Tchaikovsky's transitions are removed. The performance is one of lyricism, honesty, and force. The Maestro holds the structure firm with a perfect sense of pacing, builds his climactic passages with care, and generally makes this work far better than you ever imagined possible. The master tape is filled with good sound. This ought not to have been taken from us.

RESPIGHI

Roman Festivals
Recorded December 12 in Carnegie Hall.
LM-1973

High fidelity had really arrived when this was made. When told that the final section of the work might overload the recording equipment, Toscanini shouted: "I don't care! Break everything, but get it on!" What we have, then, is a thrilling performance of a score that is good picture music but not much else, recorded as a decibel champion of its day.

WAGNER

Die Götterdämmerung: Dawn and Siegfried's Rhine Journey
[concert version by Toscanini]
Recorded December 22 in Carnegie Hall.
LM-6020

This recording, as the *Eroica* above, is analyzed in Chapter II. Of the three versions of the score, this is second best in performance, first in sound, and since the difference in this respect is very great, no doubt this is the recording the majority will want to play.

Parsifal: Prelude and Good Friday Spell
Recorded December 22 in Carnegie Hall.
LM-6020

The very low bass one hears toward the close of the first statement of the theme on the LM-6020 transfer is a Seventh Avenue, New York, subway train, from which one can conclude (a) that Carnegie Hall is not the ideal concert room—especially for making high fidelity recordings, and (b) this recording is pretty good. Both counts are correct, which is one reason why Victor used 8-H as long as they did.

The qualities of this playing, the tensile strength of the sound, the unity of the ensemble, the incisiveness of the attack, the expressive force of the inflection and accent make for a statement of the music with an impact that others almost never achieve. I find what appears to be an equal performance in the ancient recording by Karl Muck, who inherited the score from Hermann Levi, the conductor whom Wagner selected for the first production. Muck gave *Parsifal* at Bayreuth until 1931, when Toscanini succeeded him for one season. I feel it is proper to regard this dedicated performance as being within the apostolic tradition of the Festspielhaus. The brilliant playing of Harry Glantz, the first trumpet, is especially noteworthy, and the recording reproduces his unique tone very well.

1950

CHERUBINI

Medea: Overture
    Recorded during a broadcast, February 18, in Studio 8-H.
    Unreleased
Requiem Mass in C Minor
    The Robert Shaw Chorale
    Recorded during a broadcast, February 18, in Studio 8-H.
    LM-2000

That there has been in recent years a mild revival of interest in Cherubini is due in part to Toscanini, who played his music (admittedly on a modest scale) when everyone else seems to have abandoned him to the musicologists. When Toscanini revived the *Medea Overture* no one in the audience is likely to have heard the opera, but today it is not only known but recorded in full. As Toscanini plays this music it is a fascinating synthesis of explosive passion and classical reserve, but eloquence rather than vehemence dominates.

Few composers suffered from the hands of a master the way Berlioz suffered during his student days when Cherubini presided at the Paris conservatory. Yet Berlioz hailed this Requiem for its "abundance of ideas, fullness of form, and sustained sublimity of style." Toscanini makes these qualities clear in a wonderfully transparent, spacious, and sympathetic realization of the score, and the recording captures these qualities splendidly. It is rewarding to have it, but we ought to have the *Medea* as well.

MOZART

Symphony No. 40
   Recorded March 12 in Carnegie Hall.
   LM-1789

Of the nine Toscanini recordings of Mozart by the electrical process which have been commercially distributed this is the second best. I recommend it, the 1947 *Divertimento,* and the 1938 *Magic Flute Overture* without reservations, and the 1947 *Bassoon Concerto* is satisfactory. The remaining four items are either inferior performances or sonically obsolete. Thus, this single item is all we have of Toscanini Mozart on high fidelity.

Taubman quotes Toscanini as saying of Mozart, "He was too perfect. . . . Some of his music I find cold. . . . But he was a unique genius." And going on to recall how his first experiences of this symphony (in Italian performances) sounded as if it went "tweet, tweet," so only after Puccini reported to him how von Bülow played it in Berlin, with "bite in the strings" and "the first theme . . . strong and passionate" did he realize, "that was the way for me."

None the less, as the chapter following documents, Toscanini never explored the Mozart symphonies adequately in concert, and although he studied them in score and read Mozart's life and letters, he still did not always grasp his musical language with a sense of security which would have permitted him to prepare the more distinctive of his great works with a proper approach to their unique expressive content.

Similarly, it must be noted that this is not German Mozart (for that listen to Furtwängler's fine recording) or the unique Mozart of Sir Thomas Beecham, but Toscanini Mozart, played with a passion, intensity, and sense of "blood" that is appropriate to Italian music, but is not required for music as delicate and subtle, and yet as seemingly unlimited in its expressive range, as that of the Salzburg master. What is offered here is a deeply felt and impelling performance that avoids the excess of tension and the demoniac qualities of the older recording, but still must be regarded as a personal interpretation of the score. It is artistically honest, and convincing, but I am not certain yet that it is in every way what Mozart intended.

SCHUBERT

Symphony No. 8 [Unfinished]
    Recorded March 12 and June 2 in Studio 8-H.
    LM-9022

This was the last Toscanini recording to be issued on 78 rpm disks in the United States. It preserves a reading of the score that is unusually impassioned (some moments could actually be described as fierce) even for the Maestro, who had, on other occasions, given it a more relaxed and lyric statement. Those who think of the work in terms of *Blossom Time* will find this completely uncongenial, and others, who do not find this quite so unsympathetic, may prefer a more romantic approach. Since this is a work I have studied with some care, I confess that I find Toscanini's heroic portrayal of the young artist more in keeping with my own feeling for the music than the more relaxed, romanticism of other conductors.

DUKAS

The Sorcerer's Apprentice
    Recorded March 19 in Studio 8-H.
    LM-2056

One of the most enjoyable of the lighter works in the supposedly serious repertory, given a delicious performance that is far more lyric, relaxed, and enjoyable than the 1929 version.

SMETANA

The Moldau
Recorded March 19 in Studio 8-H.
LM-2056

Does this river flow into the Elbe or the Adriatic? The performance has a clarity and drive that one rarely hears, and the inner voices are beautifully revealed, but the spirit could not be less Bohemian and the scanning of the excerpt of folk music is completely Italian in manner.

VERDI

Falstaff
Principals: Herva Nelli, soprano; Teresa Stich-Randall, soprano; Nan Merriman, mezzo-soprano; Cloe Elmo, mezzo-soprano; Giuseppe Valdengo, baritone; Frank Guarrera, baritone; Norman Scott, bass; with the Robert Shaw Chorale
Recorded during broadcasts, April 1 and 8, in Studio 8-H.
LM-6111

Falstaff is frequently cited as Verdi's masterpiece. It might well be regarded as Boito's finest work and Toscanini's most distinguished operatic interpretation. For many years connoisseurs of Italian opera have insisted that *Falstaff,* more than any other score, drew forth Toscanini's most remarkable achievements in the opera house. It was natural that one would hope for a recording, and eventually it appeared—just as the announcement of a 1955 performance at the opening of La Piccola Scala suggested a second opportunity to record the work and the possibility of an even finer cast. Unfortunately, after thus whetting the sense of anticipation, the 1955 production failed to materialize.

Once more time had given us perspective, and although

there are things about this performance which one would like to have seen improved, it is faithful to the Maestro's conception of the score and presents it with such force that one is inclined to overlook weaknesses elsewhere.

Again it is the cast that fails to come up to the virtuoso standard of the instrumental playing. Valdengo seems to have been coached to within an inch of his life. As I have grown more accustomed to his Falstaff I view it somewhat more favorably, but at best he was miscast, and his achievement is a tour de force in an uncongenial role. He does create a character, and if he does not give him particularly great depth, he makes him live and hold our interest.

Of the female singers, Cloe Elmo is outstanding and walks away with the opening scene of Act II without even a struggle. Mesdames Nelli, Merriman, and Stich-Randall have been attentive pupils at the Maestro's school and deserve high marks (they often are quite charming), but the diligent student and the accomplished actress are two different things. Bardolph and Pistol emerge as distinctly subdued ruffians, and although Ford has moments of personal force, one feels his impact could be greater. The chorus is excellent.

I find the recording bright, clear, and agreeable. The sound is clearly that of a studio (our venerable friend 8-H), happily without added resonance, so one must be prepared for the compression of sound that it provides.

Whatever its limitations, this must count as one of the great Toscanini recordings.

ROSSINI

The Italian Woman in Algiers: Overture
Recorded during a broadcast, April 14, in Carnegie Hall. Unreleased

This comes from the New York concert which launched the 1950 Toscanini tour of the United States. The work certainly deserved a re-recording from the Maestro, and the performance here is just as attractive as the famous one of 1936. Moreover, it is well recorded.

DEBUSSY

La Mer
Recorded June 1 in Studio 8-H.
LM-1833

If the American tour of the N.B.C. Symphony was Toscanini's greatest triumph of the 1949-50 season, this recording surely comes second. *La Mer* is the work he played fifty-three times in his twenty-nine seasons as a symphonic conductor in the United States, and although there had been several efforts to record it, the best known of which was (once more) during the 1942 Philadelphia sessions, none had yielded a version with the clarity and perfection of detail which he demanded. Even the Philadelphia recording, the first movement of which was so fine he said it was "just like reading the score," failed to please him because of errors in the later pages, and it is possible that, had the electroplating accident not taken place, it still would not have been approved.

Made in the final recording sessions held in 8-H, this was a performance prepared for the tour and polished by a series of six concerts before the recording was made. Some say that the final concert performance, in Philadelphia, was even finer than this. I didn't hear it, so I can't comment, but if it was better, I can't imagine how. This is one of the miracles of orchestral virtuosity. The two things which are the most striking are the phenomenal clarity (*everything* sounds) and the cohesion of the parts, each of which is perfectly executed —but always in proper relation to the whole and the other strands of sound.

Toscanini edited this score with great care, doubling lines in the subtlest fashion when necessary to make them sound, and his text should be printed for general use, now that he no longer requires it. These changes were made with Debussy's permission.

If you buy this recording these days you will have to take it with "enhanced sound." A current master, E1-LRC-0241 41S, enhances the original tape the way Hollywood enhances fading film beauties, by softening the focus with a silken haze and thus obscuring our view of both what is faulty and what is fair. The distressing thing is that this is not necessary. My copy of the original edition, LM 1221, is a better recording. Unfortunately this transfer is long out of print, and so is the first "enhanced" edition for which I confess a passing preference. It sounded better than the original on the equipment I was using in England seven years ago, but since I have acquired more sensitive pickups and a more flexible preamplifier the greater merits of un-enhanced sound have become clear. I therefore recant my former judgment and hope that we may someday have an *urtext* transfer of the tape.

SAINT-SAËNS

Danse Macabre
    Recorded June 1 in Studio 8-H.
    LM-2056

That Toscanini could in the same recording sessions perform both a transcendent masterpiece and this work poses a baffling question on the mentality of genius, quite as if Cézanne had paused between his two greatest canvases to turn out a crudely voluptuous pin-up. What can one say? It is a fine performance, well recorded. Who cares?

DEBUSSY

Images, Third Set [for orchestra—sets 1 and 2 are for piano solo]: *No. 2 Ibéria*
    Recorded June 2 in Studio 8-H, and incorporating corrections from the broadcast performance of March 27, 1948.
    LM-1833

The three *Images* for orchestra are (1) *Gigues*, (2) *Ibéria* —in three movements, the final two played without pause, (3) *Rondes de printemps*. Heard as a work of three contrasting parts they have an effect which cannot be duplicated if they are played singly, but, in fact, in all his American career, Toscanini never played either the first or third of these three works, although *Ibéria* became one of the core items in his repertory. I can offer no explanation for this, save that the expressive medium of the first and third of the *Images* is more deeply felt than that of *Ibéria,* and perhaps he did not understand it.

The performance is a marvel of ensemble coloring and balance, while its plastic qualities, the continuity of the pulse patterns within an expressive molding of the thematic material, reveal the fundamental strengths of Toscanini's art.

The insertion of a few bars of broadcast material into the second movement has produced a greater eruption of extravagant nonsense than anything ever done to a Toscanini recording. In the first place it was done on Toscanini's insistence, so the critic who protests sets himself up to protect Toscanini's art from Toscanini, a posture of arrogance which the Maestro found intolerable. The second point is that unless you know where the correction was made, the chances of hearing it are slight. Indeed, if your attention is where it belongs, on the unfolding of the detail of the music, I am sure you will not hear it at all—particularly in the current transfer with the stamper number 12 S.

1951

STRAUSS

Don Juan
Recorded January 10 in Carnegie Hall.
*LM-1157

During the summer of 1950 Studio 8-H was converted for television and the Toscanini concerts moved to Carnegie Hall. This was the best thing that could happen from the point of view of recording, and the technical level of the Toscanini disks from 1951-54 is significantly improved by the superior qualities of the larger hall.

The main difficulty with Strauss's *Don Juan* is that it's too popular. Everyone plays it, but most conductors play it badly, stressing the obvious effects and allowing the subtle points (the dissonant trumpet note at the protagonist's death, for example) to slip by. The Toscanini version offers a truly impassioned statement which is effective as portraiture but also has depth and an awareness of both the psychological as well as theatrical elements of the drama. This is the finest recording of the music I know, and with so many lesser versions available, it is distressing that this one is out of print. Its technical quality is fully satisfactory.

VERDI

Requiem [in Memory of Alessandro Manzoni]
  Herva Nelli, soprano; Fedora Barbieri, mezzo-soprano; Giuseppe Di Stefano, tenor; Cesare Siepi, bass; with the Robert Shaw Chorale
  Recorded during a broadcast, January 27, in Carnegie Hall.
  LM-6018

The most impressive quality of this recording is the sense of presence that it gives. Heard over equipment that can handle the large masses of sound without distortion, you can shut your eyes and seem to feel that in some magical way you have been transported to Carnegie Hall on that memorable evening. The fidelity, then, is spectacular, with the sound vivid, natural, and agreeable, and if you must contend with a few realistic coughs, you are compensated by hearing a performance that is actually *better than* the original, since the flaws have been expertly corrected in tape editing. Toscanini prepared this fine work regularly from his first New York season in 1908-09 and was here captured in a period of sustained intensity which was held in check by the urge to sing; thus even such hair- (and roof-) raising moments as the opening of the *Dies Irae* are perfectly under control and avoid any excess. Verdi's description of the Last Judgment is impressive in the manner by which, in a few powerful strokes, he paints the scene and achieves a greater effect than Mahler ever secures after pages of preparation in the *Resurrection Symphony*. The Toscanini performance is dramatic rather than liturgical in feeling, but it is not operatic, and the work is held together in a firm grip that does not allow the movements to appear to break up into episodes. Unfortunately, although the orchestra plays with amazing virtuosity and precision, the force of that master hand sometimes makes the soloists appear trapped in the unyielding framework of Toscanini's concept of the score. It is the splendor of that concept that makes this set the marvel that it is.

BEETHOVEN

Symphony No. 4
Recorded during a broadcast, February 3, in Carnegie Hall.
LM-1723 and LM-6901

I have listened to a copy of the original tape and can report that the disk reproduces the sound of the source recording well, though it is not less cramped and dry for that. Toscanini was driving the orchestra very hard and obviously wanted clarity and dramatic force, which are here preserved at the cost of tonal splendor. The more relaxed 1939 performance is the one to have.

ROSSINI

Semiramide: Overture
Recorded September 28 in Carnegie Hall.
LM-2040

Before writing this, I played the 1936 recording and tried once more to answer the question: "Why is the earlier one better?" in terms that would exclude sentimental bias for a set that was once, by the going standards, exceptionally beautiful, that thrilled me again and again, and that still preserves with remarkable force the wonderful sound of the Philharmonic of nearly two decades ago. My answer is that, although the 1951 version is superior in sound and presence, the 1936 recording is played more lightly and delicately, with subtler inflections and greater verve, and that, in contrast, the 1951 version seems mechanical, less expressive, and well drilled rather than deeply felt.

WEBER (*Orch,* BERLIOZ)

Invitation to the Dance
Recorded September 28.
LM-2056

DONIZETTI

Don Pasquale: Overture
Recorded October 5.
LM-6026 and Tape *AC-27
Recorded in Carnegie Hall.

Both of these are modern duplications of older recordings which offer polished and propulsive versions of scores Toscanini played extremely well. The Donizetti is almost the identical performance as that of thirty years before, and the Weber, with the prelude and postlude stated in the beautiful tone of Frank Miller's 'cello, is a charming synthesis of precision and grace. Since the postlude is usually lost under premature applause (as happened to Toscanini in the broadcast concert of December 13, 1953), a record is about the only chance one has to hear it.

PROKOFIEV

Symphony No. 1 [Classical]
Recorded October 15 in Carnegie Hall.
LM-9020

Has this symphony a slow movement? Toscanini decided that it did, and his tempo for the *Larghetto* is quite a bit slower than that of other conductors. It is convincing, but the great Koussevitzky performance (which never got on to modern records) was convincing, too, though quite different. An unusual and effective reading of a fine score, then, well worth some thought.

WAGNER

Lohengrin: Preludes to Acts I and III
Recorded October 22 in Carnegie Hall.
LM-6020

Two more modern duplications of older recordings which have the life and strength of the originals. There is a noticeable (but inoffensive) tape splice near the beginning of the *Prelude to Act I;* both preludes could use a little more solidity and bass.

Siegfried: Forest Murmurs
Recorded October 29 in Carnegie Hall.
*LRM-7029

Of all the raw and bleeding fragments of Wagner which reach the concert room, this one reaches the level of "groveling imbecility" according to Tovey, whose judgment I second with a lusty *aye!*

The American 45 rpm matches the level of the music: after twenty-four seconds of *Forest Murmurs* there is a break to the side following! Those who can stand the piece with its lack of form and silly climax (how could Toscanini tolerate it?) will find it beautifully played here.

WEBER

Euryanthe: Overture
Recorded October 29 in Carnegie Hall.
LM-6026 and Tape *AC-27

This recording inaugurates the famous trio of Weber overtures in Toscanini performances of unique clarity and vigor. This performance in particular—with its freedom from the rhetorical excesses that often pass as "German style"—is particularly welcome. The sound is not quite so full as I would like, but otherwise very good.

BRAHMS

Symphony No. 1
Recorded November 6 in Carnegie Hall.
LM-1702 and Tape *CC-8

Although some works of Brahms are clearly the product of a great composer's use of materials he can command with ease and utilize in the construction of large, solidly built compositions, others disclose faulty construction and the kind of pretension that invariably follows when one tries to make fairly ordinary things appear to be terribly significant and profound. Weingartner was aware of this, and in his book *The Symphony Since Beethoven* (Boston, 1904) went after Brahms quite soundly for his "mannerisms" and the fact that "entire sections of his works" are "built up."

I confess that I do not like the Brahms *First Symphony*, even though I am aware that millions of people do and that performances which stress the very pretentious qualities which repel me, arouse many admirers of the work to rapturous enthusiasm. The portions of the score which I am able to hear with pleasure, most of them in the final movement, Toscanini states with dignity and exemplary good taste, and the crude, crosscut-saw effect in the exposition of the first movement is, with similar good taste, minimized. The score, thus, is beautifully played and beautifully recorded here, and for those who enjoy the rest of the work, it is expertly done.

BEETHOVEN

Symphony No. 7
> Recorded November 9 in Carnegie Hall.
> LM-1756 and LM-6901

Toscanini was pleased with his 1936 recording of this work and failed to see the necessity to do it again. "Why do you need a new one?" he kept asking. The answer, of course, was high fidelity. Fifteen years had passed since the earlier version had been put on disks, but you will not find fifteen years of improvement in this 1951 recording, which is technically not up to the best work Victor was doing in the early 'fifties. When we consider the two performances it becomes clear that at eighty-four Toscanini could not duplicate what may have been his greatest achievement with this music. Even with its dated sound, the 1936 version sounds more impressive in the early pages, and as the work advances the Philharmonic version continues to score point after point on the N.B.C. edition. However this 1951 set remains an exceptional *Seventh*. It took a Toscanini to beat a Toscanini.

BERLIOZ

Romeo and Juliet, Dramatic Symphony: Part II, Queen Mab Scherzo
> Recorded during a broadcast, November 10, in Carnegie Hall.
> LM-6026

Sheer orchestral sorcery from beginning to end, this music was finally recorded and approved by the Maestro. For those who had been waiting ever since word leaked out that it had been done with the Philadelphia Orchestra in 1942, its release was a long-anticipated pleasure.

Dvořák

Symphonic Variations on an Original Theme

Recorded during a broadcast, November 17, in Carnegie Hall.

Unreleased

Toscanini was fonder of this piece than the Dvorak symphonies (the *New World* excepted), presumably because it was more easily approached as pure music and presented him with no grave stylistic problems peculiar to the Czech idiom. The work is not an especially familiar one, which makes a recording of this quality particularly deserving of an audience.

Tchaikovsky

The Nutcracker, Ballet: Suite No. 1

Recorded November 19 in Carnegie Hall.

LM-1986

Certainly the most remarkable of the two "Toscanini" versions of this score is the one made without him, in October, 1954, to be used as a gift to those who contributed to his former orchestra under its new incorporation as the "Symphony of the Air." Although they had not played the work under Toscanini since the day they made the 1951 recording, nearly three years previously, they duplicated the performance as well as any musician can duplicate a performance, showing to anyone who was interested that once a Toscanini taught them a piece they could play it forever if necessary. However, by slowing down the tempo twenty-five per cent with the Springer device one finds that they played with much heavier inflections under the Maestro, and their performance without a conductor is lighter and more sensitive both melodically and rhythmically.

This work was on the program of Toscanini's first symphony concert in 1896; fifty-five years later he was playing it with a freshness, zest, and degree of attention to balance, and coloring such as it rarely has been given. A thoroughly delicious performance that transforms a score that one is probably tired of into a delightful musical experience once more.

BEETHOVEN

Septet (Op. 20)
Recorded November 26 in Carnegie Hall.
LM-1745

This is chamber music played with orchestra forces, but the sound is still delicately scaled and the textures are those of an ensemble of—if not seven—few players. The work is a sort of divertimento in a relaxed, youthful style reminiscent of the *Second Symphony* at times. Extremely popular when it was written, it was soon overshadowed by the mature Beethoven, and although one finds it fresh, melodic, and romantic, none of the matters of which it treats are particularly weighty. It is pretty Zerlina rather than Donna Anna.

WAGNER

Die Meistersinger: Prelude to Act III
Recorded November 26 in Carnegie Hall.
LM-6020

The third act *Meistersinger* prelude is one of the most intensely human and deeply felt passages in Wagner. Toscanini was supreme in revealing these qualities, and we must rank this among his most important Wagner disks.

BRAHMS

Symphony No. 4
Recorded December 3 in Carnegie Hall.
LM-1713

The most perfectly conceived work of Brahms and one of the supreme masterpieces of the nineteenth century, this work has been audible in Toscanini performances which ranked as the finest reading of the score to be heard. From the siren song of the opening bars to the towering heights of the concluding passacaglia the work is filled with traps for the unwary conductor of dubious musicianship or taste, and Toscanini invariably navigated the course without slipping into them. Particularly, he gave us a reading of the final movement in which, by holding the tempo steady, *as it must be* (and as it almost always is *not*), he achieved the great climactic passage at the close of the variations in a manner which could serve as the paradigm for all who play the score.

When I first heard this recording I was sorry that we had been given one of the Maestro's more reserved treatments of the music instead of a warmer, more radiant account such as he had also presented from time to time. Happily, we now have the best of all possible worlds, since the Philharmonic performance of 1952 is the ideal compliment to this, thereby providing us with the two faces with which a great conductor presented one of his greatest achievements to the public.

ELGAR

Variations on an Original Theme [*Enigma*]
Recorded December 10 in Carnegie Hall.
LM-1725

To the British, Elgar is a great composer, although I doubt if he holds this reputation in any other country, certainly not in the United States where his *Pomp and Circumstance No. 1* is the invariable processional at secondary school graduations, but his larger works are unheard except for occasional performances of the violin concerto and these variations. This is the only work of Elgar which Toscanini performed with any regularity, and his recording commands our attention, for it is a lovely score, played here with obvious affection, and containing a wealth of fine moments. The recording is excellent.

RESPIGHI

The Fountains of Rome
Recorded December 17 in Carnegie Hall.
LM-1768 and ME-2409 (stereo reprocessed version) Tape
*DC-51 and FTC-2083 (stereo reprocessed version)

Contrary to a story that has been told in recent years, Toscanini was never scheduled to give the world première of this score, but you can well speculate what might have happened to it had he not taken it up after its disastrous first performance under another conductor. No one ever matched him in making its evocations as rich as possible or its pages as filled with life as Rome itself. The monophonic version is well recorded, and I prefer it to the stereo reprocessing where a certain amount of distortion enters along with the special effects.

BEETHOVEN

Symphony No. 1
  Recorded December 21 in Carnegie Hall.
  LM-6009 and LM-6901

Within the style imposed (a severe, unyielding classicism) this is a consistent and cogent reading of the score. Some may prefer a warmer and broader performance, such as that of 1937. For myself, this is a more distinctive and distinguished treatment of the music, and I give it my fullest admiration. The recording is excellent, and the whole totals up to one of the best of the Toscanini Beethoven series.

CHERUBINI

Anacréon: Overture
  Recorded during a broadcast, December 22, in Carnegie Hall.
  Unreleased

This was the first number of a benefit concert, the balance of which was broadcast. The performance is a model for conductors. For once the rhythm is right and the full effect of the score is achieved. This was the Maestro's favorite Cherubini overture. It shows.

1952

WAGNER

Die Götterdämmerung: Siegfried's Death and Funeral Music
  [concert version by Toscanini]

Recorded January 3 in Carnegie Hall.
LM-6020

This powerful statement of the hero's death is slower and more dramatically paced than the *echt* German version by Muck. It is one of the basic Toscanini repertory items.

Die Walküre: Prelude to Act III [*The Ride of the Valkyries*]
Recorded January 3 in Carnegie Hall.
*ERA-249

I dream, at times, of a nonexistent Spike Jones recording of this work with a background of high wind, thunder, pelting hail, and rain, a chorus of Valkyries fair overflowing from their cups, and a great many horsy effects. Unfortunately, this is a straight performance.

WEBER

Der Frieschütz: Overture
Recorded January 3 in Carnegie Hall.
LM-6026

One of the great works of German romanticism given a performance and recording which fully reveal its lyric and dramatic qualities.

FRANCK

Psyché No. 4: Psyché and Eros
Recorded January 7 in Carnegie Hall.
LM-1838 and Tape *CC-16

This would make a better effect if it did not tail the sensational *Pictures at an Exhibition* and reveal the big difference in Victor recording between early 1952 and a year later. The only Toscanini recording of Franck's music, it offers an agreeably melodic excerpt from a longer score. Bass requires an extra boost.

WAGNER

Tristan und Isolde: Prelude and Liebestod
Recorded January 7 in Carnegie Hall.
LM-6020

In Alma Mahler's biography of her husband, we learn of Mahler's misgivings about Toscanini's performances of *Tristan* in the 1909-10 season at the Metropolitan Opera, when they both conducted there. I share Mahler's reservations. The performance (there is no reason to believe it changed greatly in the intervening years) is over-refined, the antiseptic souvenir of passion rather than that its full-blooded actuality. In *Tristan* this will not do, although it is easily understood when we see that these two works rank fourth and fifth in frequency in Toscanini's repertory: they have had all the life played out of them. There is a noticeable break in continuity in bar 55 of the *Liebestod,* right after the strings have played a wonderful phrase in a cool, polished and unfeeling manner, more appropriate to Verdi than to this period of Wagner's music.

BEETHOVEN

Symphony No. 6 [Pastoral]
Recorded January 14 in Carnegie Hall.
LM-1755 and LM-6901

There are two *Pastoral* symphonies. One is a warm, German work, relaxed and reflecting the mood of rustic poetry; the other is this, a dazzling classical landscape, brilliantly illuminated by the Mediterranean sun. Those who want the former score need only secure the recording of Bruno Walter, while for the second there are the two Toscanini recordings. The greatest marvels are in the second movement, in which the delicacy of coloring and the plastic quality of the unfolding line of sound are a unique musical experience, but the other movements are equally fine in their respective ways, and if the village band Beethoven suggests in the trio of the *Scherzo* never appears (the refined sounds one hears are no rural musicians) the storm that follows is forceful enough, and the thanksgiving sincerely conveyed.

BRAHMS

Variations on a Theme of Haydn [St. Antoni Variations]
Recorded February 4 in Carnegie Hall.
LM-1725

The sixth ranking item in frequency in Toscanini's repertory with forty performances in twenty-nine seasons. For all that, the duplication of the 1936 set is very successful (there are one or two minor differences of an expressive character), giving one a well-remembered performance in the excellence of modern sound.

Symphony No. 2

Recorded February 11 in Carnegie Hall.
LM-1731

The sound of this 1952 Toscanini series is good, but it is not so fine as that of the 1953 series, and one of the differences is that the later recordings capture the full brilliance of the brass, while these occasionally slice just enough off the top to take away its full lustre and make it seem a bit hard and coarse.

With that warning out of the way, one can remark that this is a fine performance of the symphony, well reproduced by the disk. It is of interest to me to contrast this reading of the score with that Toscanini gave with the Philharmonia Orchestra in London the autumn following. This is a disciplined performance: intensity is the predominant feeling in the work, and the propulsive force of the dramatic line carries all before it. In London the symphony had "loosened" somewhat, it was warmer and more expressive, there were variations in tempo (not all of them completely to my liking), and a more relaxed, singing quality was dominant in the performance.

CHERUBINI

Symphony in D

Recorded March 10 in Carnegie Hall.
LM-1745

Cherubini once ranked with the great and now is forgotten and all but unperformed, a process of deflation that may well affect some of the more celebrated composers of today. (I wonder, for example, what Bartók's reputation will be in fifty years.) Toscanini's revivals were welcome, and it is especially interesting to have this symphony, since it is a fine score, full of enjoyable things, even if lacking the marks of genius one finds in the music of Beethoven. Beethoven was ahead of his times; Cherubini, unfortunately, was just abreast of them.

STRAUSS

Death and Transfiguration
Recorded March 10 in Carnegie Hall.
LM-1891

Although there is no denying the popularity of this score, I find it the weakest of the six "big" Strauss tone poems of the decade 1888-98. *Don Juan* and *Till Eulenspiegel,* which flank it on either side, are both more vital not merely in thematic invention, but also in the symphonic development. The material in *Death and Transfiguration* is dangerously close to banality in its simplest form, and its treatment is frequently obvious and pretentious. The transfiguration theme is as good an instance of this as any.

The person who is fond of this score presumably admires some of its defects and, if record sales are any guide, enjoys a broad, rhetorical performance in which the melodrama is played for all it's worth. Toscanini, as one would expect, does not comply. His approach is cooler, more sublime, and also more detached. Never have I heard the opening phrase achieved with such clarity and polish, and throughout the playing is equally distinguished. I have heard part of the rejected Philadelphia recording of 1942 and can assure the reader that this performance is as fine in every way and sonically beyond comparison. If you want *Death and Transfiguration* played for all the dignity it possesses, and will accept the brilliant (and rather chilly) sound of Toscanini's strings, this is the performance without peers.

BEETHOVEN

Symphony No. 5
Recorded during a broadcast, March 22, in Carnegie Hall.
LM-1757 and LM-6901

The 1939 recording of this work was faster than I thought necessary, and this one preserves a further increase in tempo, which is thrilling, but is increasingly dubious as an interpretation of Beethoven's intentions. I feel that the work is rushed, that the slow movement is not slow enough, that the decrease in tempo required for the "second subject" of the first movement is a bad effect, causing a lessening of force, and that an excess of intensity has robbed the music of much of its communicative power. The recording does not compensate for this. The quality is inferior to that of the Verdi *Requiem* of the previous year and well below what one had a right to expect in 1952.

Symphony No. 9 [*Choral*]

Eileen Farrell, soprano; Nan Merriman, mezzo-soprano; Jan Peerce, tenor; Norman Scott, bass; with the Robert Shaw Chorale

Recorded (final movement) March 31, (first three movements) April 1, in Carnegie Hall.

LM-6009 and LM-6901 and Tape *FC-52

"I'm almost satisfied" was Toscanini's comment on this recorded performance. Undoubtedly he knew how to do it better, with angelic choirs that never sing off key or need to breathe, but in terms of human resources this is as fine a *Ninth* as we have ever been given on records. Admittedly it has weaknesses, and characteristically they are vocal. Farrell seems unable to sing a long phrase on a single breath, Peerce is too lightweight for the *Alla Marcia,* and Scott even mispronounces *Freunde* in his introductory recitative. The chorus is a fine one but rather far from the microphone, and so on.

British critics who were out to lower Toscanini's stock in favor of Klemperer's could make the most of these things, and did, so the Toscanini recording of the *Ninth* became one of the battlegrounds of that campaign. It served, if nothing else, to remind us that all criticism involves striking a balance between positive and negative elements, and to do so the critic must have the necessary judgment to know the relative importance of the flaws and merits of the works he is appraising. The important thing in this Toscanini set is that for the majority of its listeners it became the most effective statement of Beethoven's artistic intentions that they had ever heard, and if we are to match it with the Klemperer on that ground, the Klemperer must take second place simply because it is not nearly so immediate and eloquent a transmission of the substance of the work. (For those who already know the music, it may match the Toscanini in force, although I am inclined to doubt this as well.)

In short, I think we are now beyond criticism with respect to this set and in the area of fact. From its appearance to a decade later it was, for most American record collectors, *the* Beethoven *Ninth*. No other version of this music ever did so much to bring it close to a large and appreciative public, and no other recording is more likely to shape the public and critical consensus of how this music should be played. To quibble about it now is to show a complete lack of awareness of its role in recent cultural history.

A portion of the March 27 rehearsal is available on the record mentioned in the *La Traviata* listing (1946).

WAGNER

Siegfried Idyll
  Recorded July 29 in Carnegie Hall.
  LM-6020

Students of concert life in New York should note that this ends with a fanfare of automobile horns; in fact, the constant penetration of noise into the hall caused the engineers to use a "close-in" technique which lost much of the natural resonance of the auditorium. The performance is not my favorite of the three, a little chilly and lacking intimacy. The 1946 version is best. Note the midsummer recording date of this and the following; unusual for Toscanini.

LIADOV

Kikimora
  LM-2056

PONCHIELLI

La Gioconda: Dance of the Hours
  LM-1834 and Tape *BC-38

THOMAS

Mignon: Overture
  LM-6026 and Tape *AC-26
  Recorded July 29 in Carnegie Hall.

All these are "Pops" items, pleasant, but of no great musical weight. The recordings were made close-in and then given artificial resonance, the effect of which was to coarsen the sound. The playing is very lovely indeed.

BIZET

Carmen: Orchestral Suite No. 1
  LM-6026 and Tape *AC-26

CATALANI

Lorelei: Dance of the Water Nymphs and *La Wally: Prelude to Act IV*
  LM-6026

HÉROLD

Zampa: Overture
  LM-1834 and Tape *BC-38

HUMPERDINCK

Hansel and Gretel: Prelude
  LM-6026 and Tape *AC-26
  Recorded August 5 in Carnegie Hall.

Further spectacular performances of light music with the recorded sound coarsened by the needless addition of resonance. The *Carmen* is sensational. The Humperdinck has many lovely moments, particularly the first entrance of the strings.

SIBELIUS

Finlandia
Recorded August 5 in Carnegie Hall.
LM-1834 and Tape *BC-38

Until the 1940 material is made available this remains our only example of Toscanini's Sibelius. Like the other tone poems, it receives a simple, direct, and exceptionally forceful statement with a remarkable sense of drama. The recording is satisfactory.

WEBER

Oberon: Overture
Recorded August 5 in Carnegie Hall.
LM-6026 and Tape *AC-27

Toscanini was unsurpassed in the music of the early romantics, and this performance comes up to his customary standard. For delicacy and poetic charm, it is quite out of the ordinary. The recording again is excellent.

BRAHMS

Tragic Overture
Symphony No. 1
Symphony No. 2
Recorded during a broadcast, September 29, in the Royal Festival Hall.
Variations on a Theme of Haydn
Symphony No. 3
Symphony No. 4
Recorded during a broadcast, October 1, in the Royal Festival Hall.
The Philharmonia Orchestra (London)
Unreleased

This was Toscanini's farewell to London audiences and the British capital, a city which (along with New York and Milan) he always enjoyed as a residence, even on a temporary basis. For the brief time that Toscanini returned he was as popular as ever with the Londoners, but before his retirement the press and the fan club element of the audience had begun its idolatrous worship of Otto Klemperer, and a part of the cult credo was that Klemperer, who was resident in Britain, was always to be right, while Toscanini (who was an "American" conductor) was never to be right. This sort of asinine behavior was a grave injustice to two remarkable men. I do not suggest for a moment that Klemperer did anything to encourage it, but the consequences were unfortunate for Toscanini. One of them is that although tapes were made of these concerts, the material has remained in the vaults for a decade when it ought to be available to the public.

Toscanini enjoyed working with the Philharmonia, which gave him a warm tone and somewhat richer ensemble coloring than his own N.B.C. players. Toscanini also liked the hall, unlike some other conductors, since its dry qualities made for greater clarity. He was relaxed and happy, and with an audience behind him he stated these works in broad, singing phrases. In nearly every case these performances are more *gemütlich* than those with the N.B.C. My special favorite is the *Second,* but from a documentary standpoint the great thing in the series is the *Third,* since this is the only performance we have that is actually worthy of the Maestro.

In recent months there has been talk that these tapes might finally be released in Britain. I cannot think of a finer way to serve his memory or commemorate his affection for the British people.

Symphony No. 3

Recorded November 4 in Carnegie Hall.
LM-1836

Toscanini put off recording this symphony until the end of the N.B.C. Brahms series because he was uncertain how he wanted it to go. After several days of listening to tapes of his broadcasts, he put together an ideal performance (first and fourth movements of October 15, 1938, second movement of March 31, 1946, third movement of November 20, 1948). He listened to this until he thought he had it well in mind and then attempted to duplicate it in the recording session. He was unsuccessful. The "ideal version" is consistently taut, hard driving, and intense. This performance is slower and suffers, of all things, from both a lack of continuity and changes in the rhythmic pulse and scanning of phrases.

STRAUSS

Till Eulenspiegel's Merry Pranks
Recorded November 4 in Carnegie Hall.
LM-1891

The Old Man's power here is unbelievable until one has heard it for himself. Then it becomes inexplicable. The "trial scene" in particular is played as I had no idea it could be played with human resources. Yet for all the success with which the individual sections of the score are achieved, the work has a higher degree of unity and cumulative force here than in any other performance I have ever known. A bad conductor makes this work a string of episodes; Toscanini makes it a tightly integrated whole. The clarity is astonishing, and the details of the scoring, down to the striking reproduction of some very unusual instrumental timbres, are faultlessly reproduced. The violins, unfortunately, sound as if they had steel strings throughout. I would sacrifice some of the brilliance of their tone to greater warmth. Nonetheless, from every standpoint, this is one of the great Toscanini disks.

WAGNER

Tannhäuser: Overture and Bacchanale (Paris version)
Recorded during a broadcast, November 8, in Carnegie Hall.
Unreleased

Either this or the performance of April 4, 1954 (which was recorded in stereo) is available to document this score, a central work in the Toscanini repertory. In his hands it had a fire and clarity which remain notable and eminently worthy of preservation.

BEETHOVEN

Symphony No. 8
Recorded November 10 in Carnegie Hall.
LM-1757 and LM-6901

This is one of the few recordings we have ever had which gives full justice to the Beethoven *Eighth,* a work which is all too often treated as a merry quadrille, full of jolly little tunes, and by no means a serious business. So reduced in scale it provides material for commentators to develop, starting with their astonishment that Beethoven should write such a work during a period of crisis in his life. In the Toscanini performance the *Eighth* is restored to its proper stature, as a score equal in power and intensity to the *Seventh* which precedes it. I am, therefore, obliged to call this a definitive performance, in spite of the deficiencies of the sound. Note the big difference made by repeating the exposition of the first movement. In seeing the necessity for this Toscanini reveals his superb sense of form.

VERDI

La Forza del Destino: Overture
Recorded November 10 in Carnegie Hall.
LM-6026 and in LM-6041 and Tape *AC-27

A successful re-make of the 1945 disk. This is Toscanini playing his beloved Verdi with affection and sympathy. For those who enjoy the piece it is a brilliant version.

ROSSINI

Sonata No. 3 in C Major
Recorded during a broadcast, November 15, in Carnegie Hall.
Released as a 12″ 45 rpm. Private Limited Edition for Walter Toscanini and His Friends

Rossini's six sonatas for strings reveal facts of his artistic personality which do not always appear so clearly in his operas, particularly in the overtures we know. Toscanini admired this work (it is the only one of the set of six he ever played) and it belongs among his unique achievements with this composer's music. The recorded sound is splendid and the unusual speed makes sense if you hear how fine the high frequencies come through.

SAINT-SAËNS

Symphony No. 3 [with organ]
Recorded during a broadcast, November 15, in Carnegie Hall.
LM-1874

The *Third Symphony* of Saint-Saëns is the only one of his three works in this form to remain in the present-day repertory, a rather melancholy fate for one who was once known as the "French Beethoven." Indeed, even this *Third Symphony* belongs to that second division of scores that, although containing many fine pages, cannot truthfully be ranked as masterpieces. Under a sympathetic interpreter they reveal their merits, and under a less understanding artist their weaknesses predominate.

What, then, of this Toscanini performance? The rhetoric which is inherent in much of the music, and which many performers underline with varying degrees of skill and taste, is, as one would imagine, underdone rather than stressed. On first hearing, this approach may seem disappointing, unsympathetic, a typical conflict of style between Toscanini's ideas and a romantic composer's intentions. Further hearings, however, convinced me that Toscanini's approach to the score is valid and in excellent taste, and that if there are some passages where a little less intensity and a touch of rhetoric might be a good thing, there are others, often played with great rhetorical excess, that Toscanini reveals strong and firm in their inherent musical force—which needs no rhetorical underpinning.

The audience is a little noisy and coughs off the beat. (If they were in time it would not be so bad!) Otherwise the recording is excellent.

GLUCK

Iphigenia in Aulis: Overture

Recorded during a broadcast, November 22, in Carnegie Hall.
Unreleased

This program contained all the music of Gluck which played any part in the Toscanini repertory after 1926, and it seems unjust when both works were recorded with equal skill that we should be deprived of one of them. This is an excellent performance, filled with the stylistic elegance which the Maestro brought to this composer.

Orfeo: Act II

Barbara Gibson, soprano; Nan Merriman, mezzo-soprano; with Robert Shaw Chorale.
Recorded during a broadcast, November 22, in Carnegie Hall.
LVT-1041

We are in debt to Toscanini for this record. *Orfeo* is just about the oldest opera in the repertory (when older ones are produced it is usually a special revival, steeped in the spirit of antiquarianism) and the second act contains its finest music, much of which is unfamiliar and very beautiful indeed. Toscanini and the singers are perfectly in harmony and lyricism touched with the wonderful *melos* that Toscanini can (on occasion) provide is the predominant mood. Except for a tendency to harshness in some of the louder passages, the recorded sound is extremely good. No libretto is provided: an unusual omission for Victor.

1953

BEETHOVEN

Egmont: Overture
LM-1834

BERLIOZ

Roman Carnival Overture
LM-1834 and Tape. *BC-38

ROSSINI

William Tell: Overture
LM-1986
Recorded January 19 in Carnegie Hall.

Two of these are duplications of old and unsatisfactory recordings in terms of modern sound. The third item, the Berlioz, is itself duplicated on the 1954 "Symphony of the Air" disk, *sans* Toscanini. Of the Beethoven and Rossini, one can only say that the performances are spectacularly fine and the recording equal to them. The Berlioz is much more expressive here than in the conductorless version, since Toscanini plays it with subtle changes in pace and slight deviations from strict tempo which are impossible for a conductorless orchestra to duplicate (they have to be metronomic to stay together).

HAYDN

Symphony No. 94 [Surprise]
Recorded January 26 in Carnegie Hall.
LM-1789

A warm and radiant performance of a symphony in which the most celebrated of the various surprises is not the most amusing. (The best of Haydn's surprises is in fact the Great Bassoon Joke in the final movement of *No. 102*.) The theme of the minuet is unhappy at the pace Toscanini takes it; otherwise all is relaxed and beautiful.

MUSSORGSKY (Orch. Ravel)

Pictures at an Exhibition
Recorded January 26 in Carnegie Hall.
LM-1838 and LME-2410 (stereo reprocessed version) and
Tape *CC-16 and FTC-2084 (stereo reprocessed version)

When Toscanini made this recording he, in effect, took command of a work which had been commissioned by Koussevitzky and had previously been identified with the Boston conductor. Part of this change of authority came from the skill Toscanini brought to a revision of the scoring, particularly in the final movement, which made for greater brilliance and more spectacular conclusion. (However, there are arguments in favor of the Ravel original as well.) Monophonically this was one of the notable recordings of the high fidelity era. The stereo reprocessed form has its attractive features, but there are some unhappy changes in timbre (the solo trumpet, for example) which cause me to stay with the original version.

DVOŘÁK

Symphony No. 5 [From the New World]
Recorded February 2 in Carnegie Hall.
LM-1778 and LME-2408 (stereo reprocessed version) and Tape *BC-7 and FTC-2082 (stereo reprocessed version)

The traditional performance of this work contains a good deal of unrefined corn which Toscanini removes. If you like the corn, if you think it is inherent in the thematic material and the way it is developed, then you won't find this a sympathetic reading. Not being a corn lover myself, I find this remains one of the great accounts of the score.

Jack Arthur Somer, who made the stereo reprocessed version, may properly regard it as his masterpiece to date. It adds spaciousness and depth, it makes some detail stand out in relief, and in general it adds greater life and realism to what was originally a fine disk.

SCHUBERT

Symphony No. 9 [sometimes called No. 7]
Recorded February 9 in Carnegie Hall.
LM-1835

One of the greatest Toscanini performances, his reading of the last of the Schubert symphonies is also one of his most controversial, since his departure from German, Viennese (name it what you will) tradition is absolute and uncompromising. Critics invariably are obliged to comment on the clarity and virtuosity of the playing, only to raise their hands in horror at the tempi (particularly that for the *Andante con moto*) and suggest that the record collector buy an "orthodox" version by Herr Bratwurst and the Wiener Philharmoniker. Let us, therefore, look at the score and clear up this matter, if possible. Schubert writes *Andante con moto* at bar one, and nowhere else does he indicate a change of tempo. Now Schubert was no fool, and when he indicates all one tempo for the movement, he means all one tempo. What does Herr Bratwurst do? He begins slowly, *mit* Sentiment, and so dawdles along until roughly bar 160. Here the music begins to build up to an impressive climax that is the point of the whole movement. Now this must be taken at a faster tempo in order to be at all effective and remotely like Schubert's clear intentions, so Herr Bratwurst increases the tempo, gradually, suddenly, or otherwise, until bar 250, when, after the pause, the orchestra returns in the same, flabby rhythm as before. Why does Herr Bratwurst need to read Schubert's score? He has tradition to guide him! In the Toscanini recording the single tempo for the movement is set by the tempo necessary for its climax, and here (and throughout this recording) we hear, as we almost never hear otherwise, a correct statement of the composer's expressed desires. The orchestration is not good, and Toscanini's corrections are splendid. Take this, then, for a magnificent performance, magnificently recorded.

DEBUSSY

Prelude to the Afternoon of a Faun

Recorded during a broadcast, February 14, in Carnegie Hall.

Unreleased

If you should go into an art museum and throw mud on the pictures, you would, quite properly, be hauled off to jail or the psychiatric ward. But you may with impunity go into a concert hall and destroy a great musical performance with coughing or other forms of rude and needless noisemaking. This is what happened here. The achievement of the Maestro is on a level with his *La Mer* or *Ibéria,* but whooping Yahoos riddle it with their bronchial trumpeting. An alternate version, from a February recording session, is quiet, but without an audience Toscanini tightened up and replaced the supple and sensuous elements of the broadcast performance with strict metrical regularity. Moreover, Toscanini was unhappy about the need to stop at the end of the first four minute side of the proposed 45 rpm. record. Only on the third try was he permitted to play the work through, and by this time the spirit was seemingly lost for good that day. The Maestro later decided that neither performance was as fine as a recording by Inghelbrecht, and that ended the chances of either being released in his lifetime. Because of the differences in tempo, the broadcast and studio performances cannot be interspliced, which means that some day in a documentary series we may have to take the cough infested version with all its limitations.

BRAHMS (*Orch.* DVORÁK)

Hungarian Dances Nos. 1, 17, 20 and 21
    Recorded February 17 in Carnegie Hall.
    LM-1834

Brahms, of course, did not write these wonderful melodies; he collected them and arranged them for piano—a form in which they are almost never heard. Dvořák orchestrated part of them, and his versions are scored with the same mastery he gave his own collection of *Slavonic Dances*. Toscanini plays these with great bravura, but the way he places the accents in *No. 1* ought to have every last gypsy fiddler up in arms. It is wonderful. It is thrilling. But it is completely Latin!

RESPIGHI

The Pines of Rome
    Recorded March 17 in Carnegie Hall.
    LM-1768 and LME-2409 (stereo reprocessed version) and
    Tape *DC-51 and FTC-2083 (stereo reprocessed version)

When he first heard this recording Toscanini commented that "It sounds better here than the orchestra in the hall." Technically this is one of the finest Toscanini disks, and in the years since it has been made there has still been nothing to surpass it in this music either as a performance or a piece of engineering. The stereo is a tour de force. I feel, though, that the force of the original is greater.

SCHUBERT

Symphony No. 5
Recorded March 17 in Carnegie Hall.
LM-1869

Toscanini's only performance of this score in either the United States or Britain after 1925 was recorded in one of his final N.B.C. broadcasts. For the many persons who learned to admire this work through the medium of the 1938 Beecham recording, this Toscanini reading may well seem another example of the Maestro's rushed, graceless, and over-intense performances of works that call for lightness, delicacy, and, above all, lyricism and warmth. I confess, as young romantic Schubert it seems wanting, revealing more of Toscanini's tendency in a "quick study" to impose upon a work his familiar style rather than attempt to probe its own intrinsic qualities too deeply. This may be doing Toscanini an injustice. However, it seems fair to note that the opening movement is too fast. The melody is obviously in distress, requiring a more relaxed and gentle hand before it can unfold itself or reveal its full beauty. The last movement is probably that most successfully stated in this version. The slow movement is affected by the chill, and the minuet is too high powered. All in all it's fine Toscanini; unsympathetic Schubert.

BEETHOVEN

Missa Solemnis
Lois Marshall, soprano; Nan Merriman, mezzo-soprano; Eugene Conley, tenor; Jerome Hines, bass; with Robert Shaw Chorale
Recorded March 30, 31, and April 2 in Carnegie Hall.
LM-6013

I have heard an air check recording of Toscanini's performance of this work on April 28, 1935, with Rethberg, Telva, Martinelli, and Pinza in the solo parts. The pace is slower, the inflection of the melodic line more pronounced, and the power even greater, and it is tragic that we have no recording of that period. (Victor made the work in Boston with Koussevitzky.)

This is a faster performance, as lean and ascetic as an El Greco saint, with lighter-weight soloists and a single-microphone technique which puts them at a disadvantage. It is full of remarkable things, for example the perfect handling of the solo violin (which in less than expert hands can sound disturbingly like a concerto); without doubt, we have here as great a statement of the score as one is likely to hear. But its lack of rhetoric may be a little severe, particularly at the close of the *Agnus Dei* where the final chords seem an inadequate resolution of the crisis that has gone before.

With the exception of those given to the correction of the operas in June of 1954, these three recording sessions were the last Toscanini led with the N.B.C. Symphony.

STRAUSS

Don Quixote
Frank Miller, 'cello, and Carleton Cooley, viola
Recorded during a broadcast, November 22, in Carnegie Hall.
*LM 2026

This is the finest of all Strauss's large scale orchestral works and in this performance it is stated with clarity, proportion, and dramatic contrast equal to making it a sort of opera for instruments. Once more Toscanini drew upon his own orchestra for the soloists, so the result is fully integrated and completely in keeping with the Maestro's desires. Heard in the hall this was unbelievably thrilling, and the recording goes as far as it can to reproduce that effect.

BERLIOZ

Harold in Italy
Carleton Cooley, viola
Recorded during a broadcast, November 29, in Carnegie Hall.
*LM 1951

This was the only example we ever had of one of the longer Berlioz scores complete in a Toscanini performance. It is wonderfully effective, first of all because of Toscanini's skill in transmuting Berlioz's instrumentation into the most delicate shadings and contrasts of sound, and secondly because the composer's instructions are meticulously observed (for once). Again a first chair player is the soloist, which is to say Toscanini and his orchestra are the soloist throughout. The recorded sound captures all this quite well.

WAGNER

Tannhäuser: Prelude to Act III [Urtext]
Recorded during a broadcast, November 29, in Carnegie Hall.
Unreleased

Taken with the broadcast of 1952 we have here the three best known extracts from the opera in superlative Toscanini performances, well recorded throughout. It is therefore astonishing that they have never been made generally available.

BEETHOVEN

Coriolan Overture
Recorded during a broadcast, December 6, in Carnegie Hall.
Unreleased

The year after Toscanini's retirement Cantelli came to him with test pressings of a new recording he had made of this work. The Maestro was severely critical of his young friend's achievement, whereupon they started to play the Toscanini versions of the piece. They, too, were subjected to devastating analysis and—in the end—complete rejection. Nonetheless, this *Coriolan* is certainly the finest realization of this music I have ever heard; the recording is excellent; and its documentary value is of the highest order.

Symphony No. 3 [Eroica]
Recorded during a broadcast, December 6, in Carnegie Hall.
LM-2387

The *Eroica* belongs to the nineteenth century—although just barely—but it is scored for the eighteenth century orchestra that Beethoven used until he added trombones in the *Fifth Symphony*. In the *Eroica*, although we are hearing a work of double the length and five times the harmonic and intellectual complexity of *Symphony No. 104* [*London*] of Haydn, we are hearing an orchestra that differs from the one Haydn used in that work only by the addition of a horn, giving the ensemble not four (as in the *Ninth*) or eight, as Bruckner and Mahler demand on occasion, but a total of *three* horns! The textures in the *Eroica* are, therefore, not heavy, and although we expect the *Eroica* to sound rich and full and "Beethovenish," to achieve this it must be played with great force, just as a powerful and exceptional performance of the Haydn *No. 104* can make it sound like a "little *Eroica*."

Toscanini played this symphony more than any other, and it is a blessing, no less, that the final time he played it we received a recording in every sense worthy of the man and his achievement. There is a full discussion of this performance (and its two predecessors) in Chapter II. Suffice it to say here, this is one of the indispensable Toscanini disks.

MUSSORGSKY

Khovantchina: Prelude
  Recorded during a broadcast, December 13, in Carnegie Hall.
  Unreleased

A miniature tone poem of dawn rising behind the towers of the Kremlin, this proved an ideal work for Toscanini's evocative powers. The performance is well recorded and ought to be heard.

MENDELSSOHN

Symphony No. 5 [*On the Protestant Reformation*]
  Recorded during a broadcast, December 13, in Carnegie Hall.
  LM-1851

Mendelssohn is here revealed in his best Victorian parlor manner, and I confess I find the stately thumping-out of chorales and bits of chorales and the less than flamingly inspired material that connects them rather pompous and dull. The entrance of the clarinet with the fragment of *"Ein' feste Burg"* at the start of the *Allegro vivace* (right at the close of the chorale itself) reminds me of the appearance of the *Dies Irae* in the final movement of the Berlioz *Fantastic Symphony,* an association that is hard on Mendelssohn's effect. What we have here, then, is a superlative recording of a second-rate work which Toscanini nonetheless preferred to the finer *Scotch Symphony*.

1954

VERDI

Un Ballo in Maschera
    Principals: Herva Nelli, soprano; Virginia Haskins, soprano; Claramae Turner, mezzo-soprano; Jan Peerce, tenor; Robert Merrill, baritone; Nicola Moscona, bass; with the Robert Shaw Chorale
    Recorded in Carnegie Hall during broadcasts, January 17 and 24, and corrected with additional material recorded June 3 and 5.
    LM-6112

All other values apart, this recording would be of considerable historical importance, since it documents the last operatic production under Toscanini's direction. (The longest portion of the score which can be identified as coming from the final session is the duet in the second act, where the emotional effect of both the actual and the operatic situation carries Peerce and Nelli to what is possibly their highest dramatic point in the performance.)

I am at an advantage in evaluating these records, since I heard the Carnegie Hall sessions from which the greater part of the set was derived and am competent to assure the person who listens to the recording that what he hears is superior in a number of ways—particularly balance—to what one heard in the actual performance. Merrill sounds better on the records than he did in person, and everywhere the recording reveals detail that has never been so clearly set forth before. In only one place do I sense a loss. The effect of the distant, mocking laughter of the conspirators at the close of the second act, which Toscanini produced so strikingly in the hall (by having them move toward the back of the stage), is diminished. They are too close to the microphone.

Toscanini lined the singers up in front of him with the orchestral ensemble around them and the chorus to the rear of the stage. The sonic perspective of the microphone unerringly reveals the arrangement. It is not an effect one would ever encounter in an opera house, but I am not disturbed by it. The audience is quiet, and the quality of the sound, if a bit *sec* and direct, is splendid. Included in the libretto booklet is an article by the late Olin Downes in which Toscanini is reported to have said in 1939 that the strain of producing an opera of the dimensions of *Tristan* had become beyond his powers. (He was then a youth of seventy-two.) The fact that five years later he began a series of operatic presentations that eventually comprised seven major works (one of them as long and demanding as *Aïda*) is, I think, ample proof of his continuing energy. *Un Ballo in Maschera* is not one of the operas I admire above all others, but I accept this production with the deepest gratitude, for it is a miraculous thing, worthy of a conductor in the prime of life, and without the remotest suggestion that Toscanini was on the verge of complete retirement. All of his powers, including his lyric gifts, are fully represented.

Peerce took over his role at short notice, slipping out of another engagement to assist the Maestro when Bjoerling, who had been engaged for the part, was prevented from singing by illness. Peerce was on familiar ground, since the part has been his at the Metropolitan many times, although his voice is now somewhat dry and not so pleasant as Bjoerling's might have been. Peerce sings well, however, and with force and dramatic impact. The remaining members of the cast are about as one would have expected from previous Toscanini operatic productions. No one is bad or musically inaccurate, but several tend to be dull and dramatically ineffective. Nelli, Turner, Haskins, and Merrill all sing in a good musical and dramatic manner, although only momentarily do they suggest commanding presence. The Old Man and Verdi have the field pretty much to themselves.

MENDELSSOHN

Symphony No. 4 [Italian]
Recorded during a broadcast, February 28, in Carnegie Hall.
LM-1851

Here the beautiful sound and controlled intensity of a Toscanini performance is lavished upon a score worthy of it, and this is the version of the *Italian Symphony* that one is likely to regard as standard for many years. It is unfortunate, therefore, to have to add that it is marred in a way that one might expect from lesser conductors, but that is shocking from an intelligent student of form such as Toscanini showed himself to be. As I have mentioned before, Toscanini invariably observed repeats, even when other conductors failed to do so, when they were necessary for the proper exposition of the work. It is therefore with sorrow that I report that in this symphony, which more than any other needs the execution of the marked repeat for the proper statement of the first movement, Toscanini disregarded Mendelssohn's instructions.

Mendelssohn writes an exposition of 186 bars which is followed by a quiet and lovely transitional passage of 23 bars' length. Even in this quick tempo, 23 bars is a not inconsiderable amount of music. At the close of the transition one is to repeat 183 bars of the exposition, which then leads into the development section (the fugato). The Toscanini recording, by omitting the repeat, eliminates 206 bars of material which Mendelssohn intended one to hear, 23 of which were "new" and remain unplayed in this recording. The whole first movement is thus foreshortened.

In spite of the violence done to it, the first movement is miraculously well played, and the three that follow are polished and radiant.

BEETHOVEN

Leonore Overture No. 2
Recorded during a broadcast, March 7, in Carnegie Hall.
Unreleased

No other conductor could match Toscanini in this music, yet American record collectors have never had a version of it from his hand. (The 1939 set was issued in Britain only.) This one certainly would fill the gap. It is a powerful one, well recorded, but more than this, it is the last time Toscanini played any music of Beethoven. For that reason alone it has high claim to historic significance.

VIVALDI

Concerto Grosso in D Minor, Op. 3, No. 11

Recorded during a broadcast, March 14, in Carnegie Hall. Released as a 12″ 45 rpm. Private Limited Edition for Walter Toscanini and His Friends

No one expected Toscanini to include a work of baroque music in his final concerts, but he did, and the result is a master's statement of one of the major Vivaldi scores. The recorded sound is excellent.

BOITO

Mefistofele: Prologue

Nicola Moscona, bass, Robert Shaw Chorale, with the Columbus Boys' Choir, Herbert Huffman, conductor
Recorded during a broadcast, March 14, in Carnegie Hall. LM-1849

I heard this concert and can report that the presence of this recording as I first heard it, was one hundred per cent—I thought I was back in the hall. For those who don't know the music, it is an important, if less familiar work, full of beautiful and powerful things, and in this inspired performance shaped with the greatest sensitivity. Toscanini's brass, after all the times it has been recorded with a coarsened and distorted sound, is here exactly right, and the off-stage instruments, always a problem in records, are superbly placed in sonic perspective. Toscanini was always a champion of Boito. He kept it up to the end.

VERDI

Te Deum

The Robert Shaw Chorale

Recorded during a broadcast, March 14, in Carnegie Hall.
LM-1849

It is fitting that this fine work, virtually the last of his beloved Maestro Verdi, should have been played at the last
(save two) of Toscanini's New York concerts. The performance is filled with the perfection of dedication and faith in his
art, and the recording gives it to us unblemished.

WAGNER

Lohengrin: Prelude
Siegfried: Forest Murmurs
Die Götterdämmerung: Dawn and Siegfried's Rhine Journey
[concert version by Toscanini]
Recorded stereophonically during a broadcast, April 4, in
Carnegie Hall.
Unreleased

It is ironic that we should be supplied artificial stereo from
Toscanini when the real thing exists and with good quality.
Presumably the difficulty is that there is not enough here to
make up a record, but that seems a minor problem in the
light of the historic interest in these performances from the
Maestro's last public concert. (There were also stereophonic
recordings of Toscanini's performances of *The Barber of
Seville Overture* and the *Pathétique* of March 21, but in this
case the engineering and the performance were both below
standard.) Quite apart from history, however, these are fine
performances, and we ought to have them.

Chapter 4

Toscanini's Repertory

1

IF ONE WERE TO STUDY Toscanini's repertory in a thorough fashion from the beginning of his career it would be necessary to have data from his early years as well as a representative sample of his later programs. The materials for such an investigation do not exist. Toscanini himself was always indifferent to keeping records of this type, and those which his family have assembled cover only his later period and, even then, are incomplete. In making the survey on which this chapter is based I restricted myself to Toscanini's concerts in the United States from the season 1925-26 through the season 1953-54, his concerts in Britain, and his tours with American orchestras in 1930, 1940, and 1950. This gives one the programs of the field of his major activity as a symphonic conductor during the final seasons of his career, and for that period it is unquestionably valid. During that time he may have played some works in his concerts on the Continent that he did not prepare in the United States or Britain, but I do not think the additional data from these programs, if it could be secured, would have a significant effect on my conclusions.

Excluded from this survey, then, is Toscanini as an operatic conductor (although his operatic repertory is suggested in Chapter I), and the early years of his career in the concert hall. I regret this omission, but since full, accurate data could not be secured, I felt such a survey could not be attempted. My sample represents Toscanini in the role in which he was best known during the years in which he was most conspicuous to a world audience, and what follows is, therefore, the account of the music played by this celebrated artist during the climactic period of his career.

During the seasons in question Toscanini prepared *471*

works by my count. (Another count might differ by ten or twenty items, depending on how one considers parts of longer compositions when played separately.) Of this impressive amount of music, *202 works were prepared for performance only once,* that is, they were rehearsed and given in one or more symphonic programs (usually within a single week), or they were heard in a single broadcast. *One hundred and fifty-five compositions were prepared on two to four occasions,* and *a final group of 114 scores were prepared five or more times.* Of these a nucleus of sixteen works received thirty or more performances in twenty-nine seasons, and this group I regard as the core of Toscanini's repertory.

The Toscanini repertory consisted, then, of (1) a small core of works which he played repeatedly, (2) a larger group of scores which he prepared with some regularity at one time or another, and (3) a final group of compositions which were heard infrequently. Beyond this there were the scores prepared only once, which (with a few exceptions) cannot be regarded as repertory in the usual sense of that word. It should be noted that sometimes a work would be played frequently for a short period and then dropped, never to be prepared again. On inquiry, one is forced to conclude that the process by which Toscanini selected the music he was to perform was essentially emotional, based, apparently, on whatever he was interested in, or had particular feeling for, at the moment. These repertory lists should not, therefore, be taken as a basis for deducing Toscanini's relative evaluation of scores. In the very last years of his career Toscanini became more and more concerned over the possibility of his memory failing him and, thus, more and more inclined to play music he knew thoroughly. One cannot help but be sympathetic to this situation. The focus of any criticism of Toscanini's conservatism must obviously be the earlier period when his powers were unabated.

The choices recorded here are those of an honest man who usually did not play music he did not like or thought he did not understand and who was guided primarily by his inner state at the time he was called upon to select programs. He reflects as well the common tendency for a conductor as he grows older to concentrate on a small group of scores which are familiar to him rather than add significant amounts of new music to his repertory.

It will be seen that compositions which require soloists appear far less frequently than those for orchestra alone. Although his heart was always partly in the opera house, Toscanini produced opera in this period only when his conditions of perfection could be realized. Thus in these twenty-nine years he gave opera in Italy and at Salzburg and Bayreuth, but never in Britain, and in the United States only in concert form (and then on only seven occasions). New York had good choruses, however, and thus he performed the Beethoven *Ninth Symphony* eighteen times, led the *Missa Solemnis* nine times, and gave the Verdi *Requiem* on six occasions. All three of these works were heard in London under Toscanini, but on the whole he played them less frequently in Europe than America. The difficulty of finding instrumental soloists who would accept his domination of the work, including their execution of the solo part, or who were of sufficient stature in his eyes to permit them to play as they wished, resulted in infrequent performances of concerti even by composers whose works form the backbone of his repertory.

Toscanini's recordings are not a safe guide to his repertory in every instance. Strauss's *On the Beautiful Blue Danube*, which he performed in public exactly once, exists in a recorded version, while the *Tannhäuser Overture*, a staple item, still awaits release on disks. Even some of his greatest recordings, for example the Mozart *Divertimento K. 287*, are based upon performances that were heard only once or (as in this instance) twice. His Debussy, which is not likely to be equaled again for many decades, is represented by only two commercial recordings, and considering the many tries that were required to get them, we probably should be grateful that we have anything at all of that composer from Toscanini's hand.

The three lists that follow give the contents of groups (1) and (2) indicated above. Here is group (1), the works Toscanini performed thirty times or more in the seasons 1925-26/ 1953-54, with the dates of the most satisfactory recording(s) appended:

COMPOSER	WORK	RECORDING(S)
Beethoven	*Symphony No. 3* [*Eroica*]	1953
Beethoven	*Symphony No. 6* [*Pastoral*]	1952
Beethoven	*Symphony No. 7*	1936 & 1951
Brahms	*Symphony No. 2*	1952
Brahms	*Variations on a Theme of Haydn*	1936 & 1952
Debussy	*Ibéria*	1950
Debussy	*La Mer*	1950
Mendelssohn	*Nocturne* and *Scherzo* from *"A Midsummer Night's Dream"*	1947
Strauss	*Death and Transfiguration*	1952
Wagner	*Die Götterdämmerung: Dawn and Siegfried's Rhine Journey*	1936 & 1949
Wagner	*Die Meistersinger: Prelude*	1946
Wagner	*Parsifal: Good Friday Spell*	1949
Wagner	*Tannhäuser: Overture and Bacchanale* [Paris Version]	1952
Wagner	*Tristan und Isolde: Prelude and Liebestod*	1952

For sixteen works we have an equal number of recordings, all of them adequate. The frequency of Wagner in this list should be no surprise, since Toscanini was an insatiable Wagnerian from the time he was seventeen, but Strauss's banal tone poem comes as a shock, as does the absence of eighteenth century music. The most recent work on the list is *Iberia* (1908).

Here is the second group which is made up of the works played twenty to twenty-nine times, that is on an average of once a season or slightly less for the period we are considering. Again I append the dates of the preferred recordings.

COMPOSER	WORK	RECORDING(S)
Bach-Respighi	*Passacaglia and Fugue in C Minor*	1947
Beethoven	*Egmont Overture*	1953
Beethoven	*Leonore Overture No. 3*	1945
Beethoven	*Symphony No. 1*	1937 & 1951
Beethoven	*Symphony No. 4*	1939
Beethoven	*Symphony No. 5*	1952
Beethoven	*Symphony No. 9*	1952
Berlioz	*Romeo and Juliet: Queen Mab*	

COMPOSER	WORK	RECORDING(S)
	Scherzo	1951
Brahms	*Symphony No. 1*	1951
Brahms	*Symphony No. 3*	1952
Brahms	*Symphony No. 4*	1951
Debussy	*Prelude to the Afternoon of a Faun*	1953
Haydn	*Symphony No. 101 [Clock]*	1929 & 1947
Mussorgsky-Ravel	*Pictures at an Exhibition*	1953
Ravel	*Daphnis and Chloe: Suite No. 2*	1949
Respighi	*The Pines of Rome*	1953
Respighi	*Roman Festivals*	1949
Rossini	*The Italian Woman in Algiers*	1936
Schubert	*Symphony No. 9*	1953
Smetana	*The Moldau*	1950
Wagner	*The Flying Dutchman: Overture*	No recording
Wagner	*Die Götterdämmerung: Siegfried's Death and Funeral Music*	1952
Wagner	*Parsifal: Prelude*	1949
Wagner	*Siegfried: Forest Murmurs*	1950
Wagner	*Siegfried Idyll*	1946
Wagner	*Tannhäuser: Overture* [Dresden]	No recording

Of twenty-six works in this group we have twenty-four recordings, a high standard of success considering the man with whom we have to deal. Only one work of a composer belonging wholly to the eighteenth century appears: the Bach is in a transcription that is modern in feeling and instrumentation. Once more the heart of the list is nineteenth century music. If one does not regard transcriptions as new compositions, the most recent scores are those of Respighi, *Pines* (1924) and *Festivals* (1929).

The third list gives the seventy-two scores which Toscanini prepared and played at least five times; in other words, those which received five to nineteen performances in the seasons under discussion. In some instances this is only one performance more or less than that given a work listed in the previous group or assigned to the lower division (works prepared and played two to four times). The three lists taken together give the contents of the group of 114 works cited earlier as the scores Toscanini could be said to have played at one time or another with some degree of regularity, and I think from these lists we get a reliable impression of the music Toscanini admired, understood and enjoyed. Complete details of Toscanini's repertory can be found in the 1956 editions of his book.

COMPOSER	WORK	RECORDED
Beethoven	*Coriolan Overture*	1945
Beethoven	*Leonore Overture No. 1*	1939
Beethoven	*Leonore Overture No. 2*	1939
Beethoven	*Missa Solemnis*	1953
Beethoven	*Prometheus: Overture*	1944
Beethoven	*Prometheus: Adagio and Allegretto*	No recording
Beethoven	*Quartet No. 16, Opus 135: Lento and Vivace*	1938
Beethoven	*Symphony No. 2*	1949-51
Beethoven	*Symphony No. 8*	1952
Berlioz	*Damnation of Faust: Rákóczy March*	1945
Berlioz	*Harold in Italy*	1953
Berlioz	*Romeo and Juliet: Love Scene*	1946
Brahms	*Liebeslieder Waltzes*	No recording
Brahms	*Tragic Overture*	1937
Busoni	*Rondo Arlecchinesco*	No recording
Cherubini	*Anacréon: Overture*	1951
Debussy	*Nocturnes: Nuages and Fêtes*	No recording
Dukas	*The Sorcerer's Apprentice*	1950
Dvořák	*Symphony No. 5 [New World]*	1953
Elgar	*Enigma Variations*	1951
Franck	*Les Éolides*	No recording
Franck	*Symphony in D Minor*	No recording
Glinka	*Jota Aragonesa*	1943
Gluck	*Iphigenia in Aulis: Overture*	1952
Haydn	*Symphony No. 99*	1949
Kabalevsky	*Colas Breugnon Overture*	1946
Martucci	*Notturno*	No recording
Martucci	*Noveletta*	Recorded on V-Disk 1954
Mendelssohn	*Symphony No. 4* [Italian]	
Mendelssohn	*Symphony No. 5* [Reformation]	1953
Mozart	*The Magic Flute: Overture*	1938
Mozart	*Symphony No. 35* [Haffner]	1929
Mozart	*Symphony No. 40*	1950

COMPOSER	WORK	RECORDED
Mozart	Symphony No. 41 [Jupiter]	1945/46
Paganini	Moto Perpetuo	1939
Pizzetti	Rondo Veneziano	No recording
Prokofiev	Symphony No. 1 [Classical]	1951
Ravel	Bolero	No recording
Respighi	The Fountains of Rome	1951
Rossini	Barber of Seville: Overture	1945
Rossini	La Cenerentola: Overture	1945
Rossini	The Silken Ladder: Overture	1938
Rossini	Semiramide: Overture	1936
Rossini	William Tell: Overture	1953
Roussel	The Spider's Feast	1946
Saint-Saëns	Danse Macabre	1950
Scarlatti-Tommasini	The Good-humored Ladies	No recording
Schubert	Symphony No. 8 [Unfinished]	1950
Schumann	Manfred Overture	1947
Schumann	Symphony No. 2	No recording
Schumann	Symphony No. 3 [Rhenish]	1949
Sibelius	En Saga	No recording
Sibelius	The Swan of Tuonela	1940
	The Star-Spangled Banner [J. S. Smith, Toscanini orchestration]	No recording
Strauss	Don Juan	1951
Strauss	Don Quixote	1953
Strauss	Till Eulenspiegel	1952
Tchaikovsky	Manfred Symphony	1949
Tchaikovsky	Romeo and Juliet	1947
Tchaikovsky	Symphony No. 6 [Pathétique]	1947
Tommasini	The Carnival of Venice	No recording
Verdi	Requiem	1951
Verdi	Te Deum	1954
Wagner	A Faust Overture	1946
Wagner	Lohengrin: Prelude to Acts I and III	1951
Wagner	Die Walküre: Act I, Scene 3	1941
Wagner	Die Walküre: Act III, Ride of the Valkyries	1952
Weber	Euryanthe: Overture	1951
Weber	Oberon: Overture	1952
Weber-Berlioz	Invitation to the Dance	1951

In this group of seventy-two works, more than fifty have been made available in commercial recordings. This leaves us with some great Toscanini performances lost, but considering the number of years in which he took no interest in making records, plus the fact that only about sixty per cent of the music he recorded came from these lists of works most frequently played. The Victor company can be credited with having preserved a remarkably large amount of his repertory.

Looking over this final list one is again impressed by the small amount of eighteenth century music, and the almost complete omission of contemporary scores. Toscanini drew his programs from a group of nineteenth century works augmented by a small number of eighteenth century compositions and a sprinkling of scores from the early decades of this century. On the whole, he played the music he knew as a youth and had programmed from the beginning of his career.

Writing of a celebrated virtuoso, B. H. Haggin remarked, ". . . he has gone on recombining into programs of one pattern the limited group of works that he learned fairly early —a group that has included a large quantity of trashy salon and display pieces . . ." and from this he goes on to speak of the way in which Koussevitzky, apart from the preparation of contemporary music, returned constantly to the same group of older scores rather than study different works by the well-known composers, and thus ". . . ends up going over the same limited ground year after year—much the same limited ground as all conductors go over year after year" (*Music in the Nation,* pp. 4-5). This was true of the virtuoso in question, and it was true of Koussevitzky (as a study of his repertory has further convinced me), but both points were also true of Toscanini. The pattern of his programs was unchanging, the core works, listed above, returned season after season. Usually scores which were not already fixed in this familiar sequence were heard only once or twice and then disappeared in favor of other novelties which survived for an equally short time. The last new work to find a place in his standard repertory was the *Colas Breugnon Overture* of Kabalevsky, a piece of rhythmically bouncy junk which evidently appealed to him. Indeed, many works reappeared every season or so almost on the anniversary of their previous hearing, as if the new programs had simply been copied, with slight modification, from the old.

Actually Toscanini was no innovator. His programs were conservative, meat and potatoes affairs, in which one not only failed to hear any representative selection of the notable orchestral music of the present century, but one did not even hear all the major scores by the composers for whom he had a special affinity. Even forgetting Mozart and Haydn, whom he neglected in a shocking fashion, there are important works of Beethoven, Berlioz, Brahms, Wagner, and Debussy which never were given Toscanini performances, or were played only on rare occasions. He did not look for new music of high quality, and in the established works he stuck to a limited stock of standard items. Finally, it must be noted that much of the unfamiliar music he introduced was trashy, and that some of the works he played repeatedly were of inferior quality and undeserving of the pains and skill which were wasted upon their realization. There were, and are, Toscanini addicts who would listen, with awe, to anything he chose to play. I am not among their number. The best performance of the *Dance of the Hours* that anyone can conceive is still nothing I want to hear more than once or twice, and then not when my mind desires the nourishment of a significant musical statement. Unfortunately, in addition to his masterful achievements in scores of the greatest worth, Toscanini always was inclined to offer a certain number of barrel organ tunes as well.

2

Let us consider Toscanini's repertory, alphabetically by composer, from a strict set of absolute criteria (which may, for that reason, be a little severe) resting upon the idea that a great conductor ought to be capable of offering representative and adequate statements of the music of all the great composers (although, as noted earlier) not necessarily presenting the music of different periods and styles "with equal skill and understanding." Similarly, let us note in anticipation of our discussion, that Toscanini seemed to meet this absolute criterion a little less successfully than certain other conductors of his time. Scores which Toscanini played well, Koussevitzky, for example, could frequently play equally well (or nearly so), and he gave performances of Mozart, Haydn, and Bach masterpieces which Toscanini slighted. Therefore, without diminishing our respect for Toscanini's unique achievements, let us avoid the misguided statement that he had a comprehensive repertory of music of all periods. He did not.

One would think that the music of Bach, with its fine, robust themes, its harmonic solidity, and its splendid instrumental coloring would make a direct appeal to Toscanini, but it had no such effect. Of the six *Brandenburg* concerti, two appeared briefly in his programs (one for only two performances), and of the four suites, which one would consider perfectly suited to his gifts, he prepared only one, and that for merely three performances. Except for a program of excerpts in 1934, he ignored the *St. Matthew Passion* and the other great choral works, including the *B Minor Mass*. Indeed, the only music of Bach that he played at all frequently was the *Passacaglia and Fugue in C Minor* in the Respighi transcription. This was heard nine times during the season (1930-31) and was selected to display the excellence of the Philharmonic to his audiences in Milan, Turin, and Rome. Toscanini once confessed to feeling uncomfortable when there were too many intermediaries between the composer and himself, for he feared that unknowingly he might introduce elements into the performance which were at variance with the composer's artistic intentions. This accounted in part for his cool attitude toward Mozart, whose musical perfection Toscanini took as a somewhat forbidding and frigid quality, but it was even more true of the baroque masters, especially Bach. Toscanini did not trust either the musicologists or the texts they prepared, since he felt the scholars to be needlessly divorced from the performing musician and his problems. But if he did not put his faith in the texts, neither did he feel capable of correcting them himself—although he made an effort to study some music, notably the Mozart Fortieth symphony, in manuscript. "I am never really happy until I get into the nineteenth century," he once told a friend.

In the performance of the symphonies of Beethoven Toscanini had few rivals, and it is on this music, as much as any, that his reputation is founded. None the less, it is interesting

to see the large-scale works of that composer that Toscanini
played rarely, or, in some cases, not at all. Of the five concerti
for piano and orchestra, the *Fourth* achieved the record of
two preparations and four performances, while the *Third*
was heard twice, the *First* and *Fifth* [*Emperor*] only once,
and the *Second* not at all! The *Violin Concerto,* with eight
performances, triumphs over its natural rivals, the violin concerti of Brahms and Mendelssohn, which scored five and six
performances respectively. The reason for this has been suggested: Toscanini was notorious for his inability to get along
with soloists because of his unremitting demand that they
shape their performance to the pattern he cut. When Toscanini allowed a virtuoso such as Rubinstein to play with the
freedom he desired, the result often was a conflict of styles
and a poor statement of the work. Thus, of the many celebrated instrumentalists who were active in the United States
while Toscanini was directing the Philharmonic or the N.B.C.
Symphony, only Vladimir Horowitz, his son-in-law, could be
said to have played with him with any regularity. Even during
the Toscanini Beethoven Festival in London in May, 1939,
the concerts featuring concerti were, very wisely, assigned to
the direction of Sir Adrian Boult.

Actually the staples of Toscanini's Beethoven repertory were
seven symphonies and the *Leonore Overture No. 3,* to which
the symphonies *No. 2* and *No. 8,* the *Egmont* and *Coriolan*
overtures, and the *Missa Solemnis* were added from time to
time. Beyond that there is a large group of scores, many of
them of considerable interest and value (such as the *Overture
for the Consecration of the House*) which Toscanini prepared
infrequently or ignored, and, for all the brilliance of his
Beethoven performances, he could not be credited with having
revived any neglected compositions of interest or even playing
everything that other conductors were offering, such as the
whole of *Prometheus* or the *Incidental Music to Egmont.* His
beautiful performances with string orchestra of movements
from the late quartets led to the hope that he would prepare
an entire work in this manner, but he never did, although he
gave the unimportant Verdi quartet in this fashion twice.

Berlioz poses another mystery. Toscanini anticipated the

revival of interest in this master by over a decade and gave the complete *Romeo and Juliet* in 1942 when many people were only dimly conscious that the work existed. For all that, Toscanini played only a few works of the composer, and one might assume that he was satisfied to repeat the *Queen Mab Scherzo* again and again rather than prepare a different score. There is no doubt that his performance of the *Mab* was a miracle, but one cannot help wishing that the *Fantastic Symphony* and the *Requiem* had been heard under his baton, as they never were. Here is a case in which Toscanini seems to have ignored works which were ideally suited to him and which, had he chosen to do so, he could have achieved with the most brilliant success. For example, when he played the *Roman Carnival Overture* (and in twenty-nine years he prepared it only three times!) it was a performance without equal. Happily, it was captured on a modern record.

Next to his reputation as a Beethoven specialist, Toscanini was famed, and justifiably so, as a performer of Brahms. Again he centered his attention on a few scores, the four symphonies and the *Haydn Variations,* and played other major works less frequently than they appear to deserve. Thus the fine *Academic Festival Overture* was prepared only four times, while even the inferior *Serenade No. 1* received more attention. Considering the relative size of Brahms's output of orchestral music compared with Beethoven's, Toscanini gave a hearing to a somewhat more representative sample of the whole. Of the concerti, that for violin and 'cello was prepared four times, always with first desk players from the orchestra and, presumably, entirely in agreement with Toscanini's desires. The *Second Piano Concerto* received four preparations, three of them with Horowitz, the *Violin Concerto* was prepared twice with Heifetz, and Horowitz shared in the single preparation of the *First Piano Concerto*. Three times Toscanini applied himself to the dreadful *German Requiem* which, as Bernard Shaw remarked, could be "patiently borne only by the corpse," and his performances of the pretentious *First Symphony* were more numerous than those of the finer *Third,* which he always found baffling in places.

Toscanini studied the symphonies of Bruckner, and two of them were prepared, each on two occasions. What his version of the *Romantic Symphony* was like I do not know, but the majestic slow movement of the *Seventh,* heard on an old recording from the air, combined the traditional slow, German tempi with the clarity and wonderful singing quality of a Toscanini performance and made me regret that he had not played the work again at a later date or recorded his unique achievement with it. Actually, Bruckner did not figure in Toscanini's repertory after 1935. ("Bruckner's music has no sex," Toscanini is reported to have said some years later.)

Cherubini is unjustly neglected, and the Toscanini revivals of his music were welcome. Unfortunately only the *Anacréon Overture* became a steady repertory item.

Toscanini's performances of Debussy include some of his greatest achievements, and here we have special grounds for concern over his tendency to play one or two scores again and again rather than prepare new works. Thus of the set of *Images for Orchestra, No. 2, Ibéria,* was given thirty-one performances, while *No. 1* and *No. 3* were not played at all. Since they are compositions of equal merit, there seems to be no logic in such complete omission, not to mention the slight to Debussy in presenting only the central portion of a work conceived as three contrasting parts. In the twenty-nine seasons considered here there are fifty-three performances of *La Mer,* placing it second to the *Meistersinger Prelude* as the most frequently played score. In contrast, the *Prelude to the Afternoon of a Faun* was given only twenty-three times, the *Nuages* and *Fêtes* thirteen and fourteen times respectively, and apart from these there were only a few isolated performances of other works.

Toscanini prepared six compositions of Dvořák in the seasons we are examining, but the *New World Symphony* (with six performances) is the only one to be heard with any frequency, and one can fairly say that Toscanini never offered a comprehensive selection of works by the Bohemian master.

Of the many scores of Elgar, Toscanini played two, but only the *Enigma Variations* can be considered a part of his repertory. Although he played them with obvious affection, they appear to represent the limit of his interest in the composer.

Falla, a fellow Latin with an idiom one feels Toscanini would find congenial, was represented by a single score, *El Amor Brujo*, which received four preparations.

César Franck appeared regularly in Toscanini's programs, and although he never played the *Symphonic Variations*, most of the other familiar works were heard, with *Les Éolides* and the *Symphony in D Minor* heading the list. His readings of Franck were unusually sympathetic and beautiful, and it is unfortunate that only a single short work of the composer received a Toscanini recording.

The virtual omission of Grieg from Toscanini's repertory comes as no surprise, but the neglect of Handel is rather startling. Nonetheless, except for a single concerto grosso (*No. 12 in B Minor*), which he played four times, and two shorter works which received one preparation each, the master simply was not represented in Toscanini's repertory. There has never been a Toscanini *Messiah* or a Toscanini performance of the *Water Music*.

Of 104 canonical Haydn symphonies, Toscanini performed only eight: three of these were prepared only twice, and the greatest of them all, *No. 104* [*London*] only once! Until 1938 he performed the inferior *No. 88* with some degree of regularity, and *No. 98* and *No. 99* were given from time to time, although *No. 101* [*Clock*], is the only work of Haydn heard with much frequency. Since Toscanini played Haydn's music with brilliance and evident mastery, one is perplexed why more of his works did not figure in the Maestro's programs.

Certainly Honegger is not a composer one would imagine Toscanini promoting, but *Pacific 231* actually received a dozen performances from him in the period 1928-30. In 1933 Toscanini presented another score of this genre, Mossolov's *Iron Foundry*. That seemed to end his interest in musical descriptions of locomotives and industry.

Mendelssohn obviously was close to Toscanini's heart, and his performances combined affection and understanding with incandescent virtuosity. Nonetheless, Toscanini played few

Mendelssohn scores with regularity. The *Incidental Music to "A Midsummer Night's Dream"* was given, in part, often enough, and the *Italian Symphony* was frequently heard, but the *Scotch Symphony* received but one performance, while fifteen performances were lavished upon the inferior *Reformation Symphony*. There was only a single playing of the *Hebrides Overture!*

The same concentration affected Mussorgsky, whose *Pictures at an Exhibition* was a staple item, and whose other works for orchestra (few as they are) were inadequately represented.

Most surprising is the extent of Toscanini's neglect of Mozart. Of forty-one symphonies Toscanini prepared eight, but of this group three received a single preparation, reducing the Maestro's actual repertory to *five* Mozart symphonies! Of the five, *No. 38 [Prague]* was never played after 1930, and *No. 29* was prepared only twice. In fact Toscanini played *three* Mozart symphonies regularly: *No. 35 [Haffner]*, *No. 40*, and *No. 41 [Jupiter]*, although none of the three was played nearly so regularly as the dreadful *Forest Murmurs* from *Siegfried*. Apart from these works his active Mozart repertory consisted only of the overture to *The Magic Flute*. A small number of works, by no means representative and the longest way from being exhaustive, received one, or possibly two, preparations and one to four performances.

Toscanini had a reputation as a conductor of Mozart that is hardly consistent with the actual number of scores he played or the number of those performances which can be considered truly distinguished. Sir Thomas Beecham, a Mozartian of unique powers, said that "something like two hundred" of the composer's works, "are of striking originality and beauty" and he explored his scores and performed them with an enthusiasm Toscanini never shared.

In the *Divertimento K. 287* Toscanini's fine plastic sense allowed him to create an amazing structure of harmonic and rhythmic continuity within a changing dynamic pattern, and since it is a minor work, without strong feeling or the use of the most distinctive features of Mozart's style, we do not sense a lack of penetration into the composer's deeper thoughts. In the *Symphony No. 40* it is a different matter, and the old recording preserves a reading of the score that was too intense, and revealed, in its subjugation of the music to an inappropriate, hard-driving style, that Toscanini simply did not understand the work. In his 1950 recording this has changed, but his recorded version of the *Symphony No. 41* [*Jupiter*] is bad, and of his two versions of the *Symphony No. 35* [*Haffner*] the earlier, which is relaxed, is good, while the later, overly intense version is unsatisfactory. In the *Symphony No. 39*, in which Mozart's style is revealed in the purest form, Toscanini was clearly at a loss, and the disk of his single performance, in the years here considered, preserves a reading that is brutally unsympathetic and uncomprehending.

In the 1922-23 season at La Scala and at Salzburg in 1937 Toscanini prepared *The Magic Flute*, which he "always slept through" under German conductors, but which "had life" in his faster tempi. Judging from the recording of the overture, it must have been a fine performance, although able critics who heard it tell me it was disappointing, but I find no evidence of Toscanini ever preparing any other Mozart opera, nor do I believe that he ever gave the Mozart *Requiem*. The root of this neglect is not accidental but a conscious rejection of music which Toscanini found uncongenial. Italian audiences have generally preferred other operas to *Figaro* or *Don Giovanni*, and Toscanini apparently shared to a degree the blind spot of his compatriots. He was too simple, forceful, and direct to grasp the language of Mozart's *Figaro* or the emotional and intellectual content of the *Symphony No. 39*, and in these works conductors who were far from being his peer in Beethoven could put him to shame.

Of the many compositions of Prokofiev, Toscanini prepared only the *Classical Symphony*, which is stylistically the least characteristic of his works, and the Toscanini performance changed remarkably from one of the fastest to one of the slowest to be heard.

Ravel was represented in Toscanini's repertory by three works. *La Valse* received only three preparations, while *Bolero* was dropped, except for one revival, in 1934. The

Second Suite from *Daphnis and Chloe,* which one heard reasonably often, is perhaps the best of the composer's scores, but it would have been interesting to hear what Toscanini could have done with certain of the other works.

Respighi appeared in Toscanini's concerts with the three Roman tone poems and as a transcriber of Bach. His other works, among them the *Suite No. 1* of *Ancient Airs and Dances,* which Toscanini played in his American tour with the La Scala Orchestra, had been set aside.

Rimsky-Korsakov was represented by one preparation of a single minor work; Borodin had fared little better with two scores played.

Rossini was a staple in Toscanini's programs, and invariably the performances were brilliant and enjoyable. For some reason the overture to *La Gazza Ladra* was played less than it deserved. Every conductor plays a certain amount of light music, and Toscanini played Rossini. We can be grateful to him for unique performances of these scores.

Although Roussel's *Symphony No. 4* was prepared once with the Philharmonic, his appearance in Toscanini's programs was otherwise limited to *The Spider's Feast,* which, however, became a reasonably frequent item.

Of the symphonies of Schubert, Toscanini played four, although of these only the *Unfinished* and the *Ninth* were heard often enough to count as repertory items. (The *Fifth* actually received only a single preparation and performance.) There was a performance of the *Gastein Symphony* as reconstructed by Joachim from the *Grand Duo.* Even the *Rosamunde* incidental music was ignored. What, then, can we say? That the Maestro made his reading of the *Ninth* a miracle of modern orchestra performance and revealed the powerful structure of the *Unfinished* as no other conductor, but apart from this he neglected Schubert.

Schumann fared little better. The *Spring Symphony,* the opening pages of which seem an ideal vehicle for Toscanini's unique powers, never was given a Toscanini performance. The *Fourth,* which one feels would suit him perfectly, he prepared once! There were scattered preparations of the two middle symphonies and the *Manfred Overture*. The *Concerto for 'Cello* received four performances; the fine *Piano Concerto* was never played.

After this it comes as a shock to find that the Shostakovich *First* was prepared and given in four concerts during 1931 and repeated in three later seasons. The *Seventh* had its celebrated American première under Toscanini in 1942, but was never played again after that year, nor did any other music by Shostakovich figure in Toscanini's repertory.

Toscanini's final judgment of Shostakovich is best told by this incident of the Maestro's last years. Rummaging in the shelves of his music room Toscanini discovered a huge pile of photostatic copies of an orchestral score. He went through it systematically, holding the sheets before his eyes, and then turned to his son Walter.

"Walter, what is this?" he asked.

"That is the Shostakovich *Seventh Symphony*, father."

There was a long pause as Toscanini contemplated the many sheets of notes.

"I played this?" he asked.

"Yes, father," came the reply. "You gave the American première."

"I memorized all this."

"Yes, father, you did."

The pause was ominous now.

"I was a fool!"

Normally one does not think of Toscanini as a conductor of Sibelius, and, indeed, only two of the seven symphonies (the *Second* and *Fourth*) ever were heard on his programs. Two of the tone poems evidently appealed to him, the lovely *Swan of Tuonela* and the inferior *En Saga*, and one can find occasional appearances of other works, although Toscanini seems to have had no interest in offering the composer's major compositions comprehensively, and left the two finest symphonies (*Five* and *Seven*) unplayed.

Smetana, another nationalist, was represented in Toscanini's programs by two scores only, neither of which was given in anything resembling a Bohemian style under his baton.

Stravinsky, one of the few composers of our day whose high place in the history of music seems assured, apparently did not appeal to Toscanini, who prepared *Fireworks* once and offered the opening and closing tableaux of *Petrouchka* (in other words, the folk-song material) in three seasons. Of the rest of Stravinsky's music Toscanini gave us nothing.

Of the better known works of Richard Strauss, Toscanini lavished the most performances on one of the worst, *Death and Transfiguration,* and gave the fewest preparations to one of the best, *Don Quixote. Don Juan* and *Till Eulenspiegel* were heard regularly, there were a few readings of *Ein Heldenleben* (all but one with the Philharmonic), and two preparations of the *Salome's Dance.* Once more a small group of works made up the whole of his repertory, leaving major scores unperformed. *Der Rosenkavalier,* equal in its enchantment to *Figaro* and *Don Giovanni,* shared with them his frigid rejection.

Toscanini's offerings of Tchaikovsky amounted, essentially, to four works, all of which (for obvious reasons) he recorded, and one memorable but strictly occasional performance, which may be the most widely distributed of all his recordings. The latter item is the *B-flat Minor Piano Concerto (No. 1)* which he prepared with Horowitz in 1941, recorded shortly after the initial broadcast, and repeated, apparently out of patriotism, at a War Bond concert two seasons later. That his attitude was not wholly commercial is shown by the fact that he did not prepare the symphonies *No. 4* and *No. 5,* broadcast them once, make recordings, and drop them. In fact, Toscanini, to my knowledge only played one Tchaikovsky symphony anywhere at any time, and that is the *Pathétique,* which he neglected with the Philharmonic but revived with the N.B.C. and played frequently and well during his seventeen seasons with that orchestra. The *Manfred Symphony,* a fine example of large-scale musical thought in the best Tchaikovsky manner, blessed with some excellent thematic material, and brilliantly scored, Toscanini revived from the general neglect into which it had fallen and played with both the Philharmonic and with the N.B.C. In this case he can be praised for giving us a splendid work which counts as unfamiliar. The *Romeo and Juliet Overture* and *Nutcracker Suite* were also staple items.

Toscanini prepared only one score of Ralph Vaughan Williams, the *Fantasia on a Theme of Thomas Tallis*, which he played in both New York and Britain.

Verdi, whom he admired, perhaps more than any other composer, actually played a small part in his symphonic programs. The *Requiem* and *Te Deum* were frequently heard in his magnificently impassioned readings, but there was little effort to find concert excerpts from the operas, and with the exception of the two scores cited, three preparations are the maximum attention given to any of the overtures, preludes, or scenes which he extracted for broadcast purposes. His countryman Vivaldi, although stylistically close to his heart, was perhaps a bit too refined, too reserved in his classicism to appeal to a fundamentally warm-blooded animal such as Toscanini. A single concerto grosso (*D Minor*) received four preparations, and the five other works which he played were heard only once or twice.

Wagner, with twenty-eight works performed, comes second to Beethoven in Toscanini's repertory. The magic of Klingsor of Bayreuth always had the most potent effect upon him, and all but two or three of these works received, not scattered, but frequent performances. One would expect that a conductor with a sense of form as fine as Toscanini's would be sensitive to the problems involved in making cuttings from larger works, but surprisingly enough, Toscanini played a number of the worst Wagner extracts.

Taking the items in order, the *Faust Overture* is a concert work, and the overture to the *Flying Dutchman* stands well by itself. *Dawn and Siegfried's Rhine Journey* and *Siegfried's Death and Funeral Music* from *Die Götterdämmerung* Toscanini performed in his own fine concert versions (rather than the inferior, and more common, Humperdinck settings), and the *Immolation Scene* has an acceptable beginning and closes with the final pages of the opera itself. The preludes to *Lohengrin* and *Meistersinger* are frequently played by themselves, so one cannot really object, although the *Meistersinger*

Prelude certainly ends more powerfully when it leads into the first act chorale, and I am unhappy about the flat taste one gets from the third act prelude when the theme is simply carried to a resolving chord that Wagner, wisely, does not sound in the opera. The *Parsifal Prelude* can stand alone. I am not so sure about the preludes to acts two and three of that opera, and the *Klingsor's Magic Garden* episode certainly lacks a good beginning and end. As for the *Good Friday Spell,* I am more or less resigned to being alone in my preference for it with vocal parts and within the context of the drama. The *Rienzi Overture* can stand alone; I want nothing to do with it, either.

It is here that difficulties commence. The *Forest Murmurs* starts nowhere, goes nowhere, and has the next thing to no form at all, since the whole piece is scrappy cuttings (there is no such interlude in the opera, where the raw materials of this "excerpt" are separated by other passages) which are brought to a climax by the most patently trivial means. None the less, Toscanini played this patchwork twenty-eight times and carried it to twelve cities on tour. I am overcome. The *Siegfried Idyll,* in contrast, is a real piece of music, and so is the overture to *Tannhäuser*. The prelude to *Tristan* exists in a concert arrangement by Wagner which almost no one ever plays;[1] instead one hears the prelude with its operatic ending which trails off, *pp,* in the general direction of nowhere, but invariably is found to lead to the opening bars of the final scene of the opera, invariably played *p* or *mf* rather than *pp* as marked, and moving by way of a C minor splice to a system of key relations which makes no sense in terms of the A major/minor tonality of the prelude. Further, in most cases Isolde is silent, and we hear the piece without either a soprano or an instrumental double sounding the notes allotted to the lady. Toscanini accepted this situation and did nothing about it, offering the *Prelude and Love-Death* (if we are going to keep *Liebestod* we might just as well make no bones about it) as the standardized concert item that it is. The fine prelude to the third act of the opera, invariably lack-

[1] Toscanini *may* have played it with the Philharmonic; the evidence is unclear.

ing the effect in the opera house that, in a "full" arrangement (with the English horn solo), it can produce in the concert hall, he never played. Toscanini prepared the love duet from the second act on one occasion, although I don't know how he ended it, and on five occasions he prepared the final scene of the first act of *Die Walküre*, which can stand alone. This is more than can be said for the *Ride of the Valkyries*, which is absolute hash in the concert version without vocal parts; but apparently this was not enough to overcome his liking for it.

Four of the overtures to Weber's works for the musical stage were heard, although one of them was given in only a single season. Apart from these, there have been Toscanini performances of the *Invitation to the Dance* in the Berlioz orchestration.

I wish now to consider three topics: Toscanini's performances of Italian music, American music, and contemporary music.

It seems clear that if there was a school of living composers whom Toscanini elected to champion, it was the modern Italian. This was partly national pride and partly attributable to the fact that these composers use an idiom for which he had both feeling and understanding. Respighi is the most important member of the group, certainly his name comes to mind first as we think of Toscanini's repertory, but Busoni, Castelnuovo-Tedesco, Mancinelli, Martucci, Pizzetti, De Sabata, Sinigaglia, and Tommasini, along with others of the same school, have appeared in his programs from time to time. The question of who is a great composer, and who is worth playing, is, of course, a difficult one, particularly when feelings of national culture are involved. Sibelius is a great composer in parts of Northern Europe and the United States, but has slight reputation in Italy. Bernard Zweers is a great composer in his native Amsterdam, but not in New York. It must be said in all fairness that Toscanini was the only conductor to give the American audience a chance to hear the modern Italian school; but, at the same time, a great many Americans did not especially wish to make their acquaintance, particularly in preference to Hindemith, Stravinsky, and Prokofiev. Moreover, some of these works which Toscanini offered regularly with the Philharmonic and N.B.C. were not popular, simply because they were felt to be of poor quality, making use of banal thematic material, and developing it along lines which only emphasized its conventionality and inherent vulgarity.

Thus when Lawrence Gilman wrote in 1931: "There is an impression hereabouts that Mr. Toscanini as conductor of the Philharmonic-Symphony Society has performed this season an excessive amount of inferior music," he may have been thinking of at least some of these scores. Certainly Deems Taylor, writing in September, 1930, not merely as a critic but as an American composer of some status, had one specific item in mind, and with it a complaint that raises the second issue. Commenting on the recently completed European tour of the Philharmonic, he notes ruefully, ". . . about the only kind of music that [the orchestra] did not play in Europe was American music. I think this was a mistake. In the first place, it would have been tactful toward us poor Americans, whose orchestra, after all, it is. In the second place, it would have been only just. If the programs had comprised nothing but undisputed masterpieces, the exclusion of Americans would have been all too understandable. But they did not. To say that MacDowell, Chadwick, Foote, and Carpenter, for instance, have written music as good as such gaudy rubbish as Tommasini's *Carnival of Venice* variations— which Mr. Toscanini conducted [in Milan and Rome] *con amore*—is to pay them no compliment." One can go on from this and note that Toscanini made a graceful gesture by playing Kodály in Hungary, offering Elgar in Britain, and so on, and that in this light the omission of even the briefest American work from the repertory of the tour seems an undeserved disparagement of American musical creativity.

Koussevitzky felt that he had an obligation to encourage the composers of his adopted country (even when they weren't writing masterpieces), by giving a hearing to their work, and in so doing he stimulated the creative powers of a number of able persons and enriched American music with a group of notable scores. Toscanini did nothing analogous. An American composer waiting for him to play his work would have abandoned his musical ambitions for steady employment early in Toscanini's Philharmonic period when it became clear that no interest or support could be expected from the Maestro.

During his seasons with the Philharmonic, Toscanini played next to no American music, and the four composers named by Taylor, in fact, never appeared on any of his programs at any time. Ernest Schelling's *Impressions from an Artist's Life* was given, with the composer at the piano, during two seasons, the first of them as early as 1928-29. Chasin's *Flirtation in a Chinese Garden* and *Parade* were prepared in 1931. The *Symphony No. 2* of Bernard Wagenaar was played the following year, and the *Second Symphony* of Howard Hanson in 1933. Unless I am mistaken, these five works given a total of eighteen performances constitute Toscanini's cultivation of American music in eleven seasons with the Philharmonic.

With the N.B.C. the situation changed somewhat, although no American piece ever became a staple of Toscanini's repertory, and the maximum number of performances which any American score got from Toscanini was *five*. The work so honored was nothing less than Barber's fine *Adagio for Strings,* which Toscanini gave in its world première in 1938. During his South American tour with the N.B.C. in 1940, Toscanini actually played this work in two cities, which was a refreshing change from the decade before. The *Essay for Orchestra,* which had its première in the same program as the *Adagio,* only got one further performance. Copland has been represented in Toscanini's broadcasts by a single performance of *El Salon Mexico,* one of his weakest scores; however, it is basically melodic, and that, obviously, was what it took to catch Toscanini's interest. The *Choric Dance No. 2* of Paul Creston struck Toscanini's fancy momentarily in the 1942-43 season and he prepared it with three orchestras! Unfortunately illness prevented him from giving it more than four times. Three seasons later he gave a performance to that composer's *Frontiers.* Gershwin's music draws upon a style and a manner that Toscanini cannot have found congenial. He played three

Gershwin scores. The *Piano Concerto in F* and the *Rhapsody in Blue* he chose to drop after a single hearing; *An American in Paris* was prepared a second time and recorded. Henry Gilbert's *Comedy-Overture on Negro Themes* was played twice, and the *Symphony 5½* of his producer Don Gillis once. One performance sufficed for Morton Gould's *Lincoln Legend,* Griffes' *The White Peacock,* the *Third Symphony* of Roy Harris, and G. T. Strong's *The Night,* all of them better works than Grofé's trashy *Grand Canyon Suite* which was played twice and recorded. Two performances were the lot of Kent Kennan's *Night Soliloquy,* and Loeffler's *Memories of My Childhood.* One performance was given to Elie Siegmeister's *Western Suite.* Apart from these, Toscanini played three Sousa marches, *Dixie,* and *The Star-Spangled Banner.*

Twenty-seven scores (not including the national anthem) are a rather poor record for twenty-nine seasons, especially if one realizes the total number of performances of all American music are fewer than those of the pedestrian *Tannhäuser Overture* in its two forms.

Most of the important works by American composers are modern in style as well as time and may well come under Toscanini's general lack of interest in contemporary music. His taste seems to have been formed early in his life, possibly in his years at the conservatory, and it did not develop with the times. In his heart, he was devoted to Wagner, to Verdi, to the nineteenth century romantics and post-romantics, and to their impressionist successors. As we have seen above, in the core of his repertory, the newest score was by Debussy, and it was with an all-Wagner program such as few other conductors continue to give with regularity (they were common in the 'nineties) that he said farewell to his New York audience in 1954. Toscanini's understanding best encompassed what was, more or less, contemporary with his younger self, and the length of his career made evident the changes in style since he began his musical life.

With his honesty and his consistent practice of not playing works which he felt he did not understand, he studied many scores which he never prepared, for example works by Mahler. (I cannot imagine that a Toscanini performance of a Mahler symphony would have been good.[2]) For much the same reasons he chose, apparently, to ignore Bartók and Hindemith, Stravinsky (except for two items), Prokofiev (apart from the *Classical Symphony*), Berg, and others. Toscanini wanted a melodic line, relatively consonant harmony, and simple rhythmic vitality. Respighi suited him, and Stravinsky repelled him; but, unfortunately, Stravinsky remained, for all that, a great composer, and Respighi, however well played, remained commonplace.

Those who suggest that Toscanini's avoidance of modern scores was purely commercial, based upon his respect for the box office, do him an injustice. He never had any trouble filling a hall, even when he played modern Italian works that had less of a following than even the twelve-tone school. When he turned to broadcast concerts the tickets were not sold and he was free to play whatever he wished. As I have mentioned before, if Toscanini had wanted to exploit popular symphonic works, he could have performed a number of scores that he ignored.

There is a second group which suggests that we should not take exception to Toscanini's choice of scores, since his performances were of such unique quality that they were worth one's attention, whatever the music. I do not subscribe to that. Certainly it has been of interest to see what he could do with rather crude works such as the *Zampa Overture* but there is a limit to my interest in such music, however miraculously played.

Similarly, there is a limit to anyone's interest in a steady diet of the few works which Toscanini repeated, season after season. The truth is, the Toscanini repertory was superficially large and functionally small, restricted in time to about a century, in style to the varieties of romanticism, in harmony to the tonic-dominant tradition, and in the choice of programs to the familiar and well worn rather than the new or the unusual. Thus, although Toscanini gave us performances

[2] Dimitri Mitropoulos recalled that the first time he went to visit Toscanini he begged him to play a Mahler symphony, the Fourth, perhaps. Toscanini flared up and told him "Mahler's music is fit only to be used as toilet paper."

which none of his contemporaries could duplicate, he did not always play the music which the most critical and appreciative element of his public desired to hear, even when (as in the case of Berlioz) he could have played it with supreme mastery.

APPENDIX ONE

Appendix One:

Chronology of Toscanini's Life

1867	Toscanini born, March 25, in Parma, Italy.
1876/85	Student at the Royal School of Music, Parma. Graduates at eighteen with highest honors in 'cello, piano, and composition.
1886	'Cellist and assistant chorus master with Rossi's opera company in Brazil. Professional debut as a conductor in *Aïda*, June 30, in Rio de Janeiro. Italian debut in *Edmea* of Catalani at Turin, November 4.
1886/98	Barnstorming in various Italian opera houses. Premières: *I Pagliacci*, 1892; *La Bohème*, 1896; first Italian performance of *Die Götterdämmerung*, 1895; etc.
1896	Debut as a symphonic conductor, Turin, March 20.
1897	Marries Carla de Martini in Milan, June 21.
1898/1903 1906/08	Musical Director of La Scala, Milan.
1908/15	Conductor at the Metropolitan Opera House, New York. First North American appearances at age forty-one.
1913	First New York appearance as symphonic conductor, April 13.
1915/19	Living in semi-retirement in Milan.
1920/21	North American tour with La Scala Orchestra.
1921/29	Musical Director of La Scala, Milan.
1926/27	Appears as guest conductor of the New York Philharmonic during two seasons.
1927/36	Conductor of the Philharmonic-Symphony Orchestra of New York, sharing large portions of the season with Mengelberg (1927-30), Kleiber (1930-32), Walter (1931-34), Klemperer (1934-36), Rodzinski (1934-35), Beecham (1935-36), and others.
1930	European tour with the Philharmonic-Symphony Orchestra of New York.
1930/31	Conducts two seasons at Bayreuth.
1931	Attacked by Fascists, Bologna, May 14.

1934/37	Conducts at Salzburg Festival.
1935/39	London concerts with the B.B.C. Symphony.
1937/54	Conductor of the National Broadcasting Company Symphony Orchestra, engaged and trained for him by Rodzinski. Shares orchestra with Rodzinski (1937-39), Stokowski (1941-44), Cantelli (1949-54), and others.
1938/39	Conductor of Lucerne Festival (with Ansermet, Walter, and others).
1940	Tours South America with the N.B.C. Symphony.
1950	Tours the United States with the N.B.C. Symphony.
1954	Retires as conductor of the N.B.C. Symphony, April 4; leads the orchestra for the last time, June 5.
1957	Suffers stroke New Year's Day. Dies in sleep in New York, January 16. Services, New York, January 19; Milan, February 18. Burial in Milan.

APPENDIX TWO

Appendix Two:

Toscanini Recordings Discussed in Chapter Three

For reference and index purposes I here list by composer and date all Toscanini recordings discussed in Chapter Three. Excerpts are indented under the complete works. Many of these recordings are out of print and approximately fifty of them have never been released commercially, although many of this group have been circulated in pirated editions taken from the air. Arranging the material in this fashion gives a somewhat more systematic view of the Toscanini legacy than that provided by the chronological sequence in Chapter Three. The names of assisting artists are given in brackets, except in the case of complete operatic recordings.

Composer and Work	Year(s) of Recording(s)
BACH	
BRANDENBURG CONCERTO NO. 2	1938
SUITE No. 3	1947
AIR [AIR ON THE G STRING]	1946
BACH (Orch. by Respighi)	
PASSACAGLIA AND FUGUE IN C MINOR	1947
BARBER	
QUARTET, OP. 11: ADAGIO FOR STRINGS	1942
BEETHOVEN	
CONCERTO FOR PIANO No. 1 [Dorfmann]	1945
CONCERTO FOR PIANO No. 3 [Rubinstein]	1944
CONCERTO FOR PIANO No. 4 [Serkin]	1944
CONCERTO FOR VIOLIN [Heifetz]	1940
CORIOLAN OVERTURE	1945, 1953
THE CREATURES OF PROMETHEUS: OVERTURE	1944
EGMONT OVERTURE	1939, 1953
FIDELIO	1944
KOMM, O HOFFNUNG [Bampton]	1944

LEONORE OVERTURE NO. 1 — 1939, 1944
LEONORE OVERTURE NO. 2 — 1939, 1954
LEONORE OVERTURE NO. 3 — 1939, 1945
MISSA SOLEMNIS [Marshall, Merriman, Conley,
    Hines, Shaw Chorale] — 1953
OVERTURE FOR THE CONSECRATION OF THE HOUSE — 1947
QUARTET NO. 16 (Op. 135): LENTO AND VIVACE — 1938
SEPTET (Op. 20) — 1951
SYMPHONY NO. 1 — 1937, 1951
    FINALE *only* — 1921
SYMPHONY NO. 2 — 1949-51
SYMPHONY NO. 3 [EROICA] — 1939, 1949, 1953
SYMPHONY NO. 4 — 1939, 1951
SYMPHONY NO. 5 — 1939, 1952
    FINALE *only* — 1920
SYMPHONY NO. 6 [PASTORAL] — 1937, 1952
SYMPHONY NO. 7 — 1936, 1951
SYMPHONY NO. 8 — 1939, 1952
SYMPHONY NO. 9 [CHORAL] [Farrell, Merriman,
    Peerce, Scott, Robert Shaw Chorale] — 1952

BERLIOZ

THE DAMNATION OF FAUST: SCENE 7 [Harrell,
    Chorus] — 1947
    RÁKÓCZY MARCH — 1920, 1945
HAROLD IN ITALY [Cooley] — 1953
ROMAN CARNIVAL OVERTURE — 1953
ROMEO AND JULIET: DRAMATIC SYMPHONY [Swarth-
    out, Garris, Moscona, Chorus] — 1947
    ROMEO ALONE, GREAT FESTIVITIES AT THE HOUSE
        OF CAPULET, LOVE SCENE — 1946
    QUEEN MAB SCHERZO — 1951

BIZET

L'ARLÉSIENNE: SUITE NO. 1: NO. 4, CARILLON — 1943
    SUITE NO. 2: NO. 4, FARANDOLE — 1921
CARMEN: SUITE NO. 1 — 1952
    PRELUDE TO ACT IV [ARAGONAISE] — 1921
    MARCH OF THE TOREADORS — 1943

BOCCHERINI

QUINTET (Op. 13, No. 5): MINUET — 1943

BOITO

MEFISTOFELE: PROLOGUE [Moscona, Columbus Boys'
    Choir, Robert Shaw Chorale] — 1954

BRAHMS
    ACADEMIC FESTIVAL OVERTURE   1948
    CONCERTO FOR VIOLIN AND CELLO [Mischakoff,
        Miller]   1948
    CONCERTO FOR PIANO No. 2 [Horowitz]   1940
    HUNGARIAN DANCES, No. 1   1943, 1953
        Nos. 17, 20, 21   1953
    SONG OF DESTINY [Robert Shaw Chorale]   1948
    SYMPHONY No. 1   1941, 1951, 1952
    SYMPHONY No. 2   1952, 1952
    SYMPHONY No. 3   1952, 1952
    SYMPHONY No. 4   1951, 1952
    TRAGIC OVERTURE   1937, 1952
    VARIATIONS ON A THEME OF HAYDN   1936, 1952, 1952

CASTELNUOVO-TEDESCO
    OVERTURE TO A FAIRY TALE   1945

CATALANI
    LORELEI: DANCE OF THE WATER NYMPHS   1952
    LA WALLY: PRELUDE TO ACT IV   1952

CHERUBINI
    ALI BABA: OVERTURE   1949
    ANACRÉON: OVERTURE   1951
    MEDEA: OVERTURE   1950
    REQUIEM MASS IN C MINOR [Robert Shaw Chorale]   1950
    SYMPHONY IN D MAJOR   1952

CIMAROSA
    IL MATRIMONIO PER RAGGIRO: OVERTURE   1949

DEBUSSY
    IMAGES, THIRD SET: No. 2, IBÉRIA   1950
    LA MER   1942, 1950
    PRELUDE TO THE AFTERNOON OF A FAUN   1945, 1953

DONIZETTI
    DON PASQUALE: OVERTURE   1921, 1951

DUKAS
    ARIANE ET BARBE-BLEU: EXCERPTS [Concert version
        by Toscanini]   1947
    THE SORCERER'S APPRENTICE   1929, 1950

DVOŘÁK
    SYMPHONIC VARIATIONS   1951
    SYMPHONY No. 5 [FROM THE NEW WORLD] (Stereo
        reprocessing)   1953

ELGAR
 Variations on an Original Theme [Enigma] 1951
  No. 7 Troyte 1945

FRANCK
 Psyché: No. 4, Psyché and Eros 1952

GALILEI (Orch. by Respighi)
 Gagliarda 1920

GEMINIANI
 Concerto Grosso for Strings in G Minor, 1935
  Op. 3, No. 2 1935

GERSHWIN
 An American in Paris 1945

GILLIS
 Symphony No. 5 ½ [Symphony for Fun] 1947

GLINKA
 Jota Aragonesa 1945
 Kamarinskaya 1940

GLUCK
 Iphigenia in Aulis: Overture 1952
 Orfeo: Act II [Merriman, Gibson, Robert Shaw 1952
  Chorale] 1952
  Dance of the Spirits 1929, 1946

GROFÉ
 Grand Canyon Suite 1945
  On the Trail and Cloudburst 1945

HAYDN
 Sinfonia Concertante in B flat Major 1948
 Symphony No. 88 1938
 Symphony No. 92 [Oxford] 1944
 Symphony No. 94 [Surprise] 1953
 Symphony No. 98 1945
 Symphony No. 99 1949
 Symphony No. 101 [Clock] 1929, 1946
 Symphony No. 104 [London] 1943

HÉROLD
 Zampa: Overture 1943, 1952

HUMPERDINCK
 Hansel and Gretel: Prelude 1952

KABALEVSKY
    COLAS BREUGNON: OVERTURE   1945, 1946

KODÁLY
    HÁRY JÁNOS: SUITE   1947

LIADOV
    KIKIMORA   1952

MARTUCCI
    NOVELETTA   1948

MASSENET
    SUITE NO. 4 [SCÈNES PITTORESQUES]: NO. 4 FÊTE
        BOHÈME   1921

MENDELSSOHN
    INCIDENTAL MUSIC TO "A MIDSUMMER NIGHT'S
        DREAM"
        NO. 1 SCHERZO   1921, 1926, 1929
                                  1946, 1947
        NO. 7 NOCTURNE   1926, 1947
        NO. 10 WEDDING MARCH   1921, 1947
        OVERTURE, NO. 5 INTERMEZZO, NO. 12 FINALE
          [Female chorus]   1947
        OCTET FOR STRINGS, OP. 20   1947
        SCHERZO [orchestral version]   1945
        SYMPHONY NO. 4 [ITALIAN]   1954
        SYMPHONY NO. 5 [REFORMATION]   1953

MUSSORGSKY
    KHOVANTCHINA: PRELUDE   1953

MUSSORGSKY (Orch. Ravel)
    PICTURES AT AN EXHIBITION (Stereo reprocessing)   1953

MOZART, Leopold (Arranged by Haydn)
    TOY SYMPHONY   1941

MOZART
    CONCERTO FOR BASSOON NO. 1 [Sharrow]   1947
    DIVERTIMENTO NO. 15 [K. 287]   1947
    THE MAGIC FLUTE [Salzburg]   1937
        OVERTURE   1938
    SYMPHONY NO. 35 [HAFFNER]   1929, 1946
    SYMPHONY NO. 39   1948
        MENUETTO AND FINALE *only*   1920
    SYMPHONY NO. 40   1938-39, 1950

SAINT-SAENS
>   DANSE MACABRE 1950
>   SYMPHONY NO. 3 1952

SCHUBERT
>   SYMPHONY NO. 5 1953
>   SYMPHONY NO. 8 [UNFINISHED] 1950
>   SYMPHONY NO. 9 1942, 1947, 1953

SCHUBERT (Orch. Joachim)
>   GASTEIN SYMPHONY 1941

SCHUMANN
>   MANFRED OVERTURE 1947
>   SYMPHONY NO. 3 [RHENISH] 1949

SHOSTAKOVICH
>   SYMPHONY NO. 7 [LENINGRAD] 1942

SIBELIUS
>   FINLANDIA 1952
>   LEMMINKÄINEN'S HOMECOMING 1940
>   POHJOLA'S DAUGHTER 1940
>   THE SWAN OF TUONELA 1940, 1944
>   SYMPHONY NO. 2 1940

SMETANA
>   MA VLAST: NO. 2 VLTAVA [THE MOLDAU] 1941, 1950

SOUSA
>   THE STARS AND STRIPES FOREVER 1943, 1945

STRAUSS, Johann Jr.
>   ON THE BEAUTIFUL BLUE DANUBE 1942
>   TRITSCH-TRATSCH POLKA 1941

STRAUSS, Richard
>   DEATH AND TRANSFIGURATION 1942, 1952
>   DON JUAN 1951
>   DON QUIXOTE [Miller, Cooley] 1953
>   SALOME: SALOME'S DANCE 1939
>   TILL EULENSPIEGEL 1952

VON SUPPÉ
>   POET AND PEASANT: OVERTURE 1943

TCHAIKOVSKY
>   CONCERTO FOR PIANO NO. 1 [Horowitz] 1941, 1943
>   MANFRED SYMPHONY 1949

SIEGFRIED'S DEATH AND FUNERAL MUSIC
  [Concert version by Toscanini]   1941, 1952
  IMMOLATION SCENE [Opera text] [Traubel]   1941
LOHENGRIN: PRELUDE TO ACT I   1936, 1941, 1951,
    1954 (Stereo)
  PRELUDE TO ACT III   1936, 1951
DIE MEISTERSINGER [Salzburg]   1937
  PRELUDE TO ACT I   1946
  PRELUDE TO ACT III   1951
PARSIFAL: PRELUDE AND GOOD FRIDAY SPELL   1949
SIEGFRIED IDYLL   1936, 1946, 1952
SIEGFRIED: FOREST MURMURS   1951, 1954 (Stereo)
TANNHÄUSER: OVERTURE AND BACCHANALE [Paris
  Version]   1952
  PRELUDE TO ACT III [Urtext]   1953
TRISTAN UND ISOLDE: PRELUDE TO ACT I   1952
  LIEBESTOD   1942, 1952
DIE WALKÜRE: ACT I, SCENE 3 [Traubel, Melchior]   1941
  RIDE OF THE VALKYRIES   1946, 1952

WALDTEUFEL
  THE SKATERS WALTZ   1945

WEBER
  EURYANTHE: OVERTURE   1951
  DER FREISCHÜTZ: OVERTURE   1945, 1952
  OBERON: OVERTURE   1952

WEBER (Orch. Berlioz)
  INVITATION TO THE DANCE   1938, 1951

WOLF-FERRARI
  THE SECRET OF SUZANNE: OVERTURE   1921

APPENDIX THREE

Appendix Three:

The Fabulous Fifty

What Toscanini records should every serious collector try to obtain? Which of the Toscanini recordings do you think people will be playing fifty years from now, the way people still play Caruso recordings from 1902 and 1903? To answer the first question is a matter of criticism, and to answer the second calls for nothing short of soothsaying. The present list attempts both. These are the Toscanini recordings, of those released commercially to date, which best document one or more of his distinctions as a musician and do so in terms of music which can be heard repeatedly with pleasure. In all cases the sound is good enough to make the merits of the performance clear, but I have made my selections on the basis of musical quality rather than engineering. However, when two recordings seem to illustrate the same general features of Toscanini's musicianship, I have selected the one with the better sound or that which is most readily available.

Composer and Work	Preferred Recording (By year)
BEETHOVEN	
LEONORE OVERTURE No. 1	1939
MISSA SOLEMNIS	1953
SYMPHONY No. 1	1951
SYMPHONY No. 3 [EROICA]	1953
SYMPHONY No. 4	1939
SYMPHONY No. 6 [PASTORAL]	1952
SYMPHONY No. 7	1936
SYMPHONY No. 8	1952
SYMPHONY No. 9 [CHORAL]	1952
BERLOIZ	
HAROLD IN ITALY	1953
ROMEO AND JULIET: QUEEN MAB SCHERZO	1951
BRAHMS	
SYMPHONY No. 2	1952

VERDI

Aïda	1949
Falstaff	1950
Nabucco: Va, pensiero	1943
Otello	1947
Requiem Mass	1951
Te Deum	1954

WAGNER

Die Götterdämmerung: Prologue (excerpts)	1941
Siegfried's Death and Funeral Music	1952
Immolation Scene	1941
Die Meistersinger: Prelude to Act I	1946
Prelude to Act III	1951
Parsifal: Prelude and Good Friday Music	1949
Siegfried Idyll	1946
Die Walküre: Act I, Scene 3	1941

WEBER

Der Freischütz: Overture	1952